D0399414

DATE DUE

REGULATING THE MULTINATIONAL ENTERPRISE

NATIONAL AND INTERNATIONAL CHALLENGES

EDITED BY

BART S. FISHER

JEFF TURNER

PRAEGER SPECIAL STUDIES • PRAEGER SCIENTIFIC

Library of Congress Cataloging in Publication Data
Main entry under title:

Regulating the multinational enterprise.

    Includes index.
    1. International business enterprises—Government
policy—Addresses, essays, lectures. 2. Trade regula-
tion—Addresses, essays, lectures. I. Fisher, Bart S.
II. Turner, Jeff.
HD2755.5.R43   1983   338.8′84   83-11002
ISBN 0-03-063561-6

Published in 1983 by Praeger Publishers
CBS Educational and Professional Publishing
a Division of CBS Inc.
521 Fifth Avenue, New York, New York 10175 U.S.A.

3456789 052   987654321

Printed in the United States of America
on acid-free paper

Contents

1

Introduction
Bart S. Fisher

The multinational enterprise is a business entity that operates simultaneously in a number of national territories.[1] Regulation of the multinational enterprise is a two-tiered exercise, with forces being brought to bear by the country of the parent ("home country")[2] and the country of the majority-owned foreign affiliate ("host country").[3] This volume considers host-country policies toward U.S. foreign direct investment and appropriate U.S. policy responses to these national challenges.

In 1971 Raymond Vernon found that national sovereignty was at bay and that multinational enterprises would be increasingly important factors in the developing world and in the industrialized countries.[4] In more extreme versions of the sovereignty-at-bay thesis, the nation-state itself was seen as an anachronism that would be consigned to the scrapheap of history.[5]

Today U.S. companies can no longer romp around the world at will, and the sovereignty-at-bay thesis lies in shreds. National governments have turned on international companies with a vengeance. This volume analyzes constraints recently implemented by Canada, the Common Market, France, Mexico, and the developing countries against multinational enterprises. Collectively, these policies pit the reality of national governmental power and objectives against the imperative of economic interdependence. All around the world *multinationals*, with their $500 billion in worldwide foreign direct investment, are at bay, as governments have asserted their regulatory authority against foreign direct investment.

The key question is whether the trend of host-country antipathy toward multinationals can continue in the 1980s due to the current recessionary conditions in the world economy and the need for investment

1

funds. There are some signs that a tactical retreat by host governments may be in the making. Prime Minister Trudeau, for example, has recently scaled back somewhat the anti-American aspects of the Canadian Foreign Investment Review Agency and the National Energy Program; the international lending authorities are now advising host developing countries to welcome foreign direct investment; and the Common Market appears to be cutting back its directives aimed at regulating multinational enterprises.

The dimensions of this tactical retreat and whether it will continue are matters of profound importance to the United States. In 1946 the book value of U.S. foreign direct investment abroad amounted to only $5 billion; in 1981 it amounted to over $227 billion, far above second-place Britain and even farther ahead of the home countries whose foreign direct investments were rising most rapidly. The dividend repatriations by affiliates, which totaled over $30 billion in 1982, annually assist the United States in covering its trade deficit.

The United States possesses three options in dealing with foreign investment restraints—unilateral actions taken either by the Congress or the Executive Branch; bilateral cooperative efforts on dispute resolution with foreign host governments; and multilateral efforts in international organizations such as the Organization for Economic Cooperation and Development (OECD), the United Nations (UN), or the General Agreement on Tariffs and Trade (GATT).

The unilateral mode of response has been suggested in the recent congressional battle over "reciprocity" legislation. Proposals to use section 301 of the Trade Act of 1974 to secure presidential retaliation against "unreasonable" or "unjustifiable" foreign investment restraints reveal only how limited U.S. leverage is against such constraints.[6]

Most of the chapters in this volume focus on unilateral responses to the restrictive practices of foreign governments. In *Canadian Regulation of Foreign Direct Investment*, for example, Jeff Turner argues that since the U.S. government has limited leverage over the Canadian government, it should seek to solve problems through mutually advantageous, bilateral discussions. Similarly, in *The Company Law Harmonization Program of the European Community*, Steven M. Schneebaum indicates that, since the European law harmonization program is likely to continue and any retaliatory action is likely to be counterproductive, U.S. policymakers and businesses must demonstrate a greater willingness to cooperate to resolve investment-related disputes. Alison Doyle, in *The French Nationalizations: Mitterrand Confronts the Multinationals*, essentially concurs in arguing that the U.S. government should not challenge the French government's policies, but rather should respect them as the legitimate acts of a foreign sovereign. Both Claude Fontheim and Michael Gadbaw in *Trade-Related*

Investment Requirements and Mark Jacobsen in *Mexican Regulation of the Computer Industry* conclude that the U.S. government must develop a comprehensive policy designed to combat the trade-distorting effects of trade-related investment requirements.

A common thread running through these chapters is that the U.S. government has a limited arsenal of unilateral tools to counter constraints on foreign direct investment. As a result, bilateral discussions and bilateral solutions may provide the only productive avenues for solving investment-related disputes.

A promising new mode of response is the bilateral investment treaty (BIT), which has been employed by European countries for many years and has recently been used by the United States in negotiations with developing countries. The United States just concluded extensive investment accords with Egypt and Panama and U.S. officials are projecting a total of 20 treaties with developing countries and Japan in the near future. William Coughlin analyzes the possible future applications of the BIT in his chapter, *The U.S. Bilateral Investment Treaty: An Answer to Performance Requirements?*

On March 1, 1982, Ambassador William E. Brock, the U.S. Trade Representative, announced a major new multilateral initiative by the United States to expand the General Agreement on Tariffs and Trade (GATT) to cover trade-related investment issues at the November, 1982, GATT Ministerial meeting:

> Here we seek a political commitment at the Ministerial meeting to initiate a work program on investment policies with a particular focus on trade-distorting practices such as performance requirements. A multilateral agreement on a work program should first develop an inventory of investment practices that distort trade and then examine ways to strengthen the GATT rules to cover these practices. This will be the first international effort in the GATT on investment issues. We hope to broaden the work program at a later date to cover a wide range of investment practices and problems.[7]

The U.S. proposal to expand the GATT to cover investment practices was unceremoniously rebuffed by a coalition of developed and developing countries prior to the November, 1982, GATT Ministerial meeting, and no mention of the investment problem was made in the final communique of the GATT Contracting Parties. This result was not a surprise to U.S. policymakers, who were aware of the limited incentives that could be offered to our trading partners to place the issue of investments within the GATT regime. The United Nations and the Organization for Economic Cooperation and Development (OECD) apparently will remain the principal international organizations in which investment constraints are considered. Both are light-years away from possessing enforceable codes of conduct for multinational enterprises or regulating national authorities, as George Trisciuzzi indicates in his essay, *Multilateral Regulation of Foreign Direct Investment.*

What is good for U.S. multinational enterprises may not necessarily be good for the United States. Indiscriminate moves against multinationals by foreign governments, however, may result in serious losses for the United States and the world economy. The essays in this volume make an important contribution to our knowledge of what is happening to U.S. investment on a disaggregated, selected basis around the world. This knowledge is the precondition to appropriate action by the U.S. business community and U.S. policymakers.

NOTES

1. R. Vernon, Storm Over the Multinationals: The Real Issues 12 (1977). The multinational enterprise is also referred to as the transnational corporation or the international firm.

2. For a comprehensive analysis of the policy of the United States, as a "home country," toward its multinationals, *see* C. F. Bergsten, T. Horst, & T. Moran, American Multinationals and American Interests (1978); Fisher, *The Multinationals and the Crisis in United States Trade and Investment Policy,* 53 B.U. L. Rev. 308 (1973).

3. Vagts, *The Host Country Faces the Multinational Enterprise,* 53 B.U. L. Rev. 261 (1973).

4. R. Vernon, Sovereignty at Bay: The Multinational Spread of United States Enterprises (1971).

5. For an excellent analysis of the "sovereignty-at-bay" model and its various interpretations, see Gilpin, *Three Models of the Future,* in C. F. Bergsten & L. Krause, World Politics and International Economics (1975).

6. *See* Fisher & Steinhardt, *Section 301 of the Trade Act of 1974: Protection for U.S. Exporters of Goods, Services and Capital,* 14 Law & Pol'y Int'l Bus. 569 (1982).

7. Testimony of Ambassador William E. Brock, III, U.S. Trade Representative, before the Subcommittee for International Trade, Senate Finance Committee, March 1, 1982.

2

Canadian Regulation of Foreign Direct Investment

Jeff Turner

The United States and Canada, which over the years have developed a "special relationship"[1] due in part to the extensive economic and political ties between the two states,[2] are presently mired in a dispute over Canada's right to control the level and the quality of foreign direct investment in Canada. The operation of Canada's Foreign Investment Review Agency (FIRA)[3] and the possible effects of Prime Minister Trudeau's National Energy Program (NEP)[4] have increased United States-Canadian political and economic tensions. Through FIRA, the Canadian government seeks to ensure that foreign direct investment will be of "significant benefit" to Canada.[5] Under the NEP, the Canadian government hopes to increase Canadian ownership of its domestic energy industry from 30 to 50 percent in order to achieve energy self-sufficiency by 1990. At present, the industry is dominated by foreign—primarily United States controlled—energy corporations.[6] These policies of the Canadian government, which reflect nationalist economic and energy concerns, have been criticized by the United States government. In particular, the Reagan Administration and some Members of Congress have claimed that FIRA and the NEP create serious impediments to international trade and investment.[7]

Canada's efforts to increase control over foreign direct investments do not represent an isolated phenomenon within the current international economic system. Numerous other governments also are attempting to exert greater control over foreign direct investments. The general purpose of this effort is to create jobs, expand exports and therefore spur economic development.[8] Basic conflicts of national interest between host countries

A substantially similar version of this article appeared originally in 23 Harv. Int'l L.J. 333 (1982). Used with permission of the *Harvard International Law Journal Association*.

and capital-exporting countries will invariably emerge as recipient governments seek increased influence over the investment decisions of foreign commercial entities. These conflicts are aggravated by growing economic interdependence and by the failure of traditional methods of conflict resolution. In particular, there seem to be few effective international principles or institutional arrangements available to help resolve conflicts involving national control over foreign direct investment,[9] and as a result, governments more frequently are considering bilateral rather than multilateral solutions to investment and trade problems.

The Reagan Administration and members of Congress should evaluate more objectively the rationale for and the importance of FIRA and NEP in order to resolve the present economic and political differences between the two states. This chapter seeks to put the controversy into perspective. Part I reviews the origins and development of economic nationalism in Canada. Part II discusses the historical background, development and details of the FIRA and NEP, which were designed to control foreign direct investment. Part III reviews the Reagan Administration's response to the Canadian legislation. Part IV then mentions some important considerations which should be paramount in the development of United States policy toward Canada, and analyzes several options available to the United States government in responding to the Canadian policy. This chapter concludes that the two governments should pursue a bilateral approach to problem solving and maintain a flexible ad hoc willingness to deal with current conflicts as they arise. Because a special relationship exists between the United States and Canada, policymakers have a unique opportunity to demonstrate that bilateral discussions are useful for resolving disputes over foreign direct investment.

CANADIAN NATIONALISM

The Canadian government's recent efforts to exert greater control over foreign direct investments represent, in part, a manifestation of the nation's "historical search for . . . identity."[10] Indeed, such initiatives are part of a broad effort by Canadians to reduce the economic and political influence of the United States in their country. As one observer put it, Canada's nationalist movement has sought "to protect the fabric of Canadian society against the autonomous and relentless forces running 'free' in the North American market economy."[11]

Since the 1950s, Canadians have become acutely aware of and disturbed by the level and quality of foreign, especially United States, investment in Canada. Despite this, Canada and the United States maintained strong political and economic ties throughout the 1950s and 1960s. This reaffirmed the existence of a "special relationship" between the two countries, as the two neighbors sought to accommodate conflicting interests through negotiation and compromise. That relationship, however, is becoming increasingly strained due to Canadian nationalism and American misperceptions or ignorance of it.

Since his 1980 electoral victory, Prime Minister Pierre Elliot Trudeau has demonstrated his desire to decrease Canada's dependence on the United States. At the same time, he is attempting to promote national unity through the enactment of a Canadian Constitution. Trudeau has thus set a clear but formidable political agenda which seeks to decrease foreign involvement in domestic affairs and assuage long-standing federal-provincial antagonism.[12] In order to accomplish this, he must seek to contain the separatists of Quebec, constrain the efforts of other provinces to oppose increasing federal control over their affairs in general, and encourage broader acceptance of the recently enacted Constitution.

Political tension between Trudeau and the provinces has risen as the economy has deteriorated and unemployment has increased.[13] As perceived by the leaders of Canada's ten provinces, all of whom are members of opposition parties, Trudeau's Canadianization efforts have been an important factor in causing this deterioration of the economy.

The tension between Trudeau and the provinces, in addition to the political tension that exists between Washington and Ottawa, impedes Trudeau's efforts to decrease the level of foreign direct investment in Canada. For the present, however, the United States should recognize that the sentiment to decrease foreign influence in the economy is firmly entrenched among the Canadians.

CANADIAN LEGISLATION

The Foreign Investment Review Agency

In 1970, the Canadian government appointed a national commission to propose policies for dealing with foreign direct investment.[14] The result, the Gray Report,[15] identified two central characteristics of foreign direct investment in Canada. First, the extent of foreign direct investment and the degree of foreign ownership were "substantially higher in Canada than in any other industrialized country and [were] continuing to increase."[16] During the late 1960s, for example, foreign corporations controlled 74 percent of the petroleum and natural gas industry, 65 percent of the mining and smelting industry, and 57 percent of the manufacturing sector. Second, the high degree of foreign control over Canadian enterprises, especially when coupled with the strength of external market forces, had hindered the development of an "efficient, productive, well balanced and innovative [Canadian] economy."[17] The Gray Report advocated the establishment of a screening process by means of which the government could monitor foreign-direct investment.

In January 1973 the government of Prime Minister Trudeau introduced in Parliament the legislation that was to become the Foreign Investment Review Act (the Act). As the Act's language indicated, its introduction was motivated by the realization that "the extent to which control of Canadian industry, trade, and commerce has become acquired by persons other than Canadians and the effect thereof on the ability of Canadians to maintain effective control over their economic environment is a matter of national concern. . . ." One commentator has argued that the Act embodied a quest for national identity, an intent to control national affairs, and a desire to obtain the optimum benefits from foreign direct investment.[18]

The Act applies to two forms of foreign direct investment: the acquisition of control of existing Canadian business enterprises and the establishment of new businesses in Canada. Thus, the Act does not limit investment originating from the internal expansion of businesses already in operation in Canada; such investment is permissible so long as it is "related" to the current operations. The Foreign Investment Review Agency (FIRA), which was established by the Act, will approve new foreign investment only if it is, or is likely to be, of "significant benefit" to Canada.

The Act establishes a procedure whereby the FIRA examines proposed foreign investments to determine whether they will be of "significant benefit" to Canada. In general, FIRA examines every non-Canadian investor's proposed establishment of a new business in Canada.[19] FIRA, however, has oversight over about only 20 percent of foreign direct investment in Canada because most new investments are undertaken through internal expansion.[20] As a result, approximately 80 percent of foreign direct investment may proceed independently of any review by FIRA. During 1980–81, FIRA reviewed 833 applications, the majority of which were filed by American potential investors.[21]

To initiate the review process, an individual or corporate investor files a notice with FIRA outlining a proposed investment. FIRA's Compliance Branch screens the application to determine whether the proposal requires review under the Act. FIRA's Assessment Branch then analyzes those proposals requiring review. At this time the Assessment Branch may request further information from the applicant and may consult with other government departments and the province or provinces likely to be significantly affected by the investment. The Assessment Branch ultimately reports its findings to the Ministry of Industry, Trade and Commerce.

The Ministry of Industry, Trade and Commerce formally reviews the proposals, based upon the information provided by the Assessment Branch. If the Ministry finds the proposed investment to be of significant benefit to Canada, it will recommend that the Governor-in-Council (the Cabinet) approve the proposed investment. If the Ministry decides, however, that the proposal would not generate "significant benefits" or that the Ministry lacks information sufficient to make a determination, the investor will be given time to make further information and representations available. The Cabinet ultimately decides whether a proposed investment is, or is likely to be, of significant benefit to Canada.

The Act establishes five criteria by which FIRA and the Cabinet must make this determination. These criteria are applied generally, depending on the nature of the investment proposal and the industry and region or regions that will be affected. The criteria are the following:

(a) the effect of the acquisition or establishment on the level and nature of economic activity in Canada, including, without limiting the generality of the foregoing, the effect on employment, on resource processing, on the utilization of parts, components, and services produced in Canada, and on exports from Canada;

(b) the degree and significance of participation by Canadians in the business enterprise or new business and in any industry or industries in Canada of which the business enterprise or new business forms or would form a part;

(c) the effect of the acquisition or establishment on productivity, industrial efficiency, technological development, product innovation and product variety in Canada;

(d) the effect of the acquisition or establishment on competition within any industry or industries in Canada; and

(e) the establishment of the acquisition or establishment with national industrial and economic policies, taking into consideration industrial and economic policy objectives enunciated by the government or legislature of any province likely to be significantly affected by the acquisition or establishment.

Further criteria which may be considered are set forth in various regulations established by the government. The entire process is designed to be completed within 60 days.

FIRA's proceedings are closed to the public, and the agency usually does not release specific reasons for recommending acceptance or rejection of an application. Prior to entering the review process, prospective investors are thus uncertain as to the form their proposal should take or the concessions they should be prepared to make in order to secure FIRA's approval.

During the review process itself, FIRA often extracts commitments from prospective investors with regard to one or more of the five criteria set forth in the Act. Although these commitments are not mandatory, investors normally agree to them in order to obtain a positive recommendation from the Agency. If the Cabinet subsequently approves the proposal, such commitments constitute binding legal undertakings with the Canadian government. Compliance with the undertakings is monitored by FIRA; any breach may subject the investor to legal action.

In practice, FIRA approves the majority of proposals submitted. During 1980–81, for example, the agency approved approximately 75 percent of all applications in which a United States investor sought to acquire control of an existing Canadian corporation.[22] Approximately 15 percent of such applications were rejected; the remaining 10 percent were withdrawn. Where United States investors proposed to establish a new business in Canada approximately 79 percent of their applications were approved and 9 percent were rejected, while 12 percent were withdrawn.

This high approval rate, however, should be considered in light of two factors. First, many potential investors never apply for FIRA approval, either because they are certain they will be rejected or because they fear that proprietary information will be disclosed. Second, these figures do not reveal the nature or quantity of the legally binding commitments that the FIRA-approved investors must make during the review process. The high approval rate is thus misleading to the extent it fails to account for potential investors who never apply to FIRA and obscures the amount of control imposed upon non-Canadian investors whose proposals are approved.

FIRA nevertheless appears neutral in its treatment of United States and non-United States applications. Since 1974, FIRA has approved approximately the same percentage of United States applications as non-United States applications. On first impression, United States companies, therefore, do not have a legitimate complaint that they have been singled out for unfair treatment. FIRA, however, does seems to discriminate with respect to industry sectors, as it appears more reluctant to approve applications in the mining, energy, and incidental services sectors than in other areas. To the extent United States companies submit a higher percentage of applications in these industry sectors than do other non-Canadian entities, the United States companies may be able to claim unequal treatment across industry sectors. The extent of this unequal treatment, however, is unclear. In any case, some discrimination may be justified given the high level of foreign investment in those strategic sectors.

The National Energy Program

The National Energy Program (the NEP) which was announced by Prime Minister Trudeau in October 1980, guides the development of Canadian energy policy. The Canadian government, in developing this program, sought to remedy the deleterious effects of two factors that long have dominated Canadian energy policy: provincial ownership of the state's natural resources; and foreign, primarily United States, domination of the state's energy industry. The three western provinces, British Columbia, Alberta, and Saskatchewan, contain most of the state's proven crude oil and natural gas reserves. Since the provinces own these natural resources, the federal government has traditionally influenced energy policy only indirectly: through taxation and international and interprovincial trade measures. Foreign domination of the petroleum industry has limited further the federal government's control over energy policy. In addition, since foreign energy corporations control approximately 70 percent of the petroleum industry, more profits are repatriated to foreign shareholders than are reinvested in Canadian industries.

Since 1973, domestic crude oil and natural gas prices have been determined principally by Alberta, a province that has continued to push for world level oil prices. In 1979, Prime Minister Joe Clark's minority Conservative government tentatively agreed to increase prices substantially, which would have benefited primarily the three western provinces. The government also introduced a motor gasoline tax, which would have further increased consumers' motoring costs. Prime Minister Trudeau, who promised that he would hold down oil price rises,[23] has since attempted to fulfill his pledge to redistribute Canada's energy wealth. This redistribution is a concern of particular importance to the eastern consumers who supported him.

Through the NEP, the Trudeau government seeks to achieve energy security through self-sufficiency, create opportunites for increased Canadian participation in energy exploration and production, and share the energy wealth of the western provinces with the rest of the country. These goals will be achieved primarily through two measures: the Canadian Oil and Gas Act (COGA)[24] and the Energy Security Act.[25]

The immediate reaction to the NEP was quite negative in the western provinces, among the threatened energy corporations, and in the financial community. Officials in the provinces sharply derided the proposal and maneuvered not only to frustrate the federal government's control over energy policy, but also to increase the provinces' bargaining position in negotiations for revenues under the NEP. To signal their displeasure, energy firms reduced budgets, delayed or suspended projects, and removed drilling rigs to the United States. In the financial community, concern over the possible negative effects of the NEP caused a decline in the price of oil stocks and a cutback in energy-related bond issues. As the financial community recognized, the NEP would impose a tremendous burden on the country and the energy industry. These initial fears seem to have been well-founded, as evidenced by the near collapse of the heavily debt-burdened Dome Oil.

THE RESPONSE OF THE UNITED STATES TO FIRA AND NEP

Prior to the Reagan Administration, the United States did not welcome Canadian regulation of foreign investment, although it did accept its existence and adopted a policy of accommodation. Before the Foreign Investment Review Act was enacted in 1973, the Canadian government had performed many of FIRA's activities through the use of policies ranging from moral suasion to direct incentives in exchange for performance commitments. In some respects, FIRA's establishment did not alter the problems associated with doing business in Canada. In 1976, Thomas Enders, then United States Ambassador to Canada, indicated that FIRA would not be a complication to United States-Canadian relations, as long as it did not discriminate against United States investors as compared to other non-Canadian investors.

The Reagan Administration, however, has taken a harsher view of the Canadian legislation. It considers FIRA as an obstacle to the free flow of international capital and an impediment to international trade, and has adopted a policy of confrontation in response to the Canadian legislation. Its responses range from complaining about Canada's policy before multilateral forums, to holding bilateral consultations with the Canadians to the consideration of unilateral retaliatory actions.

The Reagan Administration has raised two main objections with respect to FIRA. First, the Administration considers FIRA's extracting of legally binding commitments from potential foreign investors during FIRA's review process as analogous to regulations imposing performance requirements.[26] Thus, Reagan Administration officials assert that Canada's extracting of such commitments is inconsistent with the national treatment principle of article III of the GATT, which requires that GATT member nations not discriminate between domestically produced and imported articles. Second, Reagan Administration officials also have voiced their concern that FIRA's activities adversely affect United States international trade. The Reagan Administration, for example, is worried that when FIRA requires a United States corporation with production facilities in Canada to decrease its imports into Canada and to increase its exports out of Canada, FIRA's action reduces United States exports to Canada, decreases United States exports to third countries, and increases United States imports from Canada, all of which have a detrimental effect on the United States balance of trade. Furthermore, FIRA's policies, if left unchallenged, may serve as a precedent for other nations, particularly less-developed countries (LDCs), which could hurt American investments and trade throughout the world.

The United States has challenged FIRA under article XXIII of the GATT.[27] The principal argument of the United States is based upon the national treatment principle enunciated in article III of the GATT.[28] The Reagan Administration's argument is that local content requirements, to which foreign investors often commit themselves during the FIRA's review process, violate this article by favoring the products of domestic producers. Although paragraph 5 of article III addresses the issue of local content requirements and specifically prohibits "internal quantitative" restrictions requiring the mixture or use of domestic products in specified amounts or proportions, it is arguable that the practices of the Canadian government do not violate paragraph 5.

In addition, the United States government finds FIRA objectionable under GATT because, even if a specific provision of GATT is not violated, article XXIII authorizes GATT members to complain against measures which have the effect of "nullifying" or "impairing" any treaty benefit. Performance requirements, such as the commitments which may be extracted from a non-Canadian investor under FIRA, may undermine the benefits which the United States anticipated receiving at the time tariff concessions were negotiated under the treaty.

Strictly speaking, however, FIRA's activities do not seem to violate article III of the GATT.[29] The national treatment principle is violated only when imported goods are treated differently than domestically produced goods. The FIRA, however, does not regulate the treatment of imported goods, but rather monitors and controls foreign direct investment. Admittedly, investors make legally binding commitments to FIRA, but these commitments govern primarily the production, not the importation, of goods. Since imported goods are never subject to FIRA's control, article III seems to have no applicability.

With respect to Canada's NEP, the Reagan Administration has primarily three concerns. First, the Reagan Administration objects to the program instituted under COGA which gives the Canadian government a 25 percent interest in certain lands which prove to bear crude oil and natural gas. The Canadian government has agreed to compensate firms for 25 percent of their past exploration and drilling costs incurred in developing productive wells. Since firms will not be reimbursed for nonproducing wells and since the Canadian government has arrogated to itself 25 percent of the interest in producing wells, however, the Reagan Administration regards the Canadian government's action as expropriatory. It can be argued, however, that the Canadian government has not expropriated United States-owned property or assets,[30] but rather, by providing compensation for producing wells, has given a sympathetic response to United States energy corporations. Rather than being challenged, the Canadian policy is better viewed as a reasonable compromise.

Second, the United States government objects to a provision of COGA that amounts to a "Buy Canada" requirement. This provision requires that all crude oil and natural gas producers, in order to obtain the necessary licenses and authorizations for the design and construction of production facilities, submit a "satisfactory" plan for providing Canadian manufacturers with a "full and fair opportunity to participate on a competitive basis in the supply of goods . . . used in that activity or work."[31] The Canadian government has established a Committee on Industrial and Regional Benefits to implement this procedure and to ensure that some of the benefits of major industrial projects are realized by Canadian firms. The United States, however, fears that energy firms will be coerced into buying locally since the firms must justify their selection of non-Canadian suppliers to this Committee.

The Reagan Administration views this policy as inconsistent with Canada's obligations under the GATT. Neither COGA nor the Committee, however, actually requires United States-controlled corporations to buy specified amounts or percentages of goods from Canadian manufacturers and suppliers. Furthermore, the Reagan Administration has yet to demonstrate that such discrimination has actually occurred. Thus, it has not been clearly established that GATT has in fact been violated.

Finally, the United States government objects to the Petroleum Incentives Program that was established as part of the Energy Security Act. Under this program, the Canadian government provides incentive payments in the form of cost reimbursements to energy firms for crude oil and natural gas exploration and development on Canada Lands based on a firm's level of Canadian ownership.[32] This payment scheme favors Canadian-controlled energy corporations, since these incentive payments increase with the degree of Canadian ownership of a corporation. The Reagan Administration objects to this treatment, for it does not believe that Canadian-controlled firms should be given a relative cost advantage over United States-controlled firms. However, even if some cost advantage does exist, Canada does have a legitimate interest in promoting and strengthening the Canadian energy industry.

The United States has challenged the Petroleum Incentives Program of the NEP in the Organization for Economic Cooperation and Development (OECD), arguing that it contravenes the 1976 OECD Declaration on

International Investment and Multinational Enterprises.[33] Similarly concerned about the NEP's impact, other OECD members have joined these discussions, which are taking place before the Codes Commmittee on International Investment and Multinational Enterprises. Canada's defense of its Petroleum Incentives Program may be based on its conviction that although it signed the voluntary accord in question, it did not accept the provisions aimed at liberalizing rules allowing foreign direct investment. Thus, Canada has maintained that the NEP is consistent with its obligations under the OECD. Other OECD members, however, have not accepted Canada's position.

In addition to responding to the Canadian legislation by filing complaints under the auspices of GATT and the OECD, administration officials have also held bilateral consultations concerning the FIRA's operations and the NEP's effects. These discussions have not resulted in significant modifications to either FIRA or the NEP, but they have forced the Trudeau government to reevaluate its goals. For example, in November 1981 the Canadian government announced that it would conduct a review of FIRA's activities and that it would not extend NEP-type programs to other areas of the economy. Recently, the United States Secretary of State George Shultz visited Ottawa for discussions with the Canadian External Affairs Minister, and agreed that further consultations would be appropriate.

Finally, the Reagan Administration has considered taking unilateral retaliatory action against Canada. Such action could be taken, for example, under section 301 of the Trade Act of 1974, which empowers the President in certain circumstances to suspend trade agreements or to impose duties or other import restrictions. For a time, the Administration had considered declaring Canada a "nonreciprocal" nation under the Mineral Lands Leasing Act, a decision that would have denied Canadian-controlled firms the right to hold mining leases on federal lands. The Department of the Interior ruled subsequently, however, that for purposes of the Mineral Lands Leasing Act Canada will continue to be a reciprocal nation.

POLICY RECOMMENDATIONS

In evaluating the policy options open to the Reagan Administration, it is important to keep the Canadian initiatives in proper perspective. In particular, United States policymakers should be aware of the following considerations in formulating a policy which responds to the Canadian legislation.

First, and most importantly, Canada's attempt to shield itself from external, primarily United States, influence is not a temporary aberration, but rather a reflection of a deeply entrenched nationalism. As Marie-Josée Drouin and Harald Malmgren recently warned, "Attempts to deal with [the Canadian effort] as if it were novel or a passing outburst—the tendency in Washington today—only aggravate the tensions. . . ."[34] Foreign investment long has dominated the Canadian economy, and it is reasonable for Canada to take steps to decrease such foreign influence. Furthermore, United States policymakers should realize that inflamed attacks, confrontational strategies, and retaliatory actions may only further entrench the nationalist sentiment in Canada.

Second, just as Canada regulates foreign investment, the United States regulates or bans foreign direct investment in certain sectors of the economy deemed important to the national interest.[35] Like many other countries, the United States discriminates against certain forms of foreign direct investment as a means of promoting national objectives.[36] Canada seeks to do much the same thing through FIRA and the NEP. Particularly in the energy sector, a sector of vital national interest to most countries, Canada seeks only to increase its ownership level to 50 percent, which would still leave United States-controlled corporations as the dominant outside investors in the Canadian energy industry. It is clear that the United States would never tolerate such a high level of ownership of the United States industry by foreign interests.[37]

Third, the interests of the United States are not always synonymous with those of United States corporations. Although the government should seek to promote the development of an international economic and political environment conducive to United States direct investment abroad, it also should seek to promote and maintain United States national security and other political interests. Thus, the United States must be careful not to unduly jeopardize or undermine its longstanding special relationship with Canada in its efforts to protect certain firms which find that doing business in Canada is more expensive as a result of demands made by FIRA or the restrictions imposed by the NEP.

Fourth, Canadian restrictions on foreign investment actually may have caused significant economic problems within Canada, thus making investments in the United States relatively more attractive. Canadian capital has been flowing into the United States at least in part because Canadian investors feel that better investment opportunities exist in the United States market than in the Canadian market.

Finally, despite the economic problems in Canada, and in particular despite the restrictions imposed by the Canadian government, it has been argued that investment in Canadian markets does still remain viable.[38] The Canadian restrictions are relatively fewer in number and less restrictive in operation than those imposed by most other industrialized nations. Since the NEP covers only "Canada Lands," the majority of current and future crude oil and natural gas investments will not be governed by the NEP. Furthermore, since FIRA does not have jurisdiction over most expansions of presently existing companies in Canada, most foreign direct investment within and outside the energy sector will remain free of FIRA review. Thus, in general, foreign direct investment in Canada should remain open and profitable.

The Reagan Administration essentially must choose from among five different policy options to determine how best to respond to the Trudeau government's actions. First, the Administration might adopt a policy of inaction, based on the assumption that any active response only will increase tensions and bolster Canadian nationalism. Second, the Administration might propose the establishment of a joint United States-Canadian commission to deal with economic and political differences in a formal, bilateral setting. Third, the Administration might attempt to bring United States-Canadian differences to the attention of a multilateral forum, such as the GATT or the OECD. Fourth, the Administration could confront Canada openly and forcefully, using or threatening some sort of retaliatory action. Finally, the Administration could deal with the issues as they arise on an ad hoc basis.

If the Administration pursues the first option, adopting a policy of inaction, it would buy time for further consideration and development of a long-term approach. This option, however, poses several problems. First, it might allow Congress and the private sector to seize the initiative in responding to Canada, thereby weakening the Administration's ability to guide the development of United States-Canadian discussions in the future. In addition, a policy of inaction may send a signal to other countries that the United States either is not concerned about foreign regulation of foreign direct investment or does not have an effective means of dissuading countries from adopting such policies. Finally, it would leave unresolved the issue of the extent to which a nation should be able to control foreign direct investment.

Under the second option, the Administration might work with the Trudeau government to establish a commission composed of political and public figures, businessmen, labor leaders, and economists to review current problems and propose future policies. Two recent proponents of this view, Marie-Josée Drouin and Harald Malmgren, argue that such an approach is viable and practical:

Such a framework would force issues to be seen in a broader perspective, and give the leaders of the two nations a device for demonstrating partnership rather than confrontation. It would indeed give the two parties an equal partner status, which in itself would improve Canadian attitudes toward Washington's demands and reduce fears of its global power.[39]

Although this approach is commendable in theory, it ignores the fare of prior attempts to settle disputes with such commissions. The joint commission established as part of the United States-Canadian maritime boundary agreement, for example, has remained moribund.[40] Similarly, a joint consultative committee established in 1979 to review energy issues failed to fulfill its purpose. Given these and other past failures, the Canadian government may have limited interest in forming another commission. Without active Canadian interest and support, a new commission cannot effectively resolve the issues separating the two countries.

As a third option, the Reagan Administration might attempt to pursue further multilateral discussions in the GATT, the OECD, or another forum.[41] This approach would complement its decision to file a case against Canada in the GATT under article XXIII and to enter into discussions with Canada in the OECD. One can argue, however, that multilateral forums have remained an ineffective tool for the resolution of international conflicts, partly because many nations, including the United States, have been unwilling to accept negative determinations by multilateral bodies.[42]

As a fourth possibility, the Administration might opt for challenging the Canadian government openly and retaliating against it. The President, for example, might consider invoking section 301 of the Trade Act of 1974. If he determines that the Canadian government's actions are "inconsistent with the provisions of, or otherwise deny benefits to the United States under, any trade agreement, or [are] unjustifiable, unreasonable, or discriminatory and burden or restrict U.S. commerce. . . ," the President may, among other actions, suspend trade agreement concessions or impose duties or other import restrictions. Such a policy has its risks, however. By threatening to invoke section 301, the President might induce the Canadian government to modify its policies. On the other hand, though, such action might only embitter the Canadians and more firmly entrench nationalist sentiment in Canada. Indeed, the Trudeau government might welcome such a confrontation, for it would allow Trudeau to focus Canadian attention on the United States and away from the economic problems created by his recent initiatives. Furthermore, such retaliation might impose serious economic costs on the United States. Since Canada is the largest trading partner of the United States, both states would be affected adversely by a further deterioration in trade relations. Invoking section 301 is thus an inappropriate response not only because its invocation might affect United States interests adversely, but also because its use might encourage the false perception that foreign direct investment problems are susceptible to speedy, but crude, resolution through a statutory remedy.

Given the undesirability of the foregoing options, the Reagan Administration instead should consider pursuing an ad hoc approach for resolving the problems posed by the Canadian government's actions and for resolving future disputes that may arise with other countries. To establish the structural framework for conducting such a policy and implementing it as new disputes arise, the Administration should establish a cabinet-level group headed by the United States Trade Representative and subcabinet-level working groups headed by assistant secretaries from the Departments of State, Treasury, and Commerce and other departments, as specific disputes arise. The Administration should also suggest that the Trudeau government establish counterpart groups. In implementing this approach, the Administration should regularly consult with the Congress so that members of Congress can better appreciate the problems posed by the issue of foreign direct investment.

As a gesture of good faith, the United States might consider quietly withdrawing the case it has filed against Canada in the GATT. This step would surely put the early activities of any bilateral consultations on a solid footing and would cost the United States little. Issues which would have been dealt with in the GATT forum could then be addressed during such consultations. In any case, pursuing the case in the GATT could be damaging to the Reagan Administration regardless of the outcome. If the United States loses the case, the Administration's credibility may be damaged; and if the United States prevails, Canada might refuse to obey the decision, which would only further undermine the GATT's authority.

Pursuing this approach may pose some risks for the Administration. Like the approach of inaction, this approach may delay resolution of pressing issues, making an ultimate solution more difficult to achieve. It may also seem to signal to other countries that, although the United States government is concerned about foreign regulation of foreign direct investment, it will not vigorously pursue the options it has available for countering such treatment. Finally, it might seem politically unattractive not to confront and respond to the Canadian challenge openly and forcefully.

Nevertheless, this approach does provide a framework not only for improving United States-Canadian relations, but also for resolving problems with other countries that may arise in the future. This framework provides several advantages in finding politically acceptable and practical solutions to the vexing problems the Administration may face.

First, this approach will help to defuse the present political tension between the United States and Canada, while providing a means for resolving the policy disputes that divide the two countries. Given the tension that exists, the Administration should pursue an option that depoliticizes the issues. Furthermore, if similar problems arise in the future with respect to other countries, it may be advantageous to have a framework established in which the political aspects of the dispute can be downplayed and the substantive issues focused on.

Second, this approach provides a means for seeking compromises with the Canadian government. In addition to FIRA's activities and the NEP's operation, numerous other issues, including acid rain, fishing rights, and bilateral tax treatment, may arise in the coming years. By developing an approach that links discussions of these issues, the Administration can better make tradeoffs as it seeks to resolve these issues. The Administration, by focusing on these issues, can begin developing a bureaucracy with expertise for anticipating and resolving future disputes with Canada, and with other countries.

Third, this approach preserves the Administration's flexibility while providing a politically acceptable short-term solution. At the present time, the Administration has little leverage over the Canadian government. Any retaliatory actions are likely to hurt the United States and further entrench nationalist sentiments. Given this situation, the Administration should concentrate on understanding the issues and learning how they can be linked in the future. Furthermore, by keeping Congress abreast of current developments, the Administration should increase congressional awareness of the complexity of the problems, which should decrease congressional propensity to overreact to future problems.

Fourth, this option provides the Canadian government with a means for achieving a politically acceptable resolution of issues between the two countries. This past year, the Trudeau government signalled its willingness to compromise by agreeing not to extend NEP-type policies to other areas of the economy. Despite the boost that sentiment against the United States gives to Trudeau's Canadianization effort, it distracts Trudeau from other important goals: gaining the provinces' acceptance of the new Canadian Constitution, and redistributing the nation's energy wealth. The establishment of working groups provides him with a way to assure Canadians that he will not be deterred from his Canadianization effort, while at the same time it will allow him to devote this attention to his pressing domestic agenda.

Finally, this approach would confirm that the Administration is prepared to negotiate on a substantive, depoliticized basis in order to resolve trade and investment disputes. Given that similar disputes may arise in the future, the Administration should demonstrate its willingness to resolve such disputes pragmatically and on a bilateral level. By engaging in continued negotiations and seeking compromises with the Canadian government, the Reagan Administration can better accomplish that objective.

CONCLUSION

The challenge posed by the Canadian government's attempt to control foreign direct investment is typical of the nature of the problems that the United States government may have to face in the coming decade. With foreign governments increasingly attempting to maximize their states' share of the scarce funds available for foreign direct investment, conflicts may well develop as the United States seeks to protect the interests of its corporations. Although the United States does not share with other states the same special relationship it has with Canada, by capitalizing on that special relationship, the Reagan Administration can demonstrate that bilateral negotiations are a useful means for resolving disputes involving foreign direct investment.

NOTES

1. For an excellent account of the development of the special relationship as well as recent developments in United States-Canadian relations, see Drouin & Malmgren, *Canada, the United States and the World Economy,* 60 Foreign Aff. 393 (1982).

2. The economic interdependency of the United States and Canada is illustrated by the two-way trade between the two states, which in 1981 totaled approximately U.S. $87 billion. This accounted for 70 percent of Canadian world trade. *Issues in United States Economic Relations, Hearings Before the Subcomm. on International Economic Policy and the Subcomm. on Trade and Inter-American Trade of the House Comm. on Foreign Affairs,* 97th Cong., 1st Sess. 2 (1981) (statement of David R. MacDonald, Deputy U.S. Trade Representative). Canadian exports to the United States generate 15 percent of Canada's gross national product and provide one-half of Canadian jobs in goods-producing industries. Moreover, the Canadian market is the largest recipient of United States foreign direct investment. Kirton, *Canada and the United States: A More Distant Relationship,* 79 Current Hist. 117, 117 (1980). In addition, key public and private officials of the two states have held frequent, informal discussions and bargaining sessions on political issues. Finally, the two states have created more than 20 joint entities to address specific aspects of their relations.

3. FIRA was established by the Foreign Investment Review Act of 1973. Act of Dec. 12, 1973, ch. 46, § 2(1), 1973–1974 Can. Stat. 620, *amended by* ch. 52, 1976–1977 Can. Stat. 1274.

4. The National Energy Program includes a wide range of measures designed to achieve energy security and increase the extent to which Canadians control their oil and gas sectors. The Minister of Energy, Mines & Resources Canada, The National Energy Program Update 1982 (1982).

5. Act of Dec. 12, 1973, ch. 46 § 2(1), 1973–1974 Can. Stat. 620, *amended by* ch. 52, 1976–1977 Can. Stat. 1274.

6. Corrigan, *"Canadianization" a Red Flag to U.S. Firms and their Friends in Congress,* 13 Nat. J. 1369, 1371 (1981).

7. *See generally Extension of Margin Requirements to Foreign Investors: Hearings Before the Subcomm. on Banking, Housing, and Urban Affairs,* 97th Cong., 1st Sess. (1981); *Impact of Canadian Investment and Energy Policies on U.S. Commerce; Hearings Before the Subcomm. on Oversight and Investigations and the Subcomm. on Telecommunications, Consumer Protection, and Finance of the House Comm. on Energy and Commerce,* 97th Cong., 1st Sess. (1981); *House*

Economic Hearings, supra note 2; *U.S. Policy Toward International Investment, Hearings Before the Subcomm. on International Economic Policy of the Senate Comm. on Foreign Relations;* 97th Cong., 1st Sess. 224 (1981); Kirkland, *War of Words,* Fortune, Apr. 5, 1982, at 35–36.

8. Other objectives might include increasing managerial control of domestic corporations by a state's nationals, reducing foreign cultural influences, or redistributing income away from traditionally entrenched elites who may have close ties to foreign investors.

9. For instance, the rules established through the General Agreement on Tariffs and Trade (GATT), which govern only disputes involving goods, seem to have no immediate applicability. Given the inherent differences between trade and investment, establishing new international principles will be exceedingly difficult.

10. Drouin & Malmgren, *supra* note 1, at 399.

11. Rottstein, *Canada: The New Nationalism,* 54 Foreign Aff. 97, 115 (1976). This perception of the control exerted by the United States over the Canadian economy has not been illusory. Currently, 58 percent of the manufacturing sector and 61 percent of the top 100 corporations in the resource production and utility fields are controlled by foreign entities. Over 75 percent of the capital employed in oil, natural gas, and other major industries is foreign controlled. Significantly, four-fifths of this "foreign" control is American. Moreover, about 52 percent of the Canadian trade union movement reports to American-based headquarters.

12. The Trudeau government's efforts have been complicated by the relationship in Canada between the federal government and the provinces. Profound differences between the western, central, and eastern provinces, as well as between independent-minded Quebec and the national government, reflect long-held philosophical disagreements about the most appropriate federal-provincial relationship. Canadian provinces, particularly the western provinces, long have used their political power to chart separate courses. As one author has noted, "[t]hey often [have done so] with little regard for each other, and less for Ottawa." Meyer, *Canada's Nationalism Exacts a High Price,* Fortune, Aug. 1976, at 179. The proper allocation of the revenues from Canada's vast energy resources, which lie primarily in the western provinces, also long has been an irritant in the federal-provincial relationship. *See generally* Helliwell, *Energy in Canada,* 79 Current Hist. 125 (1980). Furthermore, the language difference between Quebec and the other provinces has remained an emotional and divisive political problem.

13. Currently, unemployment stands at a record 12.2 percent in Canada, and inflation is 10.6 percent. Between January and September of 1982, 8,074 businesses went bankrupt, the worst rate since the 1930s. Gross domestic product dropped 7.8 percent in the period June 1981 to June 1982. Foreign debt has risen from $23.1 billion in 1970 to $73.3 billion last year, of which $54.6 billion is owed to the United States, Time, Nov. 8, 1982, at 46.

14. For a historical review of the Canadian Government's attempt to control foreign direct investment in Canada, *see* J. Fayerweather, Foreign Investment in Canada (1976); S. Globerman, U.S. Ownership of Firms in Canada: Issues and Policy Approaches (1979); Rothenberg, *The Impact of Affluence: Restrictions on Foreign Investment in Canada,* 9 Am. Rev. of Can. Stud. 72 (1979).

15. H. Gray, Foreign Direct Investment in Canada (1972).

16. *Id.* at 5.

17. *Id.*

18. J. Fayerweather, *supra* note 14, at 137.

19. For an explanation of how the Foreign Investment Review Agency carries out its mandate, see American Bar Association, Current Legal Aspects of Doing Business in Canada 3–58 (1976); Spence, *The Foreign Investment Review Act of Canada,* 4 Syr. J. Int'l L. & Com. 303 (1976); Letter from Elmer Staats, Comptroller of the United States to Rep. Benjamin S. Rosenthal (Sept. 6, 1979).

20. Koehler, *Foreign Ownership Policies in Canada: "From Colony to Nation" Again,* 11 Am. Rev. of Can. Stud. 77, 89 (1981).

21. *See* Foreign Investment Review Agency, 1980–1981 Annual Report (1981). The average asset value of new acquisitions was $122 million, an increase over the $91 million average of the prior year. Most of the new business cases involved businesses with initial investments of less than $2 million.

22. *Id.*

23. *See generally* The Minister of Energy, Mines & Resources Canada, The National Energy Program (1980).

24. The Canada Oil and Gas Act, ch. 81, 1980–81 Can. Gaz. 2655. This Act governs only the leasing of "Canada Lands." Canada Lands, which must be distinguished from provincial lands, include the areas off Canada's coasts, the Yukon and Northwest Territories, and small areas scattered throughout Canada. These lands may in the future provide the greatest source of yet undiscovered crude oil and natural gas reserves.

Under COGA, the Canadian government will automatically receive a 25 percent interest in any Canadian Lands that begin production of crude oil or natural gas after December 31, 1980. After pressure was applied by the United States government and United States energy corporations, Canada, in May 1982, agreed to compensate firms for 25 percent of their past exploration and drilling costs incurred in developing productive wells.

25. This act includes the Petroleum Incentives Program, which will provide government subsidies to energy firms for crude oil and natural gas exploration and development on Canada Lands based on a firm's level of Canadian ownership. These incentive payments increase with the degree of Canadian ownership of the corporation. Petroleum Incentives Program, ch. 107, §§ 8–10, 1980–82 Can. Stat. 3131.

26. Two types of commitments commonly extracted from foreign investors are export requirements and local content requirements. Export requirements are commitments that governments impose on an investor to export a fixed percentage or a specified minimum quantity of the goods produced. Under local content requirements, governments require that a specified percentage of the value added to the final output be either obtained from local sources to be produced locally or by the foreign investor. For criticism of performance requirements and their perceived deleterious effects on trade, *see* Fontheim, & Gadbaw (chapter 5 of this book).

27. In February 1982, the Administration held official consultations with Canadian officials under article XXII procedures of GATT, which provides in part, that

> Each contracting party shall accord sympathetic consideration to, and shall afford adequate opportunity for consultation regarding, such representations as may be made by another contracting party with respect to any matter affecting the operation of this agreement.

General Agreement on Tariffs and Trade, *opened for signature,* Oct. 30, 1947, art. XXII para. 1, 61 Stat. A3, T.I.A.S. No. 1700, 55 U.N.T.S. 187. In March 1982, the Administration announced that it would present a GATT case against Canada pursuant to article XXIII, under which a multilateral panel was convened to investigate and report on the United States' complaints against Canada over FIRA. Article XXIII empowers the GATT Council to authorize member nations to suspend the application of concessions or other obligations under the GATT to particular member nations when the Council considers such retaliatory actions to be appropriate.

28. The basic principle of article III of the GATT is set forth in paragraph 1, which provides that internal regulations "should not be applied to imported or domestic products so as to afford protection to domestic production."

29. *But see* Fontheim & Gadbaw, *supra* note 26.

30. The real issue is not whether Canada has expropriated United States property, but rather whether it has adequately compensated the energy firms under the 25 percent "back-in" provision. Although these firms must pay 26 percent of the royalties from producing wells to the Canadian government, such a situation is analogous to the United States decreasing the oil depletion allowance or increasing the corporate tax rate. In all three situations, the value of the crude oil or natural gas in the ground has decreased relative to its prior value (since a greater share of the firm's revenues must be paid to the government), but the firm's crude oil and natural gas have not been expropriated.

31. Canadian Oil and Gas Act of Dec. 18, 1981, ch. 8, § 3.2(2), 1980–81 Can. Gaz. 2655.

32. Petroleum Incentives Program, ch. 107, §§ 3–10, 1980–82 Can. Stat. 3131. To be eligible for the minimum incentive payment, corporations are required to have at least 50 percent Canadian ownership at the time exploration or development costs are incurred. Canadian ownership of at least 75 percent is required for the maximum incentive payment.

33. The principle underlying the declaration is one of national treatment: foreign owned or controlled enterprises operating within a member nation ought to be accorded treatment no less favorable than that accorded to domestic firms. Declaration on International Investments and Multinational Enterprises, Organization for Economic Cooperation and Development, Press/A(76)20, art. II, para. 1, June 21, 1976. It should be noted that the United States has not challenged FIRA under the OECD declaration since the declaration explicitly states that it does not apply to member nations' right to regulate the entry of foreign investement. *See* Declaration on International Investment and Multinational Enterprises, art. II, para. 4.

34. Drouin & Malmgren, *supra* note 1, at 399.

35. For a compilation of U.S. restrictions on foreign direct investment in the United States, see Marans, Williams & Griffin, Foreign Investment Under United States Law (1979). Numerous laws and regulations ban, limit, or require disclosure of foreign direct investment in the United States. *See, e.g.,* 7 U.S.C. §§ 3501–3508 (Supp. III 1979) (foreign purchases of agricultural land must be reported); 14 U.S.C. § 11 (1976) (a vessel loses its right to U.S. registry if its corporate owner is foreign); 47 U.S.C. § 222(d) (1976) (telegraph companies are not to be more than 20 percent foreign owned).

State governments also have placed limitations on foreign ownership of land and corporations within their borders. Recently, state governments have actively engaged in promotion efforts designed to attract foreign investment funds, acting in much the same way as the foreign governments challenged by the U.S. government. For a concise review of these activities, *see* Driscoll, Incentives to Foreign Direct Investment in the United States (1981) (Congressional Research Service Report No. 81–76E).

36. For a review on the restrictions imposed by other nations, *see* Price Waterhouse & Co., Investment Policies in Seventy-three Countries: A Survey (1981).

37. Congress showed this in the summer of 1981 when it attempted to block Canadian takeovers of U.S. energy corporations. These takeover opportunities came about because of a decrease in the stock value of many energy corporations due to the announcement of the NEP and because of the limited flexibility of many United States-controlled energy corporations to sell their Canadian assets or defend themselves against takeover attempts due to the existence of FIRA. For a full discussion of the factors contributing to this merger activity, *see* Corrigan, *supra* note 6, at 1369–72.

38. *See, e.g.,* Comments of Dome Petroleum Corp. on Canadian Reciprocity Under the Mineral Lands Leasing Act (Dec. 31, 1981) (document on file with U.S. Department of Interior). As counsel for Dome Petroleum recently indicated, "Even after all the proposed 'restrictions' of Canada's National Energy Programs are in place, Canada will still provide U.S. investors with among the greatest opportunities for oil and gas investments, and the greatest net returns on such investment of any major energy producing country in the free world."

39. Drouin & Malmgren, *supra* note 1, at 112–13.

40. *See* Kirton, *supra* note 2, at 148.

41. Multilateral forums will not always be suitable forums in which to discuss trade or investment problems due to the nature of their memberships. Mexico and Taiwan, for example, are not members of the GATT, and thus the GATT dispute resolution mechanism is not available for problems involving these major U.S. trading partners.

42. The controversy over the DISC legislation in the GATT highlights the extent to which nations, including the United States, will block multilateral resolution of disputes involving favored national legislation. In 1971, Congress amended the U.S. tax code so that corporations could defer indefinitely the tax on half of their export profits by setting up domestic international sales corporations (DISCs). In 1972, the European Community challenged the DISC legislation in the GATT, arguing that it was an export subsidy. The United States responded by challenging the territorial tax practices of France, Belgium, and the Netherlands. A GATT panel found all four taxes in violation of the GATT, but final action in the GATT was blocked by the four countries. Since then, the issue has remained a constant source of tension between the United States and the European Community. *See* 13 Nat'l J. 278, 278–81 (1981). Professor John Jackson describes the DISC episode as "one of the greatest failures of the GATT system throughout four Administrations and various changes of policy." 405 U.S. Export Weekly (BNA) 106, 107 (Apr. 27, 1982).

3

The Company Law Harmonization Program of the European Community

Steven M. Schneebaum

INTRODUCTION

For most non-Europeans, the establishment and evolution of the European Community (EC)[1] have been subjects of no more than academic interest. Many have noted with genuine satisfaction the growing interdependence of the ten Member States of the EC[2] nations whose cultures, languages, and histories differ widely and fundamentally. The development of a true economic union of nations which, within the lifetimes of their leaders, have fought two World Wars is little short of a miracle. Nevertheless, few non-Europeans, including those with significant business interests in Europe, have heeded the emergence of a comprehensive and increasingly complex EC legal order.[3]

Recent proposed EC legislation affecting companies located in, or with subsidiaries located in, member countries has, however, caused many executives of U.S. multinational corporations for the first time to consider the impact of the EC's efforts on their activities. Many U.S. businesses have begun crash-courses in EC law and politics in order to counter what they perceive to be serious threats to their methods of operation in Europe and, ultimately, in the United States as well.

This chapter discusses proposed EC legislation to encourage the "harmonization" of certain diverse aspects of corporate operations, including disclosure of information, capitalization, mergers, public offerings of securities, qualifications of auditors, relationships within "groups" of com-

---

A substantially similar version of this article appeared originally in 14 Law & Pol'y Int'l Bus. 293 (1982). This version of the article is based on developments as of January 1, 1983. Used with permission of *Law and Policy in International Business*.

panies, and the rights of employees. After outlining the concept of harmonization and the procedure for its attainment, the chapter reviews EC initiatives which have already been promulgated, which are in the process of being adopted, and which have not yet been formally proposed, and will indicate those aspects of the program which should especially concern U.S. industry. Although not strictly part of the company law harmonization program, the Vredeling Proposal, a proposed directive requiring that management disclose certain information to and consult with workers' representatives, and a model corporate charter for the Societas Europea, are also discussed. Finally, the concluding section presents a critique of the harmonization program together with an assessment of its current status and prospects, and suggests resolutions to some of the most frequently disputed issues it raises.

THE CONCEPT OF HARMONIZATION

One essential aspect of the European Community's goal to permit the free movement of persons, services, and capital among Member States is what the Treaty of Rome terms "the right of establishment." This right comprises, *inter alia*, the freedom of a company organized in any Member State to establish or maintain a business in any of the other Member States. To enable EC institutions to realize the freedom of establishment, the Treaty of Rome grants them power to "coordinat[e] to the necessary extent the safeguards which, for the protection of the interests of members and others, are required by Member States of companies or firms . . . with a view to making such safeguards equivalent throughout the Community.[4] The program of company law harmonization has been constructed on this foundation. The principal component concepts of harmonization—coordination, safeguards, protection, and equivalence— are immediately apparent in this enabling language. Legislation of Member States designed to protect shareholders and "others," (creditors, customers, potential investors, and workers) by reducing their exposure to unacceptable risk is to be harmonized throughout the EC.

In order to achieve harmonization, the Treaty of Rome gives the EC Council of Ministers the power to issue "directives" to the Member States.[5] A directive is not legislation per se; rather, it is an order issued by the Council to Member States requiring that they bring their national legislation into conformity with the directive. A directive is binding "as to the result to be achieved, upon each Member State to which it is addressed, but shall leave to the national authorities the choice of form and methods."[6] Thus, harmonization does not necessarily apply the law of any one Member State directly to the European Community at large.

The process by which the Council adopts directives is complex. The Commission of the EC, which is, in essence, the civil service of the Community, and which is composed of members who, with their staffs, do not represent their individual countries, is responsible for proposing draft directives to the Council.[7] On all proposed directives, the Council must seek the advice of the European Parliament,[8] and of the Economic and Social Committee (ECOSOC) if the proposal concerns matters within its purview.[9] Any changes in the text suggested by Parliament or ECOSOC must be duly considered by the Commission. The Commission normally responds to these suggestions in writing, whether or not it elects to amend its proposal to include the revisions.

The Council of Ministers, representing the Member State Governments, conducts the final level of consideration, and normally operates in three stages. First, a "working party" of technical experts representing appropriate ministries of the Member States reviews the draft in detail, with a view to accommodating or eliminating any technical barriers to the Council's ultimate acceptance. Second, the Committee of Permanent Representatives (COREPER) assesses the political acceptability of the proposed directive. COREPER, which includes representatives of ambassadorial rank from each of the Member States,[10] may appoint staff panels to consider especially detailed or controversial proposals. Finally, the Council of Ministers itself, comprising the Foreign Ministers of the Member States,[11] has the power officially to issue directives having full legal effect. Because the Council generally takes action only if it has unanimous approval,[12] after the two earlier stages of review have produced an acceptable text, it rarely must expend much time over directives that do not involve the most important issues of Community policy.

A directive may set a time limit within which implementing national legislation must be adopted. If a Member State does not observe such a time limit, or, in the absence of an express limit, if it does not enact legislation within a reasonable period of time, the Commission has the power to bring the offender before the European Court of Justice, which can order the Member to comply forthwith.[13]

The Commission and the Council normally conduct their deliberations in private,[14] although they may and often do consult affected industry or labor groups. Parliamentary and ECOSOC debates are public, and Parliament often holds committee hearings with public witnesses on proposals under consideration.[15] Those parts of the legislative process that are open to the participation of the private sector do not discriminate against comments, suggestions, or interlocutors from outside the European Community. It is therefore extremely important for U.S. and all non-EC businesses to understand the EC system, as well as its results which promise or threaten to regulate their operations. A well-reasoned supporting or opposing viewpoint is generally welcomed. Participation by U.S. businesses in the EC legislative process in no way challenges or denigrates the power of the Community to make laws; indeed, such participation manifests a sincere and healthy respect for the maturity of the developing EC institutions.

THE COMPANY LAW HARMONIZATION PROGRAM

The program to harmonize the company laws of the EC Member States encompasses ten directives.[16] Five of these have been issued by the Council, three have been proposed by the Commission and are in the legislative "pipeline," and two have not yet been submitted. In addition to these, two other legislative initiatives that would significantly affect the operations of companies in the European Community are under consideration: the Vredeling Proposal on the dissemination of information to and consultation with workers' representatives, and a model charter of an EC corporation, the Societas Europea.[17]

The Directives Already Promulgated

The First Company Law Directive was issued in 1968.[18] Although significant controversy greeted its issuance as the Member States explored the new territory of company law harmonization, the First Directive is substantively neither radical nor onerous. It has been implemented in all of the Member States.

The First Directive covers three distinct issues: public disclosure, the validity of corporate acts, and the "nullity" of companies. It requires that companies[19] publish their articles of incorporation or charters and all subsequent amendments, their balance sheets and profit-and-loss statements, and various juridical acts which could affect creditors or shareholders.[20] Member States are ordered to record this information in central registers.[21] Although the First Directive expressly requires that these matters be published, it lacks specific detail concerning the form of their publication: the Fourth Directive addresses this issue.

The First Directive protects third parties relying on apparent corporate acts against a defense of ultra vires, by preventing a de facto corporation from declining to assume obligations arising from its acts, and by assigning responsibility and legal liability to the individuals who performed them.[22] When a company purports to act in excess of its charter, an innocent third party may still hold the company liable for its actions.[23]

Finally, the First Directive provides that companies may be declared "null," that is, void or voidable, in certain limited circumstances. Declarations of nullity are permitted only upon judicial decree entered for failure of legal capacity or prescribed formalities, or for violation of law or contravention of public policy. A declaration of nullity may be contested,[24] and does not affect the validity of the company's obligations.[25]

Promulgated in 1976, the Second Directive[26] deals with the formation, maintenance, increase, and decrease of capital in the form of shares of public stock companies, the payment of dividends, and the acquisition of assets. It effectively precludes the creation of small stock companies by setting certain minimum levels of capitalization as a prerequisite for incorporation or authorization to do business.[27]

Although the Second Directive contained a time limit of two years for implementation,[28] after more than five years, only the United Kingdom and Germany have implemented it. The apparent reluctance to adopt the appropriate legislation probably stems not from ideological rejection, but from the view that specific national laws were already in advance of the EC "reform."

Adopted in 1978, the Third Directive[29] regulates mergers, including those formed by acquisition and those formed by the creation of a new company. It requires that certain draft terms of the merger be published and be publicly available at least one month prior to the approval of the merger, and requires management to report the effect of any merger on the workforce. Perhaps most importantly, it gives workers' representatives the right to address shareholders' meetings considering the merger.[30] The Third Directive attempts to protect the interests of shareholders by requiring an evaluation of the draft terms by independent experts. The report of the experts must specifically include an evaluation of the fairness and reasonableness of the proposed share exchange ratio. The Third Directive required implementation before October 1981,[31] but no Member State has met the deadline.

The Fourth Directive[32] establishes the technical requirements for the publication of corporate data required to be published by the First Directive. The Fourth Directive is by far the most technical and most controversial of the company law directives yet in effect. It is currently in the process of implementation by the Member States.[33]

The Fourth Directive guides accountants in presenting, auditing, and verifying balance sheets, annual reports, profit-and-loss accounts, and notes. The most significant aspects of the Fourth Directive are:

1. The Directive sets only minimum standards for the Member States; through implementing legislation a particular Member State may impose stricter accounting rules.[34]
2. The Directive relies upon the accounting concept of a "true and fair view"[35] of corporate financial status, although the precise meaning of this

notion varies among the Member States.[36] The Directive does not attempt to legislate a standard interpretation.

3. The Directive contains detailed instructions on layout, valuation methods, means of publication, and audits.[37] It will, however, have no significant tax implications since it recognizes the sharp variations among the systems of taxation of the Member States.[38]

4. The Directive permits derogation in the cases of "small" and "medium-sized" companies.[39]

5. The Directive does not apply to "dependent companies" of "groups" whose "dominant companies" are organized under the laws of a Member State, pending adoption of the proposed Seventh Directive.[40]

6. Except as noted in (5) above, and with certain other extremely limited exceptions, the Directive applies on a company-by-company basis.[41] Thus, if a non-EC multinational corporation has subsidiaries in the Community that satisfy the requisite size criteria, each subsidiary is independently responsible for complying with the Fourth Directive.

Although the Fourth Directive has engendered serious controversy and much public discussion, from a jurisdictional point of view it is unassailable. Fourth Directive obligations are imposed only upon *European* limited liability companies.[42] The Directive is neither discriminatory nor extraterritorial. Government control over the format of required financial disclosure is exercised in many countries, including, of course, the United States.[43]

The most recent company law directive to have been approved by the Council of Ministers is the Sixth Directive.[44] It attempts to create a standard format for the prospectus issued by a company on its first public offering of shares, and it has caused hardly any controversy. The Sixth Directive requires implementation by the Member States by September 1982.

The Directives in the Legislative Process

One of the most radical and far-reaching initiatives in the company law harmonization program, the Fifth Directive[45] was proposed by the Commission to the Council in 1972. According to the usual constitutional procedures, the Council promptly referred the Directive to the Parliament where it lay dormant for nearly a decade.

The Commission text of the proposed Fifth Directive would generalize to the entire European Community a structure of corporate governance now in use only in Germany and The Netherlands.[46] It would require that companies establish a two-tier board system in which a supervisory board would appoint and oversee a management board actually to run the company.[47] Under the Directive, enterprises with more than

500 employees would be required to reserve at least one-third of the seats on the supervisory board for representatives chosen by employees or their unions.[48]

The Fifth Directive raises a host of juridical problems. First, its requirements run counter to traditional corporate forms in English and U.S. law.[49] For example, the Directive's provision for corporate control by individuals who neither have an ownership interest nor are answerable to the owners is inconsistent with the power of shareholders ultimately to decide the course of the company.

Supporters of the Fifth Directive do not shy away from charges of radicalism. They assert that in today's complex and troubled economies, the "pure" form of corporate governance is an anachronism. Large companies have social responsibilities; they have become public actors in control of the lives of their employees, and often of their communities as well. Thus, they argue, the modern age requires more social control over corporations. The debate over corporate control is, of course, fundamental. Regardless of the specific content of the Fifth Directive, if any variant of it is enacted, this debate will continue within the EC. In a significant development, the European Parliament, in April 1981, adopted a report calling for increased control of multinationals, including mandatory information disclosure and more diligent enforcement of rules regulating competition and the protection of employees' interests.[50] The adoption of this report indicates that there is at least a good measure of support for the policy behind the Fifth Directive.

The commission draft of the Fifth Directive also contains provisions concerning the selection, independence, and payment of outside auditors. As is apparent from consideration of the Seventh and Eighth Directives, EC institutions view the harmonization of audit practices as an essential component of the company law project.

On May 11, 1982, the European Parliament adopted a motion for a resolution officially endorsing the Fifth Directive as amended and transmitting it to the Council for consideration.[51] The amended text significantly alters the Commission version by converting the mandate to establish two-tier boards into an option. Thus, the parliamentary text contemplates the continuation of the various practices regarding corporate governance now in use in the Member States: two-tier boards, works councils, unitary boards, and so on. While companies are allowed the facility of selecting their form of organization, however, the parliamentary text does require that disclosure must be made to worker-directors (or members of the works council) that may far exceed what is routinely disseminated today. The question of the scope of disclosure to such persons is likely to vex the Council for some time, with the United Kingdom and Ireland unlikely to permit the elevation of workers' representatives to a level of information higher than that of nonexecutive directors under current law.

The Commission response to these proposed amendments is expected in February 1983. It is generally assumed that it will be a ringing endorsement. Thus, the Fifth Directive will be laid before the Council and referred to its working party, in all likelihood, before the beginning of the German Presidency on July 1, 1983.

The Commission first proposed the draft Seventh Directive to the Council in 1976.[52] After review by Parliament[53] and ECOSOC,[54] the Commission revised the proposal in late 1978.[55] By establishing procedures for the consolidation of accounts of "groups" of companies in the EC, the Seventh Directive would regulate enterprises not covered by the Fourth Directive. The drafters of the Seventh Directive maintain that only if consolidated reports are filed can an accurate picture of the role of related enterprises in the Community be derived.[56]

The consolidation requirements of the Seventh Directive create an obvious problem for multinational corporations not headquartered in the EC. The consolidation of separate subsidiaries of foreign parents would be both difficult and misleading, if, for example, those subsidiaries were in different industrial sectors, were managed independently, and shared only their ultimate parentage and their location in EC Member States. Nevertheless, in its original versions, the draft made no special allowance for the compliance problems of foreign multinationals. It simply required EC-wide consolidations to include all related enterprises located in or controlled from the Community. As might be expected, non-EC chambers of commerce and employers' federations objected strenuously to this requirement, claiming that compliance would be extremely costly and of little value.[57]

Partly as a result of these vehement protests, the working party of the Council proposed certain compromises. Member States would be permitted to allow non-EC enterprises to produce either European Community subconsolidations or worldwide consolidations at their option. The working party, however, added one proviso: worldwide accounts would have to be "comparable" or "equivalent" to the consolidations required of EC companies by the Directive.

Commission officials have repeatedly assured U.S. multinational corporations that Form 10-K, regularly filed with the U.S. Securities and Exchange Commission, would satisfy Seventh Directive obligations as set out in the amended text. Those assurances should be viewed, however, as subject to two caveats. First, the Commission cannot guarantee that Member States in their implementing legislation will take as lenient a view of foreign filings as the Commission does.[58] Proponents of the Directive respond that Member States, inclined to impose onerous disclosure requirements on foreign companies doing business in their territory, do not need an enabling EC directive; they are free to adopt such legislation, whatever the law imposed at the Community level.[59] Second, the worldwide consolidation option is of little use to privately held companies outside the Community which are not required to disclose worldwide accounts even in their countries of incorporation.[60] This consideration has evidently left Commission officials unmoved, perhaps because of the very small number of foreign closely held corporations operating in Europe, as well as because of the not uncommon but erroneous mistrust of the privately held company.

Compliance difficulties encountered by closely held companies exemplify an even more fundamental challenge posed by the various drafts of the proposed Seventh Directive. A subsidiary corporation generally has no legal right to demand access to information held by its parent.[61] Although in practice the kinds of information to be provided by foreign companies under the Seventh Directive—for example, worldwide accounts—are commonly available to European subsidiaries, such disclosure is not required as a matter of law.

A publicly held company is unlikely to object to an EC requirement that a few more copies of its annual report or its Form 10-K be printed.[62] In contrast, the obligation imposed upon subsidiaries to present worldwide information concerning their parent could be viewed as an example, albeit perhaps a technical one, of extraterritoriality that is impermissible under principles of international law. While a nation may not, in general, mandate or proscribe activities by aliens outside of its borders, most states recognize an exception to this rule when foreign conduct causes direct domestic effects.[63] Both the United States and the EC[64] recognize such a rule, along with its limited exceptions. Even the doctrine of direct effects, however, does not provide a basis for ongoing extraterritorial regulation of foreign business operations.

In response to the charge that the Seventh Directive would apply extraterritorially, EC officials argue that worldwide consolidation is simply an option offered for the convenience of foreign companies, and that non-EC companies may, if they choose, produce only EC accounts. They assert that because the operations of foreign parents directly affect the European economy, any extraterritorial reach is justified, and that it is inappropriate for businesses in the United States, the extraterritoriality of whose laws in the area of competition has long been criticized, to raise this objection.[65] Nevertheless, the proposed Seventh Directive does differ from the directives already enacted, whose obligations affect only companies incorporated in the Member States. Some commentators, therefore, see the Seventh Directive as evincing an underlying fundamental distrust of multinational corporations, which expresses itself by requiring full disclosure as the price of doing business in Europe.[66]

Whether that distrust would in fact be reduced by the Seventh Directive is unclear. The many weaknesses in the language of the various drafts have created uncertainty about its actual meaning and potential impact. Numerous key terms—"group," "consolidated account," and "EC subgroup,"—are left undefined, or are defined only in unhelpful ways. As it has been drafted, the Directive would require that the "equivalence" of foreign filings be certified by auditors in each Member State, thus creating the potential for different consolidations to be required in different countries.[67] Nor does the Directive contain specific instructions concerning currency valuation or language, and this too could lead to anomalous and onerous results for companies.

The accounting and technical problems in the text of the Directive have led to an unusual development in the legislative process. The working party of the Council terminated its work in December 1981 without having agreed upon a single, definitive text to refer to COREPER. Instead, it proposed alternative solutions to several important questions, including: whether "actual control" of one company by another, absent unified management or substantial shareholding, creates a "group" relationship; whether small groups should be exempted, and if so, how such an exemption should operate; whether parent companies that are not limited liability companies should be included; and whether to require or permit the inclusion of single EC companies actually managed as groups together with companies outside the EC.

The inability of the working party to reach agreement has posed extremely technical problems for COREPER. COREPER has, therefore, had to appoint its own working group in order to resolve these matters, and the transmittal of a final text to the Council will thus be delayed. At present, few observers believe that the Seventh Directive will be issued before the end of 1983, even if the questions that are still outstanding are resolved rapidly by compromises rather than by extensive rewriting.[68]

First submitted by the Commission to the Council in April 1978, the Eighth Directive has since been revised, and the current text was published in December 1979.[69] The proposal, which concerns the professional qualifications of auditors, would not create a general cross-border right to practice,[70] but it does set out conditions under which auditors qualified in one Member State would be able to conduct audits in another. This capability would be especially important upon adoption of the Seventh Directive, because it would avoid the unnecessary, potentially confusing, and extremely costly duplication of audit reports. An auditor certified under the Eighth Directive could issue a single opinion for a group or subgroup consolidation that would be accepted by all Member States requiring such a report. For example, once an auditor has certified accounts as satisfying the requirements of the Seventh Directive, separate certification should not be necessary in the other Member States.

The draft Eighth Directive also would require Member States to maintain official registers of qualified auditors, would provide for the independence of auditors, and would specify the forms of business association available to them. These provisions have engendered considerable controversy within the accounting profession and could be responsible for the delay in the Directive's adoption, which originally had been expected in late 1981.

The Directives Not Yet Formally Proposed

Of all the legislative proposals included in the company law harmonization program, the draft Ninth Directive, which concerns the organization of groups of companies, is, by general consensus, the most radical. Although no final text has yet been submitted by the Commission to the Council, the Commission's working draft, together with a lengthy analytical commentary, has been widely circulated in Europe since January 1981.[71]

The Ninth Directive would attempt to encourage parent companies to conclude "control contracts" with their subsidiaries. A control contract— a creature known only to German law and not widely seen even in the Federal Republic[72]—is an agreement whereby the parent guarantees certain obligations of the subsidiary vis-a-vis third parties, such as employees, creditors, and minority shareholders. Control contracts are designed to protect third parties against default by a subsidiary, by requiring the parent to issue certain guarantees in exchange for the right of management. Minimum capitalization requirements for the dependent company are normally waived, because an injured third party would have recourse to the parent's assets.

The debate over the Ninth Directive has so far been characterized by the absence of public statements of strong support for the initiative. Unlike other parts of the company law harmonization program, it has received little support even from the trade unions.[73] Because parent companies have not, in the past, manifested any pattern of willingness to tolerate defaults by their subsidiaries, it is not likely that control contracts would reduce the frequency or mitigate the effects of such defaults.

Opponents of the Ninth Directive have objected vehemently to many of its provisions.[74] The greatest amount of criticism has been directed at the means it uses to coax companies toward the control contract model.

Since the purpose of control contracts is to provide a form of guarantee by the parent company of certain of its subsidiary's obligations, the Commission draft legislates comparable guarantee where the control contract has not been used. The draft provides that when management undertakes actions that inure to the detriment of the subsidiary, not only is the parent company liable to those who may be injured, but the members of the parent's board must bear joint and several unlimited liability. That a decision affecting the subsidiary may substantially benefit other companies in the same group is not a defense. Nor is directors' liability in any way conditioned upon their failure to meet any recognized standard of prudence or of business judgment.[75] Thus, under the Ninth Directive, foreign multinationals would confront an impossible dilemma: either to elect the unfamiliar and cumbersome control contract, or to submit their directors to potential personal liability. Neither option is palatable; nor, on the available evidence, is the need to make such a choice in any way justified.

Other Ninth Directive requirements are equally extraordinary. The draft requires public notice whenever blocks of shares in companies are acquired by other enterprises,[76] and periodic reports detailing all activities undertaken by a subsidiary for the benefit of its parent, including actions which have failed to benefit the subsidiary. A shareholder, creditor, or employees' representative may protest any notice or report, and may call for an independent audit to be conducted at the company's expense. Should the auditor—who has subpoena authority—uncover allegations that the subsidiary has been "influenced" and thereby "damaged," the courts would have authority to prevent or mitigate the damage by a variety of means, including suspending directors or issuing injunctions against further "damaging measures."[77] The only way for a company to avoid these results would be to institute a control contract form of organization.

The Directive purports to guarantee the position of minority shareholders, by assuring them of the right to be bought out, either in cash or through annual "equalization payments," based upon estimated future earnings.[78] All calculations of proper values to be offered may be challenged in litigation, which may result in an injunction against the proposed valuation or transaction, and/or the removal of the board members.

The Ninth Directive is aimed, as some would argue the entire harmonization project is aimed, at the decentralization of corporate management. Its language is facially inconsistent with the obligation of a board of directors to defend the interests of its company or group of companies, an obligation upheld by the French courts, for example, in *Fruehauf Corporation* v. *Massardy*.[79] In *Fruehauf*, the *Cour d'appel* of Paris sharply delineated the overriding responsibility of directors to their company in ordering a

French subsidiary of a U.S. company to perform a contract allegedly barred under U.S. law. The court pointed to "the interests of the company rather than the personal interests of any shareholders even if they be the majority."[80] Indeed, the *Fruehauf* case, which concerned the application of the U.S. Trading with the Enemy Act of 1917, demonstrates that directors' obligations can differ even from the interests of the shareholders. Directors are obligated to act in a fiduciary capacity with respect to their company. As long as they act prudently and faithfully, they are protected from personal liability. Prudent and faithful directors may determine, and in some cases may even be required to determine, that one part of their company must be harmed in order to benefit the whole. Directors must be free to pursue the interests of the company, or group of companies, with whom they have assumed a fiduciary relationship.

The Ninth Directive was to be submitted by the Commission to the Council in the autumn of 1981. Because it has met a firestorm of opposition, mostly from European sources, the Directive has been so delayed that it has not yet been finalized. Rumors abound that the project has been returned to the Commission staff for substantive revision. The Ninth Directive is likely to be amended further before publication. It is of course possible that it will never be submitted, or that, after being issued by the Commission, it will be left in suspended animation as was the Fifth Directive. Nevertheless, that such a proposal has even been put forward is significant. EC institutions have demonstrated a willingness to propose fundamental changes in the operation of companies outside the Community, if they perceive such changes as somehow beneficial to companies within their jurisdiction. They are not seriously deterred by the doctrine of extraterritoriality, or by the charge that their proposed initiatives are impermissible according to principles of international law and comity.

An intelligent reaction to a proposal such as the Ninth Directive must include an acknowledgement that the EC is, at present, confronting an extraordinarily harsh economic and political climate. Unemployment has reached levels undreamed of since World War II and is continuing to climb. The voters of France and Greece have elected socialists as national leaders, and since January 1981, the governments of Ireland, Denmark, The Netherlands, Germany, Italy, and Belgium have fallen. The United Kingdom has once again vehemently protested what it sees as its excessive contribution to the Community in the annual budget review. In short, there are fundamental problems in maintaining the political and economic unity that has been attained by the European Community. It is not surprising, then, that EC officials may assign to the survival of the Community an importance greater than that given to traditional, and arguably outdated, precepts of corporate law.[81]

OTHER MEASURES RELATED TO COMPANY LAW HARMONIZATION

The Vredeling Proposal

More than any other EC initiative, the so-called Vredeling Proposal[82] has been responsible for the sudden increase in awareness in the United States of developments in European law. The Proposal is named for its originator, the Dutch Socialist Henk Vredeling, whose term as Commissioner for Employment and Social Affairs ended on December 31, 1980.[83] If adopted, the Vredeling Proposal would impose three distinct obligations upon multinational corporations operating in the European Community. First, MNCs would be required to provide workers' representatives, on a periodic basis, with "a clear picture of the activities of the dominant undertaking and its subsidiaries taken as a whole."[84] This "picture" must include information relating to matters described, all too vaguely, as "the economic and financial situation, . . . the employment situation and probable trends, [and] all procedures and plans liable to have a substantial effect on employees' interests." However difficult it may be to define these terms, what is actually to be disclosed under the Vredeling Proposal would certainly be subject to negotiation and compromise. Few companies would be unwilling to circulate an information sheet to their employees, describing in general terms the present state of the company and its plans for the future.

Second, the Vredeling Proposal would require disclosure of information to workers when "the management of a dominant undertaking proposes to make a decision concerning the whole or a major part of the dominant undertaking or of one of its subsidiaries which is likely to have a substantial effect on the interests of its employees." The parent company must disclose such information to the management of its subsidiary no less than forty days "before adopting the decision," and it must then be communicated "without delay" to employees' representatives whose opinion must be sought within thirty days. The disclosure must include the "grounds for the proposed decision," its consequences for employees, and "the measures planned in respect of" affected workers. Decisions triggering these obligations include plant closings or transfers, substantial "modifications" to a company's activities or to its organization, and the introduction or termination of cooperation with other enterprises.

According to the Commission draft, information about a decision must be disclosed, *before* a decision is formally adopted.[85] This poses a number of potential problems concerning the effect of such disclosure on competition and on share prices and, in the case of U.S. parent companies, raises the prospect that the "insider trading" rules of the Securities and Exchange Commission may be violated.[86] If management must disclose certain future plans to workers' representatives in the EC, this information might arguably be required to be publicly disseminated, in order to prevent its misuse.

Finally, the Vredeling Proposal would require that the consultations with workers' representatives be "with a view to reaching agreement on the measures planned in respect of them." It is unclear whether agreement must actually be reached, or just what is meant by the words "with a view to." Should the management of the subsidiary fail to carry out such consultations, employees' representatives would be authorized to consult with management of the parent.

The Vredeling Proposal would impose these requirements on parent companies located outside the EC as well as on EC companies. This, however, poses an enforcement dilemma. The EC's writ does not run outside its borders, and although foreign parents might comply voluntarily, provisions for sanctions against enterprises that do not comply might well not be recognized or enforced by non-EC authorities.[87]

The Commission's proposed solution to the problem of enforcement is the "hostage company" provision, which reads as follows:

> Where the management of the dominant undertaking whose decision-making centre is located outside the Community and which controls one or more subsidiaries in the community does not ensure the presence within the Community of a [sic] least one person able to fulfil the requirements as regards disclosure of information and consultation laid down by this Directive, the management of the subsidiary that employs the largest number of employees within the Community shall be responsible for fulfilling the obligations imposed on the management of the dominant undertaking by this Directive.[88]

Thus, while the information sought may be located outside the EC, the Vredeling Proposal would require enterprises within the Community to obtain and then to disclose it. By adopting this expedient, the EC would avoid imposing legal obligations directly upon foreign entities.

Even if the "hostage company" provision does succeed in restricting the Vredeling Proposal's legal obligations to European enterprises, the practical effect of the clause could be more far-reaching. A foreign parent would have two available options before making a decision subject to disclosure and consultation under the Proposal. The parent might designate a person in Europe to consult with workers' representatives, ensuring that this person has been fully briefed on the background of the decision, or it might communicate sufficient information to its largest subsidiary[89] to allow that company's management to conduct the required consultations.[90] In any event, however, the foreign parent must make significant decisions affecting its internal structure, including when and to whom potentially very sensitive information will be distributed within the company.

Although the dissemination of the information required by the Seventh Directive and under the periodic disclosure provisions of the Vredeling Proposal would probably not pose problems of sensitivity or confidentiality in the vast majority of cases, discussion of proposed decisions before they are adopted may threaten to compromise important corporate interests.[91] Not only would the security of potentially confidential future plans be in doubt but, in addition, all of the complex commercial and financial relations contingent upon the proper timing of public announcements would be at risk. It is not inconceivable that, under the Proposal, secret designs, marketing strategies, and information on new lines of business could be demanded by employees' representatives.

Many commentators have stressed that the Vredeling Proposal lacks the kind of protections for confidential information that would allow management to countenance its disclosure to workers' representatives. Those gaining access to such information are directed only to treat it with "discretion," and Member States may provide for "appropriate" penalties.[92] Industry spokesmen generally believe that this provision is inadequate, and some fear that confidential information might be held to ransom by trade union leaders. They note that should such information be disclosed, no sanction could restore their companies to the competitive position they would thereby have lost.

Another frequently voiced objection to the Vredeling Proposal concerns its relation to the Guidelines for Multinational Enterprises adopted by the Organization for Economic Cooperation and Development (OECD) on June 21, 1976, and to the "Declaration of Principles Concerning Multinational Enterprises and Social Policy" of the International Labor Organization (ILO). Both the OECD and ILO statements, adopted with the concurrence of the EC Member States, call for multinational companies to consult with their workers on a voluntary basis, with due consideration of questions of legality, competition, and the overall health of the enterprise.

U.S. business organizations have been in the forefront of those opposed to the Vredeling Proposal.[93] Their principal objections have been those outlined here: the competitive impact of premature disclosure, extraterritoriality, the inadequate protection of confidential data, inconsistency with other international agreements, and the practical difficulties with the disclosure and consultation requirements. They argue that such cumbersome obligations to disclose and consult over decisions of perhaps only tangential relevance to Europe can only make the EC a less attractive place for new or continued investment.

At the very least, they say, compliance with the Vredeling Proposal would be confusing and costly. The draft text of the Proposal does not indicate how to resolve conflicting views between workers' representatives in two Member States, or at two sites in the same State concerning a proposed decision. The Proposal fails to specify what, if any, remedies might be available to European workers who believe that a company's decision to open a plant in Brazil harms workers in Italy. It does not address the policies of companies which prefer in principle to make decisions at a low level of the corporate hierarchy, as close as possible to the workplace affected.

Perhaps all these criticisms are best summarized in the position paper of the National Foreign Trade Council: "More broadly, the directive would deter corporate management from innovative changes and initiatives, thereby reducing the productivity and competitiveness of European Community enterprises in comparison with companies in other parts of the world." Granting that such a concern on the part of U.S. industry is not wholly altruistic, neither is it entirely selfish. U.S. companies do, after all, have the option of doing business wherever they deem the atmosphere and opportunities most suitable and accommodating.

The Vredeling Proposal was sent to Parliament and ECOSOC in 1981, and three parliamentary committees reviewed it and prepared reports. The Committee on Social Affairs and Employment, which had primary responsibility, supported an amended version of the Vredeling Proposal.[94] Both the Commission text and the Committee's proposed revisions were laid before the plenary session of Parliament, meeting in Strasbourg in September 1982. The Members of the European Parliament tabled nearly 250 amendments in addition to those contained in the Committee report.

Parliament voted in September, after six hours of debate, to defer detailed review of the Proposal until the October session. In October, Parliament approved a text which contains some significant alterations to the original draft. These include, inter alia, the following:

1. the minimum size of an enterprise to "trigger" obligations under the Proposal would be 100 employees in a given EC facility *and* 1,000 employees in the group as a whole;
2. workers' representatives must be freely elected by the workforce;
3. in lieu of holding the largest EC subsidiary of a company "hostage," disclosure and consultation obligations would be imposed upon management of the local subsidiary affected by the decisions;
4. the scope of consultation obligations would be clarified;
5. it would be made clear that consultations are limited to the effects of a proposed decision on the workforce, and need not consider the decision itself;

6. it would limit the so-called "bypass" provisions that give EC workers' representatives access to the parent company's management, granting the right to make a written demand for information only when the subsidiary is unable to comply; and
7. it would exempt business and trade secrets, including information which could have an impact upon share prices, from mandatory disclosure.

The endorsement of such a text by Parliament did not, however, conclude its role in the legislative process. In October, Parliament pointedly declined to adopt a "motion for a resolution," the "vehicle" that transmits the text of a proposed directive to the Council and completes the consultation required under the Treaty of Rome.

Parliament's intention was to force Commissioner Richard to bring his revisions in draft back to Strasbourg, so that their conformity to the parliamentary amendments could be assessed. It invited Richard to attend the November session for this purpose. Tom Spencer, MEP, the rapporteur for the key parliamentary committee reporting on Vredeling, even threatened legal action were the Commission to place before the Council a version different from that recommended by Parliament. The weight of this argument was borne by the slender constitutional reed of the Treaty requirement that Parliament be consulted before the directive may be adopted.[95]

At the November session, Richard arrived with a policy statement accepting most of the proposed changes, but Spencer and his colleagues were able to keep the motion for a resolution off the floor. They sought the unprecedented appearance of a Commissioner ready to commit his support to the specific text endorsed by Parliament, with a promise that any deviation would be submitted for parliamentary review.

Hardly surprisingly, this gambit failed. At its session of December 1982, Parliament was again asked by Richard to free its hostage by adopting the motion for a resolution. Richard committed himself publicly, on behalf of the Commission, to incorporating at least some of the parliamentary amendments. He would not agree, however, to mandatory free elections of representatives from among the workforce, or to the exclusive right of management to define confidentiality. He also insisted that the text make clear the right of representatives to consult before a decision is adopted, and not just before it is implemented.[96] Richard would not accept Parliament's insistence that its version be controlling. To do so, the Commissioner argued, would be to subordinate his constitutional role to that of Parliament.

Richard had suggested in November that he prepare a new complete draft of the Vredeling Proposal by the first quarter of 1983. It was widely expected that at the December session in Strasbourg, Parliament would defer further action on the motion for a resolution until Richard's revision could be analyzed.[97]

These predictions were incorrect. On December 14, 1982, Parliament adopted the motion for a resolution,[98] transmitting its advice on the Vredeling Proposal to the Council and terminating its constitutional role with respect to the Proposal.[99] The new Commission text is anticipated in March or April 1983, and that text will be referred to the Council working party, to COREPER, and finally to the Ministers themselves, for further modification and eventual adoption.

As in the case of the Ninth Directive, it is necessary for persons of all ideological persuasions to see the Vredeling Proposal in the appropriate context. Plant closings have been a serious problem in several European countries. Unemployment is reaching catastrophic proportions. The national legal systems of the Member States have been inadequate to prevent these problems. Whether the Vredeling Proposal in any form would ameliorate these conditions is uncertain. What is certain, however, is that there is a very significant movement in Europe which firmly believes that it would.

The debate over the Vredeling Proposal has significant political implications as well. It would be extremely impolitic, given the economic climate, for the EC to deny the trade union movement any remedial measures that might protect jobs. To do so would be to increase the alienation of labor from Community institutions, and to stiffen the resolve of opposition to membership in the EC among such groups as the British Labour Party.

Charter of the "Societas Europea"

In 1970, the EC Commission proposed a regulation recognizing a new form of corporate organization, to be called the "Societas Europea" (S.E.).[100] This proposal has provoked considerable academic discussion in Europe and the United States, but the political process has moved slowly. Parliament has not given its opinion, and the regulation is probably years away from enactment.[101]

The draft S.E. Charter presents in microcosm many of the concerns seen in the company law harmonization program. It calls for a two-tier board,[102] with worker participation in the supervisory board, comprising, in equal numbers, shareholder representatives, employee representatives, and representatives of "general interests." It regulates company "groups," defined in terms of actual control even in the absence of equity ownership,[103] and would protect outside shareholders and creditors in the manner of the proposed Ninth Directive.[104] As the regulation is currently drafted, non-EC companies could not create a Societas Europea, although their EC subsidiaries could. There would, however, be special guarantees imposed for the protection of outside shareholders when ultimate control of the S.E. was outside the Community.[105]

The S.E. would be no more than an option available for doing business in Europe. It is envisaged as a kind of "federal corporation," designed to have the maximum flexibility in cross-border dealings within the Community. Such flexibility would endow S.E. companies with a significant advantage, and therefore, non-European industry should carefully follow the emergence of the S.E. concept. Also, because of the similarities between the S.E. charter and the company law harmonization program, developments with respect to the former illustrate the concerns and objectives of EC officials with respect to the harmonization program as a whole.

CONCLUSION

It is essential for non-European business interested in the European Community to see what the company law harmonization program is, and also what it is not. The program is conceived as a comprehensive attempt to protect workers, creditors, minority shareholders, and the public against certain risks arising from the conduct of corporations. It is not the opening salvo of a socialist revolution or of major economic warfare with the United States.

Many commentators, including the author of this article, believe that the proposals currently under consideration suffer from serious defects, both in their drafting and in their underlying principles. Many argue that the proposals are inadequately designed to achieve their stated objectives, and that they will neither provide the desired security nor, ultimately, increase employment or economic welfare.

Certainly investment relations between the United States and the EC are not now at their best. Charges and counter-charges of impermissible extraterritorial jurisdiction are frequent. The United Kingdom's Protection of Trading Interests Act 1980,[106] and France's Loi No. 80-538,[107] have been enacted specifically to limit the effect of U.S. antitrust laws overseas.[108] Prompted in large part by the Vredeling Proposal, Representative Thomas Luken (D-Ohio) and Senator Steven Symms (R-Idaho) introduced bills in the U.S. Congress, patterned after the U.K. law, to protect U.S. companies from allegedly extraterritorial EC legislation.[109] The Luken and Symms Bills, both entitled "The Protection of Confidential Business Information Act," would require or permit U.S. businesses subject to foreign regulations that compel disclosure to protect the information sought if it is in fact confidential.[110] The two bills are retaliatory legislation, in that, if either were enacted and had its provisions triggered by a demand for disclosure under the Vredeling Proposal, U.S. and Member State government agencies would immediately be at loggerheads. U.S. companies would, under certain circumstances at least, be directed by U.S. law not to comply with obligations apparently imposed upon them by European law. The probable resolution of such a conflict is difficult to determine.

In addition, the 97th Congress was confronted with several bills to reform section 301 of the Trade Act of 1974,[111] and these are likely to be resubmitted. Some of these proposals[112] would enable the President to retaliate against foreign unfair investment practices or against the failure of foreign nations to observe reciprocity in their treatment of investments by U.S. nationals. At least one has been expressly linked by its sponsors to the Vredeling Proposal and other EC initiatives.[113]

Despite these attempts to retaliate in kind against what may be perceived as over-regulation of business outside national boundaries, it is probable that the European legislative project will continue. The introduction of bills in Congress, however, may well serve the critical function of directing the focus of policymakers on both sides of the Atlantic to the international, and essentially the bilateral, character of the company law harmonization program. U.S. business, with $80 billion invested in Europe, is a major constituent of any program that is responsible for the economic future of the Community.

Resolution of differences of opinion on a bilateral basis will include many aspects: diplomatic contacts between U.S. and EC officials at the appropriate working levels; ready accessibility between EC policymakers and foreign business representatives; maximum transparency of the EC legislative process; and the elimination of harsh rhetoric that inflames passions and dulls reasoning. Non-Europeans must be aware of the important economic and political considerations that underlie the harmonization program; Europeans must recognize that the creation of an atmosphere hostile to business would destroy the kind of society that the program is apparently designed to create.[114] Each side must be far more receptive to, and understanding of, the legitimate concerns of the other. Such understanding is, after all, the very essence of cooperation, and if the United States cannot cooperate with its oldest and closest allies, the economic future of the Western Alliance seems grim indeed.

NOTES

1. Treaty establishing the European Economic Community, *done* Mar. 25, 1957, art. 85, 298 U.N.T.S. 3 [hereinafter Treaty of Rome]. This article uses the term "European Com-

munity" or "EC" in accordance with the resolution of the European Parliament urging the adoption of that nomenclature. Resolution of February 16, 1978, 21 O.J. EUR. COMM. (No. C 63) 36 (1978). In July, 1967, the substantive duties of the three councils and Commissions of the "Common Market"—the European Economic Community (EEC), the European Atomic Energy Community (EURATOM), and the European Coal and Steel Community (ECSC)— were combined and vested in the newly created Commission of the European Communities. Treaty Instituting a Single Council and a Single Commission of the European Community, Apr. 8, 1965, art. 9, 10 O.J. EUR. COMM. (No. C 152) 2 (1967). For all practical purposes, the three Communities now share all of their institutions and have become a single entity.

2. The six original Member States were Belgium, the Federal Republic of Germany, France, Italy, Luxembourg, and The Netherlands. On January 1, 1973, Denmark, the Republic of Ireland, and the United Kingdom joined the Community. Greece became the tenth member on January 1, 1981. Spain and Portugal are scheduled to join, possibly as early as 1985.

3. There is one notable exception to this generalization. The development of EC antitrust law, pursuant to the Treaty of Rome, arts. 85, 86, received considerable attention in this country. See, e.g., HAWK, UNITED STATES, COMMON MARKET, AND INTERNATIONAL ANTITRUST: A COMPARATIVE GUIDE, chs. 7–13 (1981).

4. Treaty of Rome, art. 54, para 3(g). Perhaps the most immediate consideration behind this provision was that Member States would find it difficult to remove the traditional restrictions or special formalities imposed upon foreign companies and to admit and treat them as domestic companies unless they met certain standards with respect to the protection of their creditors and shareholders.

5. Article 54(2) states:

> In order to implement this general programme, or in the absence of such programme, in order to achieve a stage in attaining freedom of establishment as regards a particular activity, the Council shall, on a proposal from the Commission and after consulting the Economic and Social Committee and the [Parliament] issue directives, acting . . . by a qualified majority.

6. Treaty of Rome, art. 189. By contrast, a "regulation" is of direct effect and is legally binding in its entirety. Verbond Van Nederlandes Ondernemingen v. Inspecteur der Invoerrechten en Accijnzen, 1977 E. Comm. Ct. J. Rep. 113, 1977 Comm. Mkt. L.R. 413. See also Van Gend en Loos v. Nederlandse Administratie der Belastingen, 1963 E. Comm. Ct. J. Rep. 1, 1963 Comm. Mkt. L.R. 105.

7. The independence of Commission members and their staffs from Member State influence is established in the Merger Treaty, supra note 1, art. 10(2).

8. Since June 1979, the citizens of the Member States have directly elected the members of the Parliament. See 19 O.J. EUR. COMM. (No. L 278) 1 (1976).

9. The Economic and Social Committee has advisory status, representing employees, workers, and various professional and consumer interests. The Committee's 156 members, appointed for four year terms, have jurisdiction over, inter alia, approximation of laws, art. 100, labor, art. 49, social issues, art. 63, and the right of establishment, art. 52.

10. In practice, the day-to-day work of COREPER is conducted at the level of the members' deputies. The actual decision making, however, cannot be delegated to COREPER. The power of the final decision remains in the hands of the politically "responsible" Council of Ministers. With the exception of the Permanent Mission of Luxembourg, which consists of three persons, each Permanent Mission maintains a staff of 25 officials drawn mostly from the Ministries of Foreign Affairs, but also including officials on detached service from Ministries of Economic Affairs, Finance, and others.

11. The Merger Treaty provides only that the Council include "members" of the Governments of the Member States. The Council of Ministers should not be confused with the "European Council," consisting of the ten Prime Ministers, or with the Council of Europe, another organization altogether.

12. The Treaty of Rome authorizes the adoption of company law harmonization directives on the basis of a qualified majority. The qualified majority system is designed to require that a proposal obtain the assent of at least two of the four larger members (France, Germany, Italy, and the United Kingdom), but that those four must be joined by at least one smaller Member State for a proposal to be passed. *See* K. SIMMONDS, B2 ENCYCLOPEDIA OF EUR. COMMUNITY L. ¶ B10-337 (1973).

Since the adoption of the Luxembourg Compromise in 1966, however, the Council defers a vote in the absence of unanimity. The Luxembourg Compromise directs the Council to reach unanimous agreement on any issue as to which it is represented that "very important interests of one or more Members are at stake." Extraordinary Session of the Council (January 1966): Second part of the session (28 and 29 January 1966), 3-1966 BULL. OF THE EUR. ECON. COMMUNITY 5, 8 (1966). Although the Luxembourg Compromise has no legal effect, the practice of the Council since 1966 has been to require unanimous approval of most significant decisions.

Recently, however, the Luxembourg Compromise itself has again become an object of controversy. Angered over the refusal of the Council to revise its budget contribution, the United Kingdom attempted to veto the annual farm price review in the spring of 1982. Invocation of the Compromise was ruled out of order, and the council proceeded to adopt the Commission proposals on a qualified majority basis.

The Treaty explicitly requires unanimous adoption decisions affecting the basic structure of the Community, such as admission of new members.

13. *See, e.g.,* Comm'n of the Eur. Communities v. Italian Republic, 1980 E. Comm. Ct. J. Rep. 3635 (Italy's failure to implement a Council Directive on the approximation of laws, relating to the certification and marketing of wire-ropes, chains and hooks, constituted a failure to comply with an obligation incumbent upon it under the Treaty); Comm'n of the Eur. Communities v. Kingdom of Belgium, 1980 E. Comm. Ct. J. Rep. 1473 (Belgium's failure to implement a series of directives on the approximation of laws relating to type-approval of motor vehicles and of agricultural tractors, constituted a failure to fulfill its obligations under the Treaty).

14. The Commission's Rules of Procedure require that meetings of the Commission be closed to the public, and that all discussions be confidential. R. P. COMM'N, ch. 1, art. 8, 6–17 J.O. COMM. EUR. 181/63 (1963), 1974 O.J. EUR. COMM. 11 (special ed., 2d series).

15. Rule 89 of the European Parliament's Rules of Procedure requires the publication of the minutes of parliamentary proceedings in the *Official Journal of the European Communities*. In the past, Parliament's committees traditionally met in private. Since direct election of the Parliament in June of 1979, however, the public has been admitted to some committee meetings. A number of committees have organized public hearings to obtain the testimony of expert witnesses, or have routinely opened their doors to the public. *See* M. PALMER, THE EUROPEAN PARLIAMENT 87 (1981).

16. *See* Ficker, *The EEC Directives on Company Law Harmonization*, in HARMONIZATION OF EUROPEAN COMPANY LAW 66 (C. Schmitthoff ed. 1973) (descriptive analysis of the various company law directives proposed as of 1973).

17. The basic policy of the EC regarding company laws and multinational enterprise was enunciated in a 1973 Commission report. *Multinational Undertakings and Community Regulations*, BULL. OF THE EUR. COMMUNITIES, SUPP. 15/73 (1973) (communication from the Commission to the Council). HARMONIZATION OF EUROPEAN COMPANY LAWS: NATIONAL REFORM AND TRANSNATIONAL COORDINATION (1971).

On the subject of EC harmonization generally, see STEIN; THE HARMONIZATION OF EURO-PEAN COMPANY LAW (C. Schmitthoff ed. 1973); Berger, *Harmonization of Company Law under the Common Market Treaty,* 4 CREIGHTON L. REV. 205 (1971); Schmitthoff, *The Success of the Harmonisation of European Company Law,* 1 EUR. L. REV 100 (1976); Silkenat, *Efforts Toward Harmonization of Business Laws Within the European Economic Community,* 12 INT'L LAW. 835 (1978); Stein, *Assimilation of National Laws as a Function of European Integration,* 58 AM. J. INT'L L. 1 (1964).

18. First Council Directive of 9 March 1968 on coordination of safeguards which, for the protection of the interests of members and others, are required by Member States of companies within the meaning of the second paragraph of Article 58 of the Treaty, with a view to making such safeguards equivalent throughout the Community, 1968(I) O.J. EUR. COMM. (No. L 65) 41 (special ed.)

19. The First Directive specifies the types of company organizations in each Member State to which the Directive applies and includes most of the common forms: the French, Belgian, and Luxembourgeois societe anonyme (S.A.), the German Aktiengesellschaft (A.G.) and Gesellschaft mit beschraenkter Haftung (G.m.b.H.), the Italian societa per azioni (S.p.A.), and the Dutch and Belgian naamloze vennootschap (N.V.). It also includes forms akin to the U.S. limited partnership. Upon accession of the United Kingdom and Ireland, most companies of limited liability in those countries were also included. For country-by-country discussions of the various forms of business organizations in the EC, see DOING BUSINESS IN EUROPE, COMMON MKT. REP. (CCH).

20. Such acts include transfer of corporate headquarters, dissolution, certain judicial decisions, and details concerning liquidation.

21. All documents and particulars subject to the disclosure requirements of the Directive must be kept in a file in a central register, commercial register, or companies register. Such information must also be published in the national gazette. Copies of the documents may be obtained at cost by written application.

22. The First Directive mandates the imposition of joint and several liability upon persons who act in the name of a company before the company has acquired legal personality, unless otherwise agreed.

23. The First Directive states that acts by the company shall be binding upon it "even if those acts are not within the objects of the company, unless such acts exceed the powers that the law confers or allows to be conferred on those organs." The Directive, however, allows Member States to hold such acts not binding upon the company where the third party knew or should have known of their ultra vires character.

24. Where the law of the Member State allows a third party to challenge the decision of nullity, the Directive requires that the third party do so within six months of public notice of the decision.

25. The Directive states that nullity "shall not of itself affect the validity of any commitments entered into by or with the company without prejudice to the consequences of the company's being wound up."

26. Second Council Directive of 13 December 1976 on coordination of safeguards which, for the protection of the interests of members and others, are required by Member States of companies within the meaning of the second paragraph of article 58 of the Treaty, in respect of the formation of public limited liability companies and the maintainance and alteration of their capital, with a view to making such safeguards equivalent. 20 O.J. EUR. COMM. (No. L 26) 1 (1977).

27. The Second Directive sets a minimum capital requirement of 25,000 European units of account (EUA) for a company to be incorporated or to obtain authorization to commence business. If the equivalent of the European unit of account in national currency is altered so that the value of the minimum capital in national currency remains less than

22,500 European units of account for a period of one year, the Commission will order the Member State to amend its legislation to comply with the 25,000 EUA standard within one year. The Directive provides for the periodic review of the minimum level required, in light of economic and monetary trends in the Community.

28. The Second Directive required implementation by the Member States within two years of its adoption, *i.e.*, by December 13, 1978. The Directive provided, however, longer time limits in certain specified cases, such as application of particular provisions to companies already in existence, and application to unregistered companies in the United Kingdom and Ireland.

29. Third Council Directive of 9 October 1978 based on article 54(3)(g) of the Treaty concerning mergers of public limited liability companies. 21 O.J. EUR. COMM. (No. L 295) 36 (1978).

30. This is the first use of Article 54(3)(g) of the Treaty of Rome specifically to protect employees, although the language appears neither to contemplate nor to preclude such use.

31. The Third Directive required implementation by the Member States within three years of its adoption. It provided exceptions to this time limit, however, in certain specified cases, such as application to unregistered companies in the United Kingdom and Ireland, and application of particular provisions to certain holders of convertible debentures and convertible securities.

32. Fourth Council Directive of 25 July 1978 based on article 54(3)(g) of the Treaty of the annual accounts of certain types of companies. 21 O.J. EUR. COMM. (No. L 222) 1 (1978).

33. As of April 1982, the United Kingdom, Belgium, the Netherlands and Denmark had enacted implementing legislation.

34. "The Member States may authorize or require the disclosure in the annual accounts of other information as well as that which must be disclosed in accordance with the directive."

35. Article 2, paragraph 3 provides: "The annual accounts shall give a true and fair view of the company's assets, liabilities, financial position and profit or loss." Paragraphs 4 and 5 cover the circumstances in which compliance with other provisions of the directive is incompatible with or insufficient to meet the requirement of paragraph 3. Where the provisions are found not to be sufficient to give a true and fair view, additional information must be given. Where a provision is incompatible with the presentation of a true and fair view, that provision must be departed from. Departure from the provisions must be noted and explanations offered for both the reasons for the departure and its effects on assets, liabilities, financial position and profit or loss. Thus, the true and fair view requirement has precedence over the other provisions of the Directive.

36. Tax laws in several Member States require that annual accounts reflect some balance sheet and profit-and-loss account items in accordance with specific requirements of their tax treatment rather than in accordance with generally accepted accounting principles. *See* M. CLAYTON, D. COMM & J. HINTON, HANDBOOK ON THE EEC FOURTH DIRECTIVE 4 (1979). To mitigate any impairment of a true and fair view caused by use of different accounting systems, the Directive requires disclosure of the effects of using tax-based valuation rules on the accounts.

37. Section 2 of the Directive, which includes articles 3–5, is entitled "General provision concerning the balance sheet and the profit and loss account;" section 3, articles 8–14, covers "Layout of the balance sheet;" section 4, articles 15–21, sets out "Special provisions relating to certain balance sheet items;" section 5, articles 22–27, covers "Layout of the profit and loss account;" section 6, articles 28–30, contains "Special provisions relating to certain items in the profit and loss account;" section 8, articles 43–45, comprises "Contents of the notes on account;" section 9, article 46, is entitled "Contents of the annual report;" section 10, articles 47–50, deals with "Publication;" and section 11, article 51, concerns "Auditing."

38. The Directive details reporting and disclosure requirements. It does not seek to change the tax law of any Member State; rather, it attempts to have a true and fair view presented even where different tax accounting systems are used. *See* arts. 2, 9, 10, 23–26, 30, 33, para. 2(a), 43, para. 1(10).

39. Article 27 provides: "The Member States may permit companies which on their balance sheet dates do not exceed the limits of two of the three following criteria: (1) balance sheet total: 4 million EUA, (2) net turnover: 8 million EUA, [or] (3) average number of employees during the financial year: 250, to adopt [simplified layout requirements]."

40. Article 57, paragraph 1, provides that "[u]ntil the entry into force of a Council Directive on consolidated accounts . . . the Member States need not apply to the dependent companies of any group governed by their national laws of the provisions of this Directive concerning the content, auditing and publication of the annual accounts of such dependent companies [under certain conditions]." Similarly, article 58 provides an exemption with respect to the auditing and publication of the profit-and-loss accounts of such dominant companies.

The Seventh Directive would govern preparation of, *inter alia*, accounts and annual reports of groups much as the Fourth Directive does for individual companies. Proposal for a Seventh Directive pursuant to Article 54(3)(g) of the EEC Treaty concerning group accounts (submitted to the Council by the Commission on 4 May 1976), 19 O.J. EUR. COMM. (No. C 121) 2 (1976) [hereinafter Proposed Seventh Directive].

41. The Directive lists exactly what types of companies are covered by it in each of the Member States.

42. The Fourth Directive expressly applies only to certain listed "types" of companies. All these "types" include only enterprises organized under the laws of one of the Member States. For instance, companies covered in the United Kingdom are "public companies limited by shares or by guarantee [and] private companies limited by shares or by guarantee." By contrast, draft versions of the Seventh Directive would assign certain consolidation and disclosure obligations regarding the "dominant undertakings" of EC companies, whatever their form and whatever the system of law that governs their incorporation or operations.

43. *See, e.g.*, 17 C.F. R. § 210 (1981) (form and content requirements for financial statements required by U.S. securities laws).

44. Council Directive of 17 March 1980 coordinating the requirements for the drawing up, scrutiny, and distribution of the listing particulars to be published for the admission of securities to official stock exchange listing, 23 O.J. EUR. COMM. (No. 1 100) 1 (1980). Since the adoption of this Directive, there has been a redesignation of certain parts of the harmonization program. A directive on scissions (that is, splitting of limited liability companies) has been redesignated as the Sixth Directive. It is generally "the opposite side of the coin" from the Third Directive on mergers, and was adopted in December 1982. 25 O.J. EUR. COMM. (No. L 378) (1982).

45. Proposal for a fifth directive to coordinate safeguards which, for the protection of the interests of members and others, are required by Member States of companies within the meaning of the second paragraph of article 58 of the Treaty, as regards the structure of societes anonymes and the powers and obligations of their organs, 15 O.J. EUR. COMM. (No. C 131) 49 (1972). For a discussion and analysis of the Fifth Directive, see Comm'n of the Eur. Communities, *Proposal for a Fifth Directive on The Structure of Societes Anonymes*, 32 BULL. E.C., 1 (Supp. 10 1972) (article by article analysis of the Fifth Directive); Conlon, *Industrial Democracy and EEC Company Law: A Review of the Draft Fifth Directive*, 24 INT'L & COMP. L.Q. 348 (1975) (describing influence of German company kawa); Lang, *The Fifth: EEC Directive on the Harmonization of Company Law*, 12 Common Mkt. L.R. 155, 325 (1975) (discussing Fifth Directive in relation to British and Irish law).

In May 1982 Parliament completed its deliberations on the proposed Fifth Directive.

The parliamentary text suggested that numerous amendments to the Commission version. Its thrust is to eliminate the mandatory character of the original proposal so that, for example, unitary boards will still be permissible in countries, such as Ireland and the United Kingdom, where they have been the tradition. The impact of Parliament's text on multinationals headquartered outside the EC is still unclear. 25 O.J. EUR. COMM. (No. C 149) 17 (1982).

46. *See* Ottervanger & Pais, *Employee Participation in Corporate Decision Making*, 15 INT'L. LAW. 393, 398 (1981). The Fifth Directive would apply only to certain types of companies in the Member States, *e.g.*, in Germany, the Aktiengesellschaft, in Belgium, France, and Luxembourg, the societe anonyme, in Italy, the societa per azioni, and in Belgium and The Netherlands, the naamloze vennootschap.

47. Note that this analysis is based on the Commission's proposed text, and not that recommended by Parliament. The Commission is expected to respond formally to the latter in early 1983.

48. An alternate approach under the Fifth Directive for companies with 500 or more employees is to allow the supervisory organ to appoint its own members subject to objection by the general meeting or representatives of the workers on the grounds that the appointee lacks the ability to carry out his duties or that a particular appointment would cause an imbalance in the composition of the supervisory organ with regards to the interests of the company, the shareholders or the workers.

49. As long ago as Lord Coke, it was well established that a corporation was a company of persons "made into one body," and, at least in legal fiction, manifesting a single identity. The Case of Sutton's Hospital, 10 Co. Rep. 32b. U.S. law similarly views the corporate form not as a forum for exchange of social views but as a legal entity, existing for the purposes set out in its charter. *See* Dartmouth College v. Woodward, 17 U.S. (4 Wheat.) 518, 636 (1819).

50. The so-called Caborn Report was adopted by Parliament on April 15, 1981, notwithstanding Parliament's right-of-center majority. *Report on Enterprises and Governments in International Economic Activity,* [1981–82] EUR. PARL. DOC. No. 1–169.

51. 25 O.J. EUR. COMM. (No. C 149) 17, 44 (1982).

52. Proposed Seventh Directive, *supra* note 40.

53. 21 O.J. EUR. COMM. (No. C 163) 60 (1978). Parliament suggested that the Seventh Directive be changed. In particular, it urged the adoption of the worldwide consolidation option for non-EC parents, and the deletion of obligations to publish subgroup consolidations when the dominant undertaking itself must publish a consolidated report.

54. 20 O.J. EUR. COMM. (No. C 75) 5 (1977). ECOSOC, like Parliament, endorsed the draft "in principle" but proposed numerous technical and textual changes.

55. 22 O.J. EUR. COMM (No. C 14) 2 (1979).

56. The preamble to the Amended Proposed Seventh Directive recites that "annual accounts of companies belonging to a group cannot by themselves give a true and fair view of their position."

57. *See* American Chamber of Commerce in Belgium, Memorandum on the Amended Proposal for a Seventh Directive Pursuant to Article 54(3)(g) of the EEC Treaty Concerning Group Accounts, Sept. 13, 1979. The Chamber asserted that the requirement for Community consolidations will present an "unacceptable burden" to groups dominated by non-EC companies, and questioned the ultimate usefulness of the information required. *See also* National Foreign Trade Council, Inc., Comments on Proposed Seventh Directive Pursuant to Article 54(3)(g) of the EEC Treaty Concerning Group Accounts, Apr. 14, 1980. The National Foreign Trade Council asserted that the proposed reporting requirement, insofar as it related to non-EC based multinationals, was deficient in two major respects: the envisaged consolidations would fail in certain circumstances to reflect economic reality; and developing the necessary information would present substantial technical accounting difficulties.

58. Under the Treaty of Rome, the Member States would be free to select the "forms and methods" of achieving the directive's "result." It is unlikely that the European Court would hold Member State legislation which required information substantially different from that included in a Form 10-K to be an abuse of that freedom.

59. If it is within the sovereign authority of a Member State to enact legislation in response to a Community directive, it must be within that State's authority to enact such legislation on its own initiative. The Treaty of Rome does not expand the Member States' legal powers to regulate trade or business within their own borders, or with respect to their own citizens.

60. SEC filing requirements, for example, are not generally applicable to privately-held companies but are triggered by the number of a company's shareholders. *See* 15 U.S.C. § 78 1(g) (1976).

61. *See* H. HENN, HANDBOOK OF THE LAW OF CORPORATIONS (1961). A parent corporation and its subsidiary are generally treated as separate and distinct entities, even if the parent owns all the shares in the subsidiary and the two enterprises share directors and officers.

62. Of course, it may object if it is required to translate the language or the currency of the form. Whether such translation might be required is unclear.

63. See the discussion of the territorial and nationality principles in Jacobs, *Extraterritorial Application of Competition Laws: An English View*, 13 INT'L LAW. 645, 647 (1979). It is arguable that the Seventh Directive contravenes these principles since the information sought is located outside the EC and no one in the community has a legal *right* of access to it. Those who allege that the Directive operates extraterritorially assert that any "direct effects" in Europe caused by multinational companies are produced through EC subsidiaries which are themselves already subject to the Fourth Directive.

64. Judge Learned Hand formulated the "direct effects" doctrine in U.S. law: "It is settled law . . . that any state may impose liabilities, even upon persons not within its allegiance, for conduct outside its borders which the state reprehends." United States v. Aluminum Co. of Am. 148 F.2d 416, 443 (2d Cir. 1945). Some U.S. courts first balance matters of comity before examining the directness of effects on the United States. *E.g.,* Mannington Mills v. Congoleum Corp., 595 F.2d 1287, 1297–98 (3d Cir. 1979). *See generally* H. STEINER & D. VAGTS. TRANSNATIONAL LEGAL PROBLEMS 932–1085 (2d ed. 1976); Garvey, *The Foreign Trade Antitrust Improvements Act of 1981*, 14 LAW & POL'Y INT'L. BUS. 1 (1982); Note, *Antitrust Law: Extraterritoriality* 20 HARV. INT'L L.J. 667, 670 (1979). For a discussion of EC law, *see* STEINER & VAGTS, *supra*, at 1394–1405, 1417–19; Imperial Chemical Industries Ltd. v. Commission of the European Communities, 1972 E. Comm. Ct. J. Rep. 619, 11 Common. Mkt. L.R. 557 (EC formulation of the "direct effects" doctrine is applied.)

65. Karl Gleichman, head of the EC Commission's multinationals department said that it was "curious to see Americans complaining about the extraterritoriality of laws. Often, it is precisely this aspect of U.S. antitrust rules which other countries complain about." Int'l Herald Tribune, Oct. 27, 1981, at 11, col. 1.

The United Kingdom and France have recently enacted legislation to combat the allegedly impermissible extraterritorial effect of U.S. antitrust laws. *See* Herzog, *The 1980 French Law on Documents and Information*, 75 AM. J. INT'L L. 382 (1981); Love, *Blocking Extraterritorial Jurisdiction: The British Protection of Trading Interests Act, 1980*, 75 AM. J. INT'L L. 257 (1981); Pettit & Styles, *The International Response to the Extraterritorial Application of U.S. Antitrust Laws*, 37 BUS. LAW. 697 (1982).

66. Senator Symms apparently perceived such distrust when he introduced "a bill to provide protection from requirements and prohibitions imposed upon citizens of the U.S. by foreign nations concerning the disclosure of confidential business information and for other purposes." S. 1592, 97th Cong., 1st Sess. 1, 127 CONG. REC. S9230 (daily ed. Aug. 3, 1981).

The Senator said that "the European institutions are trying to compel U.S. companies to make public and ultimately to subject to European control their every move—worse, their every contemplated move." 127 CONG. REC. S9230 (daily ed. Aug. 3, 1981) (remarks of Sen. Symms).

67. The unpublished final draft of the EC Council Working Party, art. 7a, para. 4(a) (Aug. 1981) substituted the word "equivalent" for the word "comparable" used in the Amended Proposed Seventh Directive.

68. Recent unofficial reports indicate that the COREPER working group may decide to delete article 7a, which would have affected EC subsidiaries of foreign parents. The committee is said to have removed the obligation of publishing "artificial horizontal subgroup consolidations" by companies which are not actually managed by—or in conjunction with—other enterprises in the EC. If independent subsidiaries of non-EC parents are exempted, the option of producing parents' worldwide accounts falls as well, since it was offered as a facility for complying with the EC consolidation requirement. Only foreign companies actually managing groups from within the EC would be affected by the remaining requirement of vertical consolidation.

If these reports are correct, the most likely result would appear to be that subsidiaries of foreign parents must annotate their Fourth Directive accounts to reflect intra-corporate transactions, including the sharing of overhead and expenses. Exactly what would be included in such annotations is still extremely unclear.

69. Amended Proposal for an Eighth Directive founded on Article 54(3)(g) of the EEC Treaty concerning the approval of persons responsible for carrying out statutory audits of the annual accounts of certain types of company, 25 O.J. EUR. COMM. (No. C317) 6 (1979).

70. The Eighth Directive does not go as far as "the effective exercise by lawyers of freedom to provide services," which permits lawyers to practice anywhere in the EC. Council Directive of Mar. 22, 1977, 20 O.J. EUR. COMM. (No. 1, 78) 17, art. 1 (1977).

71. Proposal for a Ninth Directive Based on Article 54(3)(g) of the EEC Treaty on Links Between Undertakings, and in Particular on Groups. From time to time, revisions of certain articles also have been circulated.

72. For an analysis of the German Aktien Gesetz of 1965, see Matomura, *Protecting Outside Shareholders in a Corporate Subsidiary: A Comparative Look at the Private and Judicial Roles in the United States and Germany,* 1980 WIS. L. REV. 61, 68–71. The German law applies only to the Aktiengesellschaft (A.G.) in Germany. The draft Ninth Directive is much wider and covers, for example, French and Belgian societes anonymes. Both the limited coverage of the German law and the broad scope of the Directive argue against rapid expansion without reasonable cause. That is, total EC experience with control contracts is limited to a comparatively few companies in one single Member State.

73. The European Trade Union Congress (ETUC) testified passionately and effectively at the Parliamentary Social Affairs Committee hearings in October, 1981, in support of the Vredeling Proposal. The Caborn Report is an eloquent defense of the spirit of the Vredeling Proposal as well as of the Fifth Directive. There has been no similar show of union support for the proposed Ninth Directive.

74. *See* Council of American Chambers of Commerce—European and Mediterranean, Memorandum on the Proposed Ninth Directive on Company Law (Sept. 1981); National Foreign Trade Council, Memorandum Concerning the Proposed Ninth EC Directive on Company Law (Nov. 20, 1981).

75. A member may, however, be relieved of liability if he can prove that the influence giving rise to the damage is not attributable to him.

76. The obligation to report is triggered by the acquisition of shares representing 10, 25, 50, 75 and 90 percent of a company. Whenever a shareholder owning more than 10 per-

cent of a company increases or decreases his holding by more than 5 percent, he must notify the company in writing and, until that notice is given, the shareholder may not exercise rights attaching to his shares.

77. The Directive provides that a court or authority competent under national law may, if it is necessary to protect the company, it shareholders, or employees: a) suspend management from office: b) enjoin performance of a "damaging" contract; and c) require the parent corporation to buy out the subsidiary's shareholders.

78. "Independent experts" appointed by the management will give their opinion on the appropriateness of the offers made for the stock and the method of valuation.

79. [1968] D.S. Jur. 147 (Cour d'appel, Paris, 1965). *See* 5 INT'L LEGAL MATERIALS 476 (1966). For an analysis of the case, see W. L. Craig, *Applications of the Trading with the Enemy Act to Foreign Corporations Owned by Americans*, 83 HARV. L. REV. 579 (1970).

80. "[L]e juge des référés doit s'inspirer des intérêts sociaux par préférence aux intérêts personnels de certains associés, fussent-ils majoritaires." [1968] D.S. Jur. at 148.

81. The Tenth Directive would govern the dissolution or winding-up of companies. As of the beginning of 1982, there was no information available about the Tenth Directive, which is apparently still in the early drafting stages within the headquarters of the EC Commission.

82. Proposal for a Council Directive on procedures for informing and consulting the employees of undertakings with complex structures, in particular transnational undertakings, 23 O.J. EUR. COMM. (No. C 297) 3 (1980) [hereinafter cited as Vredeling Proposal].

83. Vredeling's portfolio has been assumed by Ivor Richard, Q.C., of the British Labour Party. Richard was British Ambassador to the United Nations from 1974 to 1979.

84. References to the Proposal are, unless otherwise indicated, to the published Commission version, pending publication of a revised text after consultation with Parliament.

85. Because of the timing requirements, the decision will not yet have been taken at the time that consultations are opened. The consultation requirement is stated to apply with respect to "the proposed decision." It is probable that workers' representatives could get a court injunction against implementation of a decision as to which they had inadequate or untimely information.

86. *E.g.,* Employment of manipulative and deceptive devices, 17 C.F.R. § 240.10b-5 (1981).

87. The Vredeling Proposal provides only that Member States shall provide *appropriate* sanctions for failure to comply with the information disclosure requirements, and the consultation requirements. Workers' representatives would be entitled to go to court "to protect their interests." There is no provision excepting foreign parents.

88. In this and numerous other respects, Parliament has recommended substantial modifications to the Commission text. Thus it is by no means certain that the "hostage company" provision will be part of any directive that is eventually adopted.

89. The Commission text of the Proposal imposes the information and consultation requirements on the largest subsidiary even though it may not in any way be affected by the decision under consideration.

90. Theoretically, there is another possibility: the parent may simply ignore the Vredeling Proposal and allow sanctions to be taken against the management of one of its subsidiaries. Such a course is unlikely because of the harmful effects it would have on confidence in local management and morale in the workforce. It would also raise serious questions about the company's attitude toward its legal obligations.

91. *See generally* Continental Oil Co. v. Fed. Power Comm'n. 519 F.2d 31, 35, *cert. denied sub nom.* Superior Oil Co. v. Fed. Power Comm'n. 425 U.S. 971 (1975) (harm to competative position); Chrysler Corp. v. Schlesinger, 412 F. Supp. 171, 176 (D. Del. 1976) (disclosure

of trade secrets and commercial or financial information causing competitive harm).

92. The secrecy provisions of the Proposal are:

1. Members and former members of bodies representing employees shall be required to maintain discretion with respect to information of confidential nature. Each must take account of the company's interests in communications with third parties and shall not divulge secrets regarding the undertaking or its business.

2. Member states shall empower a tribunal to settle disputes with respect to confidentiality of information.

3. Member states shall impose appropriate penalties in cases of infringement of the secrecy requirement.

93. *See A multinational bone for Europe's hungry unions.* ECONOMIST, Apr. 24, 1982, at 73.

94. *Report on the Vredeling Proposal,* EUR. PARL. DOC. (No. 1-324)(1982) (rapporteur: Tom Spencer, M.E.P.). The Committee on Economic and Monetary Affairs and the Committee on Legal Affairs prepared their own reports and amendments which are attached to the Spencer Report.

95. *See* Treaty of Rome, art. 100.

96. This position was not significantly different from the one Richard had consistently espoused in his various public appearances on both sides of the Atlantic.

97. Some Members proposed that the motion be formally referred to the Social Affairs Committee, so that it would not be necessary to keep it in the plenary agenda until Richard completed his text.

98. The vote was 161 to 61, with 84 abstentions.

99. If the Commission text differs substantially from both the Vredeling original and the parliamentary revisions, it could be argued that Parliament must be asked for a new opinion.

100. Proposal for a council regulation on the Statute for European companies, 13 O.J. EUR. COMM. (No. C 124) (1970). The proposal was issued with explanatory notes in 1970 BULL. EUR. COMM. Supp. 8/70, *as amended by* 1975 BULL. EUR. COMM. Supp. 4/75 at 11. *See also* Derom, *The EEC Approach to Groups of Companies,* 16 VA. J. INT'L L. 565, 577 (1976).

101. On April 13, 1978, Parliament asked to be kept informed as to the progress of this regulation. 21 O.J. EUR. COMM. (No. C 108) 42 (1978).

102. The company would be managed by a Board of Management exercising its functions (represent the company in dealings with third parties; confer power on persons to represent the company; close or transfer establishments; modify activities of the undertaking; conduct long-term cooperation) under continuous supervision of a Supervisory Board. Members of the Board of Management are to be appointed by the Supervisory Board, and the Board of Management must submit periodic reports to the Supervisory Board on the management and progress of the company.

103. A dependent undertaking is a separate legal personality over which a controlling company is able, directly or indirectly, to exercise a controlling influence. A controlling undertaking and one or more dependent undertakings would constitute a group if they were under the unified management of the controlling undertaking and if one of them were a European company (S.E.)

104. After a group is formed, the controlling undertaking must offer to acquire the shares of outside shareholders for cash or, where the controlling undertaking is an S.E., in exchange for shares or convertible debentures of the controlling company. In addition, annual equalization payments calculated in proportion to the nominal value of shares must be offered. The Board of Management of the dependent undertaking must report to outside shareholders on the appropriateness of the offer and must convene a meeting to decide whether or not to accept the offer. The controlling undertaking would be liable for the debts and liabilities of dependent undertakings.

105. Where the controlling undertaking is an S.E., it must, upon the formation of a group, offer to acquire the share of outside shareholders for cash or shares, at its option. Where the controlling undertaking is not organized under the laws of a Member State, however, it must offer cash but may also offer to exchange for shares instead.

When the controlling undertaking offers annual equalization payments, its offer may be calculated as representing the average prospective earnings per share in light of previous earnings and the future prospects of the dependent undertaking. If the controlling undertaking is an S.E., it may calculate the payment by reference to the earnings per share of the controlling undertaking.

106. Protection of Trading Interests Act 1980, ch. 11 *in force* March 20, 1980. *See also* Lowe, *Blocking Extraterritorial Jurisdiction*, 75 AM. J. INT'L. L. 257 (1981).

107. Law No. 80-538, [1980] J.O. 1799 *reprinted in* Herzog, *The 1980 French Law on Documents and Information*. 75 AM. J. INT'L. L. 382 (1981).

108. President Reagan's decision extending the ban on dealing with Soviet natural gas pipeline construction to subsidiaries and licensees of U.S. companies has heightened the debate on extraterritoriality. While the pipeline sanctions crisis ended amicably with an apparent understanding concerning subsidized trade with the Eastern bloc, many Europeans were extraordinarily angered by this extension of American law to companies incorporated in their countries.

109. The Luken bill would empower the SEC to issue protective orders (generally or at the request of individual companies) against compliance with foreign orders to disclose confidential information. H.R. 4339, 97th Cong., 1st Sess. (1981) (introduced July 30, 1981). The Luken Bill was referred to the House Committee on Energy and Commerce, Telecommunications, Consumer Protection and Finance Subcommittee. The Chairman of the Oversight and Investigation Subcommittee is planning an investigation to bring the situation to public attention.

The Symms bill would require U.S. companies to inform the Attorney General when they receive such orders, so that he may direct them not to comply. S. 1592, 97th Cong., 1st Sess. (1981) (introduced Aug. 3, 1981). The Symms Bill was referred to the Senate Judiciary Committee. Its sponsors are pushing for joint hearings with the Senate Finance Committee, and are waiting to see the progress of the Vredeling Proposal. The EC directives are clearly among the intended targets of these measures. *See* 127 CONG. REC. S9230-31 (daily ed. Aug. 3, 1981) (remarks of Sen. Symms). *See also* 127 CONG. REC. H6016 (daily ed. Aug. 4, 1981) (remarks of Rep. Schulze).

110. Section 4(a) of the Luken Bill provides that the SEC shall promulgate regulations protecting U.S. citizens from extraterritorial disclosure requirements affecting such confidential material; section 4(b) empowers the SEC to issue protective orders where necessary; and section 4(c) empowers the SEC to order non-disclosure under certain circumstances. Section 4(a) of the Symms Bill requires business to notify the Attorney General of any requirement imposed by a Foreign Government for disclosure of confidential information, and section 4(c) empowers the Attorney General to order non-disclosure in certain circumstances.

111. Trade Act of 1974, § 301, *as amended by* The Trade Agreements Act of 1979, 19 U.S.C. § 2411 (1976).

112. H.R. 4407, 97th Cong., 1st Sess. (1981) (introduced by Rep. Richard Schulze (R.-Pa.)), 127 CONG. REC. H6106 (daily ed. Aug. 4, 1981) and the identical Senate version, S. 2067, 97th Cong., 2d Sess. (1982) (introduced by Sen. Symms), 128 CONG. REC. S423 (daily ed. Feb. 4, 1982).

113. It "is of great concern to this country that the European community now plans to hand over the management of business—including American businesses—to trade unions, many of them leftist or Communist dominated. . . . The so-called Vredeling proposal, now

under consideration in the European Parliament, would do exactly that." 127 CONG. REC. H7731 (daily ed. Oct. 26, 1981) (remarks of Rep. Schulze).

"[T]he legislative program of the European Communities [is unfair and unreasonable]. The seventh and ninth company law directives, and the so-called Vredeling proposal, would impose unreasonable and extremely burdensome requirements upon U.S. companies of information disclosure, consultation with trade unions, and even personal liability of U.S. directors." S. 2067 "would insure that . . . the President will be empowered to take retaliatory investment-related measures when other countries discriminate against American investments." 128 CONG. REC. S423 (daily ed. Feb. 4, 1982) (remarks of Sen. Symms).

114. The directives and proposed directives considered in this article are by no means the only proposals of the European Community which would have drastic effects upon the operations of non-European multinationals in Europe. The proposed Directive on Liability for Defective Products would establish a system of virtually absolute liability for products which cause injury, regardless of whether the article could have been regarded as defective in light of the state of scientific and technological development at the time the article was put into circulation and regardless of whether the manufacturer knew or could have known of the defect. 22 O.J. EUR. COMM. (No. C 271) 7 (1979). The proposed Directive to Approximate the Laws of the Member States relating to Trade Marks forbids in nearly all cases the use of different trade marks by the same manufacturer for the same product in different Member States. 23 O.J. EUR. COMM. (No. C 351)2(1980). Other initiatives would regulate specific industrial sectors, such as banking, pharmaceuticals, insurance, and advertising. There is no indication that the Commission staff is running out of ideas for proposed legislation affecting business.

4

The French Nationalizations: Mitterrand Challenges the Multinationals
Alison L. Doyle

INTRODUCTION

The election of a Socialist Government in France after 23 years of Gaullist rule was an event of great importance for the French economy, particularly its trade and investment components. The size of the election victory created fear among many businessmen in France and abroad. While France has a long-standing tradition of *dirigisme* (government-directed industrial policy), the Socialist campaign platform promised more far-reaching changes in French economic structure than had been attempted since World War II.

Of particular concern to American and other foreign investors in France was President François Mitterrand's promise to nationalize or otherwise take firm government control of industries important to the economic future the Socialists visualize for France. Military suppliers, the chemical industry, and the steel industry, with their poor growth record, and the computer industry and the credit sector, with their great potential for growth and support for an overall economic policy, were obvious targets for a revitalization effort. Mitterrand proposed several methods of gaining state control of the targeted sectors, of which nationalization constituted a substantial part of the package. The legislation for this policy was finally enacted in February 1982. While precise numbers are not available, the nationalizations roughly increased the French public sector from 17 percent to 30 percent of the economy, including 95 percent of all bank deposits and 30 percent of all manufacturing. Both the banks and industry were areas of heavy foreign involvement in French business.

The French experience presents one of the very rare cases of a nationalization controversy in an industrial western nation, and could have set a particularly damaging precedent for world trade and investment relations. Despite the expressed concerns of the targeted firms, the nationalizations largely were nonadversarial, in accordance with principles of French and international law.

The actual nationalization process can be instructive for U.S. policymakers today in illustrating the continuing strength of generally accepted (but rarely codified) principles of international law, and how, when matters of major domestic policy underlie largely economic shifts, they can be integrated properly into international economic relations instead of becoming a source of international conflict. As world trade becomes more interdependent, the context in which nationalization issues are raised becomes ever more complicated. In the case of France, the nationalization involved corporate and private foreign shareholders of nationalized companies, corporate joint ventures with French corporations in France and abroad, and subsidiaries of nationalized companies located abroad and incorporated under the laws of another country, usually with some non-French ownership.

While this chapter will recommend no overt response by the U.S. government to such well-handled nationalizations, it will touch upon the effects of nationalization on private parties, particularly American corporations with some presence in France. First, this chapter will briefly discuss *dirigisme* and the historical foundation underlying President Mitterrand's policies. Second, it describes the government's nationalization program and business' reaction to it. Finally, it assesses the impact of this program and concludes that the French approach should serve as a model for those nations that decide to nationalize sectors of their economies.

DIRIGISME AND NATIONALIZATION IN PERSPECTIVE

The nationalizations proposed by President Mitterrand were but one aspect of a major new industrial policy for France. In order to stimulate demand and reverse a growing unemployment trend, he proposed and the National Assembly agreed to a major expansionary economic policy, including higher wages, increased government transfer payments, low-cost easier credit, and increased public investment.[1] To keep jobs at home and maintain French power in trade, Mitterrand also proposed a new industrial strategy to maintain or regain France's competitive position in world trade, to be implemented in part with government direction through nationalization of the industries most involved in growth for the coming decades. Mitterrand's policies reflect the fundamental French belief in *dirigisme*—direct government control of the industrial sector for the benefit of the economy as a whole.[2] The French believe that industries, if left to themselves, will not (for various reasons) produce the push necessary for growth. Whether or not this perception is valid, *dirigisme* is fundamental to French economic policy.

National control in France can be traced to the days of Louis XIV and Colbert. Nationalizations, however, did not become important until the 1930s, when the Popular Front government, elected for its nationalization ideology, conducted partial nationalizations of the railroads, the munitions industry, the aircraft industry, and the Bank of France. More extensive nationalizations occurred in the wake of World War II.[3] Nationalization, then as today, was as much psychological as economic or political. Nationalization reflected a multitude of problems with and distrust of French industry, a distrust of the ability or desire of industry to work for the good of the whole.

Even when the government has not nationalized industries, it has maintained pervasive control over the French economy. Foreign direct investment in France, for example, has been subject since 1966 to "liberalized" screening procedures.[4] This case-by-case review, like nationalization, has been used to foster economic and social goals.

The *dirigiste* mentality has been manifested by various French governments. When Citroen developed financial problems in the mid-1970s, for example, Giscard d'Estaing ordered a merger with Peugeot, to the distress of both corporations, but without any significant resistance.[5] More recently, Honeywell, Westinghouse, and ITT's investments in France were significantly altered in a 1976 "Francisation" of telecommunications interests.[6] Thus, the socialist government's actions, at most, reflect a turning back to more direct economic intervention, not a stunning new development.

In fact, the corporations nationalized this year, and investors in them cannot truly claim to have been surprised. The Socialist party had promoted a strong nationalization platform since 1972, and proposed the identical nationalizations in the 1978 elections, based on the same need to establish a position in industries presumed to be engines of growth for the next decades and to reassert French competitiveness. Corporate executives should have known for a long time that nationalization was likely to occur.

NATIONALIZATION LAW AND PRACTICE

The power and right of a sovereign nation to nationalize property is clear and cannot be controverted in present international practice.[7]

Whether there is an international "law of nationalization" to be applied uniformly to all may be questioned, but a basic principle generally agreed upon among the industrialized western nations is that prompt, adequate, and effective compensation is an absolute minimum standard of behavior; moreover, nationalizations must be nondiscriminatory and for a public purpose.

The Mitterrand government was bound by numerous legal obligations in connection with its nationalization program. Chief among these is the French Constitution, which permits nationalization, but provides for equal protection and compensation with regard to property rights.[8] France is also a signatory of the GATT, the Treaty of Rome, the OECD Draft Convention on the Protection of Foreign Property, and the European Convention for the Protection of Human Rights and Fundamental Freedoms, all of which protect property rights or otherwise place constraints upon the power of nations to nationalize.[9] In the case of the rights of U.S. citizens located or doing business in France, the bilateral Convention of Establishment (like other treaties of Friendship, Commerce and Navigation) binds the French government to assure national treatment, nondiscrimination, and nonimpairment, and prompt, adequate, and effective compensation for expropriations undertaken for a public purpose.[10] France is also bound by various individual investment agreements with foreign investors which generally incorporate the domestic laws of the sovereign and often "general principles of international law."[11]

Neither these domestic laws nor general principles of international law have a settled way of dealing with a situation that is becoming more common: the presence of foreign investors. Property actually located in France clearly may be nationalized regardless of ownership, subject only to restraints the sovereign places upon itself. The modern era, however, has made the simple rule difficult to apply: 1) Must the government respect the property of foreigners located in France? Can the government, for example, nationalize and take control of more than just the bank building? Can it reach the assets or business of the foreign-owned property, not only located in France, but located in New York or in West Germany? 2) Should the nationalization apply to a U.S. or a German citizen, in his or her own country, holding a few shares of a nationalized company? 3) Can the government reach the property of French citizens or companies located abroad, such as foreign subsidiaries or joint ventures? The French government avoided the first question by excluding foreign banks explicitly from the nationalization, which in itself raised a question of reverse discrimination for French opponents of the legislation. Although no public pronouncement explained the government's decision, such a nationalization would not have served French policy of controlling domestic credit (hence no public purpose), and would surely have damaged French credibility (or credit-worthiness) abroad more than was necessary for economic purposes. The second and third issues, which are more difficult to resolve, were presented in this nationalization. Foreign subsidiaries and shares held by foreigners were nationalized and, as will be noted below, are the most likely source of any litigation. However, given the manner in which the nationalization effort was undertaken, it is unlikely that anyone will object successfully to the loss of shares in property located in France or abroad. The government also put itself in the self-contradictory position of having withheld assets located in France when Egypt nationalized the Suez Canal in 1957, declaring them beyond the reach of the power to nationalize (ironically announced by then-Justice Minister François Mitterrand), while maintaining today that the nationalizations of the stock of subsidiaries located abroad is somehow different. Nonetheless, considering the problems involved, the nationalization program was carried out very smoothly and equitably.

The Decree of Nationalization

French antipathy toward the credit sector is deep and longstanding. While opponents of nationalization decried the end of competition in the credit market and losses of customers, the government revelled in the extremely popular notion of ending the domination of the credit sector by "certain privileged interests" and in the implementation of effective control of credit. The many other industrial targets, largely profitable and not intrinsically damaging to the economy, were chosen as necessary components of the planned restructuring of industry, creating "filiales" or vertical rationalizations of production in areas of large potential growth for the next century.

The original nationalization plan, sent by the Cabinet to the National Assembly on September 23, 1981, proposed the following:[12]

Main companies of the following industrial groups to be nationalized totally:
Compagnie Générale d'Électricité
(engineering, electronics and telecommunications, founded 1848, 6th largest industrial corporation);
Compagnie de Saint-Gobain-Pont-à-Mousson
(glass, ceramics, electronics, paper, founded 1665 by Louis XIV, 5th largest industrial corporation);
Péchiney-Ugine-Kuhlmann
(chemicals, metals, founded 1855, 7th largest industrial corporation);

Thomson-Brandt
(electrical goods, aviation detection systems, telephones, computers, medical products, created in 1946 by a series of mergers, 10th largest industrial corporation); and
Rhône-Poulenc
(chemicals, textiles, pharmaceuticals, founded 1928, 8th largest industrial corporation).

36 major banks as well as the two largest financial holding companies were to be nationalized totally:[13]

Paribas (Compagnie Financière de Paris et des Pays-Bas)
(created by merger in 1972, number one financial group); and
Suez (Compagnie Financière de Suez)
(finance, investment, industrial and services, created in 1956 with assets from the Suez).

Discussions were to be held with foreign shareholders of three groups to examine a restructuring of their capital with the goal of the government becoming majority shareholder of:

Roussel-Uclaf
(57 percent German, pharmaceuticals);
ITT-France
(99 percent United States, telecommunications); and
CII-Honeywell-Bull
(53 percent United States, computers, other high-tech).

The government planned to become a major shareholder in two military suppliers:

La Société Aéronautique Dassault-Breguet
(aircraft, 28th largest industrial corporation); and
Matra-Hachette Group
(armaments).

Finally, the plan contemplated conversion of government credit into shares in the two remaining major steel companies:

Usinor (Union Sidérurgique du Nord de la France)
(produces 50 percent of French steel, 17th largest industrial corporation); and
Sacilor (Sacilor Aciéres et Laminoirs de Lorraine)
(produces 30 percent of French steel, 22nd largest industrial corporation).

As part of the nationalization plan, the government included a compensation component touted as "just and judicially incontestable . . . [in accord with] national and international law."[14] Shareholders were to be compensated with 15-year government bonds, according to a formula supposedly designed to produce the same return as would a voluntary takeover of the targeted corporations.[15]

Not surprisingly, the business community protested that such pervasive state control of credit was abnormal, even though state control in this area had long been substantial. A more substantive concern was that state participation in previously private business activities would repel customers and partners. For example, A. G. Becker, a U.S. investment bank which owned a 20 percent interest in the target Paribas, indicated that it would seek to end its relationship with Paribas upon nationalization of that interest.[16] Tosco, an independent U.S. oil driller, similarly warned that it would not proceed with plans for a joint venture in Morocco if Paribas were nationalized. Corporations also expressed concern about the confidentiality problems state employees or labor representatives on the board of directors would present.

Investors criticized the valuation method for the compensation as too low. The proposed formula made no adjustment for inflation, nor did it reflect accurately consolidated accounts, among other problems. Independent auditors, for example, valued Crédit Commerciale de France, one of the target banks, at twice the amount the proposed valuation formula would yield.[17] However, not all analysts agreed that the government's initial compensation plan was truly inadequate. Although none of the nationalized companies perceived the compensation as adequate, the valuation was certainly related to the true value of the investments. A study by French law professors and the U.S. law firm Cleary, Gottlieb, Steen & Hamilton, for example, indicated that U.S. courts would be unlikely to deem the compensation inadequate, and that all legal tests were met by it with relative ease.[18]

The involvement of foreign subsidiaries of the targets, and multinational corporations as dispossessed shareholders, also raised bothersome questions of extraterritoriality. While French citizens had no recourse in their own courts, the multinational corporations did have other avenues for relief. No precise information was available, but about 30 percent of the targeted banks' stock was held by foreign interests, largely U.S., British, and German banks, and most of the industrial targets had foreign shareholders. With so many nationalized subsidiaries located abroad, France was vulnerable to foreign process under the jurisdiction of other nations and subject to attachment should the nationalization not be respected.[19] The subsidiaries of the targets were twice vulnerable—if the host government refused to recognize the nationalization altogether, ownership of the subsidiary could theoretically be handed over to the dispossessed shareholders. Alternatively, even if the nationalization were recognized, the compensation could be held inadequate and the foreign subsidiaries liquidated to satisfy judgments against the French government. The subsidiaries also would be susceptible to retaliation by foreign governments, industries, or minority shareholders should it become apparent that they were being used to support French unemployment.

Clearly, investors were more interested in saving their original investment than owning French government bonds. The French government was properly wary of their attempts to use foreign subsidiaries to drain parent assets (into subsidiaries) and then split them off, thus justifying for practical purposes the need for the extraterritorial reach of the nationalizations. Such wariness was justified, given the protests of the nationalization targets. Paribas and Suez, for example, complained that they were losing valuable, nonfinancial foreign and domestic subsidiaries, which the government need not control to manage credit policy, and Baron Guy de Rothschild moved the remnants of his family's assets to the United States.

Illustrative of the problems of international consequences was the Paribas-Suisse affair, which occurred in October 1981. In the midst of the protestations of Paribas executives about the loss of lucrative foreign subsidiaries, and while the nationalization bill was being debated in the National Assembly and the media, Pargesa Holding S.A., a Swiss financial group (in whom A. G. Becker (US) and Power Corp. (Canada) are major shareholders and who in turn are partly owned by Paribas), made an offer of 2.3 billion Ffr ($418 million) for the controlled subsidiary Paribas-Suisse (oil and commodities trading).[20] The offer was quite tempting. Despite the corporate interconnection, the bid was probably a fair one, and illustrated the inadequacy of the government valuation offer. Although Paribas-Suisse represented only about 10 percent of Paribas' assets, the offer was closer to two-thirds the government offer for the entire group, reason enough in itself to try to split off whatever was possible. Despite the size of the offer and the obvious benefit it represented for Paribas-Suisse shareholders, the Board of Paribas, pressured by the French government (*dirigisme* at work again), opposed the bid. Amid allegations that Paribas-Suisse shares had been shuffled among other subsidiaries to disguise Paribas' activities, Pargesa successfully took over on October 26, 1981, enraging the powerless French government, and making it ever more wary of other attempts to frustrate the nationalization measures. The Paribas-Suisse incident led the government to tighten foreign exchange controls and exchanges of controlling stakes in foreign subsidiaries of targets, as well as to place government representatives in the head offices of the targets.

The government proposal also suffered from weakness on the issue of nondiscrimination, as required under both domestic law and international obligations. Although no generalized protest was made about the choice of industrial companies to nationalize, large banks complained that small banks and foreign owned or controlled banks were unfairly favored since they were not included in the nationalization of the credit sector. The proposed nationalization plan also excluded cooperative banks, three of which would otherwise have met the definition of large banks. Not surprisingly, the small banks supported nationalization and voted down any attempt by the Association des Banques Privees to mount a general anti-nationalization campaign.[21]

The public purpose issue created little open controversy. Opponents recognized the public policy arguments underlying the nationalization effort, but objected that the government gained little by nationalizing many of the target companies' subsidiaries. Paribas executives, for example, argued that control of domestic credit did not require control over Paribas' branches in 41 countries, branches which generated 40.7 percent of Paribas' net income in 1980. As the Paribas-Suisse affair illustrated, however, the government had hoped to nationalize entire companies.

Ignoring the public complaints about various aspects of the nationalization plan and over the objections of the Communists and more radical Socialists that the compensation was too generous, the nationalization bill was passed, as initially proposed, on December 18, 1981. The battle, however, did not end in the National Assembly. Passage by the Senate or repassage over its veto is required to enact a law, and the Socialists did not control the Senate. Under pressure from the large banks, the Senate voted to refer the bill to the *Conseil constitutionnel*, a body of elder statesmen,[22] which was called upon to determine the legality of the bill. The *Conseil constitutionnel* ultimately approved the nationalization plan in principle, but indicated that three important constitutional flaws needed remedying. First, the government's plan for reimbursing shareholders stemmed from an unsatisfactory method, failing to calculate the value of the consolidated group and also neglecting to take into account dividends on 1981 profits or the effects of inflation. Second, a section of the law permitting the government and heads of nationalized companies to negotiate the sale of foreign affiliates once takeovers were completed was unconstitutional because it left too much discretion in the hands of the managers. Finally, the clause defining which of France's banks were to be nationalized was declared unconstitutional on the grounds that it excluded banks of a mutualist or cooperative character. (The *Conseil* did not object to the exclusion of foreign-owned banks from the nationalization. In deference to the National Assembly, it held that such banks were distinguishable from domestic banks for purposes of the goals of the nationalizations and thus presented no problem of discrimination.)[23]

Within a week the government sent a new bill to the National Assembly which met all of the objections of the *Conseil* and which sweetened the pot considerably for investors. By meeting the *Conseil's* objections, final enactment was virtually assured and the likelihood that any foreign court would refuse to recognize the nationalization greatly reduced. The bill was passed as proposed, was sent again to the *Conseil*, was ruled constitutional on February 11, 1982, and minutes later was signed into law.

The final approval by the *Conseil* did not quell the protests. Investors continued to complain about inadequate compensation. Opposition party members lodged fresh appeals on several grounds, including international law. An unidentified "leading Paris law firm" reported almost certain legal challenges by unnamed clients in Switzerland, Belgium, Luxembourg, and West Germany, and possibly the United States, seeking attachment of assets held outside France.[24]

Foreign governments, though generally not pleased with the nationalization plan, did not consider the plan likely to create major rifts with the French government, because they generally acknowledged the right of a sovereign to expropriate domestic industries. The U.S. government's efforts were directed toward assuring that the process was fair to U.S. investors. The long-term implications of this policy probably will be assessed in order to determine whether, on policy grounds, the U.S. government should consider such actions as contrary to our national interests.

Not-Quite Nationalizations

One major, though not particularly controversial, element of the Socialist plan was to formalize the government's de facto control of the French steel industry. As in many countries, the steel industry had been struggling for decades, aided with government loans and other assistance. With little fanfare, the government debt was converted to shares.

In addition to the large industrial groups nationalized outright, the Socialists targeted several other companies in critical high-tech areas for national control. However, it was felt that in order to retain access to technology and marketing agreements, these companies could not be nationalized. This policy acknowledged that French industry did not possess the technology, the research and development emphasis, or the market to develop certain products alone. National policy for years encouraged investment and joint ventures from abroad under a requirement that the foreign corporation must share technology with a local partner. Nationalization had to be managed to retain those connections.

The nationalization plan included a declaration of intent to gain control of the wholly owned French companies, Dassault (aircraft) and Matra (armaments). Negotiations with Dassault were held in secret, with the government eventually obtaining a 51 percent interest in the company. Matra executives complained about inadequate valuation by the government, but eventually gave up controlling interest in April 1982.

More crucial to the government's strategy, especially the desire to start an information technology empire in France, were the proposed takeovers of ITT-France, CII-Honeywell-Bull, and Roussel-Uclaf. As a consequence, these companies were in a position to drive much harder bargains than had been possible for others.

ITT-France, which is a wholly owned subsidiary of ITT, controls many subsidiaries that produce telecommunications equipment. Since France desired total control of its own telecommunications but needed ITT technology and ITT needed market penetration and the competitive advantages of a local partnership, the purpose of the negotiations between ITT and the French government was to reduce ITT control but maintain its participation. ITT was not particularly surprised, having been forced to sell its telephone manufacturing subsidiary, Laboratorie Materiale Telephonique, to the state in 1977, but was in a strong position and opened negotiations in January with a demand for $65 million in compensation. In the final pact, signed in October 1982, the government obtained 100 percent ownership of two subsidiaries for approximately $30 million in francs, leaving twelve smaller subsidiaries intact.[25]

CII-Honeywell-Bull was created by the French government in 1976 in a forced merger between a Honeywell subsidiary and a French company in which Honeywell became a 47 percent partner. Honeywell bolstered its position as a technology source by incorporating a mandatory buy-out clause in the 1976 deal worth up to $290 million (in dollars) were Honeywell ever to be the victim of another takeover. Again, the French needed Honeywell and vice versa for cross-licensing agreements, market access, marketing agreements, and research and development. Honeywell had an added impetus to reduce its exposure because of CII-Honeywell-Bull's $20.7 million losses in the first half of 1981. The French government was originally worried enough to send an emissary to Minneapolis to persuade Honeywell to remain in France; Honeywell and the French government signed an agreement in June 1982, under which the U.S. company accepted a reduction to a 19.9 percent equity position in CII-Honeywell-Bull in exchange for $150 million.[26]

The planned takeover of the pharmaceuticals company, Roussel-Uclaf, was much more hostile and proved less successful for the government. The French government was in a similarly weak position in these negotiations—it needed the technology and trade links that the parent company, Hoescht AG (West Germany), provided. Hoescht adamantly opposed the takeover, and the West German government reportedly quietly backed the corporation. The final agreement was far less than France desired. Hoescht agreed in February 1982, to allow France's indirectly owned 22 percent stake (via the nationalized companies) to increase to a blocking minority of Roussel-Uclaf stock, an influential, but by no means controlling, position. Relations between the parties remain acrimonious.[27]

THE NATIONALIZATIONS IN PERSPECTIVE

The decisions of the *Conseil constitutionnel* leave no grounds for honest dispute about conformity with French law. While many shareholders no doubt remain disgruntled with their individual difficulties, the approval of the overall plan, methods, and valuation by a body made up of elder statesmen must be considered determinative.

The French government, in its extended process of developing a fair nationalization act, did much to disarm any possible reactions from abroad. The government developed a coherent national policy for domestic economic recovery and chose a tool it has found useful in the past. Under international law, nations cannot dictate internal policy choices for other nations, although growing economic interdependence makes international economic repercussions inevitable. Thus, a nation's domestic policy choice to nationalize should be beyond the reproach of other nations. This was by and large the reaction of France's trade partners, even those with disgruntled shareholder-citizens and newly nationalized subsidiaries. No doubt consultations were conducted behind the scenes, but no overt government reaction was made beyond statements suggesting that France award prompt, adequate, and effective compensation. In fact, the U.S. government had little involvement in any negotiations. The Departments of State and Treasury were reportedly kept informed by the United States corporations directly involved but did not take an active role. Participation by the West German government was not made public.

France also performed the nationalizations without raising any serious problems of discrimination. It chose its targets and methods of gaining control on solid policy grounds: major industrial groups for their economic power, banks for their credit control, and ITT-France and Honeywell for their technology sources. Groups not chosen were rationally excluded on economic and social policy grounds.

The concept of extraterritoriality raises a more interesting issue. While the government avoided much of the problem in excluding foreign banks, it created many problems with the foreign subsidiaries. As mentioned previously, the French government was in the ticklish position of having opposed a similar extension of nationalization by Egypt. While the cases arguably are distinguishable, France is at the mercy of other countries to enforce government ownership if suits are brought. This restrained form of extraterritorial application really stands or falls on the question of compensation, at least in U.S. courts. France went a long way toward assuring acceptable compensation. While the terms "prompt, adequate, and effective" are often referred to as requiring timely, sufficient, liquid compensation in the currency of one's choice, what it really comes down to is how much money (in any form) is realized. The courts of the United States, following the Act of State doctrine and case law, will simply not overturn a nationalization that provides reasonable compensation.[28] The price offered seemed reasonable in relation to the actual market value of the shares surrendered to the government, and was paid in marketable bonds, which was hardly the sort of compensation one could call clearly inadequate.

CONCLUSION

The French nationalization presents a textbook case for the exercise of sovereign authority to expropriate private property within the bounds of international law. It can be an instructive example for future nationalizations affecting U.S. interests and can add more weight to the authority of the principles of nondiscrimination and prompt, adequate, and effective compensation.

The Mexican government recently nationalized the domestic banking system. Although the situation was still in a state of flux at the time of this writing, and the influence of the French nationalization effort is difficult to ascertain, one must be encouraged that the Mexican nationalization effort seemed reasonable and well managed, although many Mexicans probably would disagree. Foreign banks are unaffected, legislation has been passed, and compensation is planned.

Greece and the United Kingdom are often considered likely countries in which nationalizations will be undertaken in the near future. Mexico, the UK, and Greece now have a modern example of a low-friction nationalization effort and the prevailing calm adds authority to this method.

At the corporate level, the French nationalization has probably been a reassuring experience in many ways. While it should not cause investors to ignore the risk of nationalization, it can at least be seen as a risk that nets out to a very low potential loss for investment in France and other industrial nations. Honeywell and ITT, for example, presumably believed their interests were adequately protected and the investments worth the risk in France, even after the 1976 reorganizations, and it would have been too costly to liquidate, given their enormous financial interests. In their cases, as in those of other foreign investors, the benefits of market access and any indirect benefits may outweigh the risk of nationalization when compensation is forthcoming.

The investment climate has not really changed in France—investment screening is unchanged and governmental interference in choice of location and equity investment is unchanged. If anything, the Mitterrand government is more warmly disposed to foreign direct investment than its predecessor. Nonetheless, the possibility of nationalization still exists.

Overall, the French government handled this nationalization quite well, though some industries remain wary of the long-term repercussions of nationalization. Fears of government restrictions on management independence seem well-founded. The banks, for example, were directed in mid-1982 to provide several billion dollars in loans to nationalized firms to cover losses as well as to fund development.

Whether the policy will really help the French economy is a separate issue. Developments in the French economy since implementation of Mitterrand's policies, including rising inflation and unemployment, devaluation of the franc, large losses by the nationalized firms, and huge government deficits, suggest the policies were not wise. To make such choices, however, remains within the province of any government.

Rather than object to nationalizations in general, the U.S. government should limit objections to foreign governments' actions in the future that directly contravene an international obligation or international law or when vital U.S. interests are directly implicated. Efforts to insulate a nation from direct exposure to unfavorable economic conditions—such as export subsidies, discriminatory government procurement policies, or protectionist barriers to trade, are all proper topics for government action. Thus, unless French policies or other governments' policies become more blatantly protectionist, unilateral swing, the U.S. government should respect such governmental actions.

NOTES

1. Int'l Trade Admin., U.S. Dep't of Commerce, International Marketing Information Series, Foreign Economic Trends and Their Implications for the United States–France (Oct. 1981).

2. Organization for Economic Cooperation and Development, The Industrial Policy of France 10 (1974).

3. The post-World War II nationalizations completed the government's takeover of the coal, gas, electricity, and some insurance companies that had begun in the 1930s. For more about other nationalized firms, see W. Baum, The French Economy and the State (1958).

4. See Torem & Craig, Developments in the Control of Foreign Direct Investment in France, 70 Mich. L. Rev. 285 (1971).

5. N.Y. Times, Feb. 19, 1978, § IV, at 3, col. 1.

6. N.Y. Times, June 4, 1976, § IV, at 1, col. 4. Westinghouse and Honeywell were forced into minority shareholder positions in their French subsidiaries, and ITT was forced to sell to the government one of its components manufacturing subsidiaries.

7. Acceptance of this principle is commonly traced to Secretary of State Cordell Hull: "The right to expropriate property is coupled with and conditioned on the obligation to make adequate, effective and prompt compensation." Expropriation of American Oil Properties in Mexico, Note from the Secretary of State to the Ambassador of Mexico, 2 Dep't of State Bull. 380 (1940).

This view of the rights of property owners is not necessarily universal. The Calvo Doctrine (remedies of foreign investors limited to local law) or the suggestion that national sovereignty over natural resources supersedes any compensation rights of producers are two current principles being touted by less developed nations. For a recent discussion of the latter, *see The Charter of Economic Rights and Duties of States and the Deprivation of Foreign-Owned Wealth*, 75 Am. J. Int'l L. 437 (1981). Since rules of international law are perforce only what all (or a great majority of) nations agree upon, no rule can be enforced when a nation chooses to ignore it.

8. *See* Constitution of October 11, 1958, *incorporating by reference* Article 17 of the Declaration des droits de l'homme et du citoyen of August 26, 1789, and the ninth paragraph of the preamble of the French Constitution of October 27, 1946.

9. GATT article XVII provides that state enterprises, though permissible in general, may not be used to create serious obstacles to trade. Article 37 of the Treaty of Rome does not prohibit nationalizations per se, but does prohibit the creation of any monopoly or impediment to the free circulation of goods and services which discriminates against EEC members. The OECD Convention enshrines prompt, adequate, and effective compensation, and the European Convention for the Protection of Human Rights and Fundamental Freedoms of November 4, 1950, gives French citizens recourse to the European Commission on Human Rights for violations of the Convention by their own government.

10. Convention of Establishment Between the United States of America and France, T.I.A.S. 4625, Dec. 21, 1960.

11. *See* Fortune, Feb. 22, 1982, at 8; Financial Times, Nov. 18, 1981, at 19, col. 3. The choice of what to nationalize made private agreements less of a factor in this case, since very little foreign direct investment was implicated. Honeywell had such an agreement with the French government after 1976.

12. For more background information, *see* 68 ABA J. 422, 424 (1982).

13. The government, however, exempted the following firms from nationalization: banks under foreign control; cooperative banks; discount banks; the SICOMI (similar to S&Ls); and small banks (less than 1 billion Ffr in deposits as of January 2, 1981).

14. New York Times, Sept. 3, 1981, § IV, at 1, col. 1.

15. Three elements comprised the compensation package: (1) average share price during 1978–1980; (2) net worth of the corporation at the end of 1980; and (3) capitalization profits (that is, tenfold average of net profits) during 1978–1980. Corporations whose shares were quoted on the Bourse were to weight these three elements 50 percent, 25 percent, and 25 percent, respectively. Corporations not traded on the Bourse were to weight the second and third elements equally (since no share price existed).

16. *See* N.Y. Times, Sept. 3, 1981, § IV, at 1, col. 1; 68 ABA J. 422, 424 (1982).

17. Economist, Oct. 31, 1981, at 93.

18. Business Week, Dec. 21, 1981, at 66; N.Y. Times, Nov. 6, 1981, § IV, at 2, col. 4.

19. The French government only assumed ownership of whatever was already owned by the targets abroad. No attempt was made to take anything more. However, the scope of this "limited" takeover was impressive: Saint-Gobain had 100 subsidiaries in 17 countries; Pechiney had 86 on 4 continents; Rhone-Poulenc had subsidiaries in Brazil, Great Britain, the United States, Switzerland, West Germany, and Spain; Thomson-Brandt had subsidiaries in over 12 countries; and both Paribas and Suez had extensive investments abroad.

20. Business Week, Nov. 9, 1981, at 55; N.Y. Times, Oct. 17, 1981, at 33, col. 5; Economist, Oct. 19, 1981, at 93.

21. Economist, Oct. 31, 1981, at 94. The odds were not quite as bad as they looked, for the targets themselves controlled a substantial number of the smaller banks. Out of the 396 banks registered in France, 170 became directly or indirectly state controlled. 68 ABA J. 422, 423 (1982).

22. The *Conseil constitutionnel* is a quasi-judicial body, average age 74, whose members serve nine-year terms. All but one of the current members were appointed by previous governments, and they were not believed to be sympathetic to the Socialist plan. Realistic commentators did not believe the *Conseil* would dare block the legislation entirely. However, given the makeup of the *Conseil*, the compensation was expected to be improved. *See* N.Y. Times, Jan. 18, 1982, at 14, col. 3; Economist, Jan. 23, 1982, at 35–6; Economist, Oct. 31, 1981, at 94.

23. Reprint of the decision of the *Conseil constitutionnel*. Le Monde, Jan. 19, 1982. The *Conseil* noted that the legislature, taking into account the risks and difficulties such nationalizations would present for the overall goals of nationalization, and that such banks were not necessary or particularly useful for those goals, could find them a separate class for purposes of this Act and thus presented no problems of discrimination.

24. Journal of Commerce, Feb. 19, 1982, at 1, col. 5.

25. N.Y. Times, Oct. 15, 1982, § IV, at 1, col. 6. The two parties also intended to sign separate technical and marketing agreements governing the two subsidiaries' future activities.

26. *See* N.Y. Times, Apr. 22, 1982, § IV, at 5 col. 1; N.Y. Times, June 9, 1982, § IV, col. 4, at 4; N.Y. Times, June 26, 1982, at 39, col. 6.

27. Financial Times, Feb. 24, 1982, at 1, col. 5; Wall St. J., Mar. 15, 1982, at 15, col. 1.

28. *See Banco Nacional de Cuba v. Sabbatino*, 376 U.S. 398 (1964). A party would first have to overcome the Act of State defense before being able to challenge the nationalization decree.

5

Trade-Related Investment Requirements

Claude G.B. Fontheim
R. Michael Gadbaw

INTRODUCTION

Trade-related requirements placed on foreign direct investments by national governments have become commonplace in recent years. These measures are commonly referred to as trade-related performance requirements (TRPRs). Governments impose performance requirements to ensure that foreign investors act in accordance with national policy objectives,[1] including regional development, the training of local workers, research and development, and technology transfers. TRPRs may take one of two forms: first, they may require foreign investors to maintain certain export levels, based either on a fixed percentage of production or a minimum quantity of goods produced; second, local content performance requirements may be imposed requiring that foreign investors obtain a certain percentage of the value of the final output from local sources or produce that level of production inputs locally.[2] The TRPRs may be imposed by statute, by regulations published in administrative documents, or by informal investment requirements implemented by government agencies. For several reasons, firms hostile to the imposition of TRPRs frequently acquiesce to them rather than locate production facilities in other countries. First, the firm may have located in the country prior to the imposition of TRPRs. Second, the host country may require local production facilities before access to the domestic market may be obtained. Third, the host country may have a natural comparative advan-

A substantially similar version of this article appeared originally as *Trade-Related Performance Requirements Under the GATT-MTN System and U.S. Law,* 14 Law & Pol'y Int'l Bus. 129 (1982). Used with permission of *Law and Policy in International Business.*

tage in the production of the good that the firm seeks to produce which outweighs the cost of compliance. Fourth, the host government may provide other benefits to induce the continued presence of foreign investors despite the cost of compliance. Thus, foreign investors continue to participate in a system which forces them to behave in ways other than they would in a free market setting.

An analysis of the economic effects of TRPRs is difficult because the politically sensitive nature of TRPRs makes parties unwilling to provide relevant data. The governments that utilize them view TRPRs as an important domestic policy tool needed to achieve national economic goals and are, therefore, reluctant to release information that would aid those opposed to the use of such measures. The foreign investors are generally unwilling to object or provide information regarding the terms of TRPRs for fear they will antagonize the host governments. This makes the economic impact and incidence of TRPRs virtually impossible to quantify. Nevertheless, TRPRs distort international trade and investment markets. The pervasive use of TRPRs, in itself, makes it likely that their effects are substantial. Furthermore, their effects are analogous or identical to the effects of other practices, such as export subsidies and import quotas, which have already been the subject of extensive economic analysis demonstrating that these practices result in a net welfare loss.[3]

The use of TRPRs violates several provisions of the General Agreement on Tariffs and Trade (GATT)[4] and the Subsidies Code negotiated during the Tokyo Round of the Multilateral Trade Negotiations,[5] and thus undermines the extensive efforts made to achieve an open international economic environment. While several international forums have addressed the TRPR issue, substantial progress has not been made toward reaching an international agreement specifically directed to the use of TRPRs, perhaps because of the general opposition of countries who perceive TRPRs as being the most effective means of achieving certain domestic policy objectives. However, U.S. efforts to apply the norms of the GATT-MTN system explicitly to TRPRs should be actively pursued both in negotiations and through the available multilateral dispute settlement mechanisms. Furthermore, although U.S. legal remedies exist,[6] they have yet to be utilized to obtain relief from the effects of TRPRs on U.S. trade.

This chapter will provide an overview of the economic and political issues surrounding TRPRs in the international setting and examine the legality of TRPRs in the GATT-MTN system of international trade rules. The chapter will then discuss the procedures for relief from the effects of TRPRs provided in U.S. statutes based on the GATT-MTN principles and argue that, since a fundamental tenet of U.S. trade policy is to promote adherence to GATT-MTN provisions, the U.S. statutes should be administered to counter practices which violate these provisions. The chapter will examine a number of strategies that the United States can employ to counter the use of TRPRs, including recourse to GATT dispute resolution mechanisms, amendments to U.S. laws to provide more effective opposition to TRPRs for private parties, who are in the best position to formulate complaints against the impact of TRPRs on U.S. trade. Finally, Canada's Foreign Investment Review Act will be discussed in the context of a brief case study of the manner in which TRPRs are implemented and the alternative approaches private parties and the U.S. government may select to combat the Act's performance requirements.

ECONOMIC AND POLITICAL POLICY ISSUES

Economic Issues

TRPRs cause distortions in the international flow of trade and capital while providing implementing governments additional economic policy tools. Certain countries implementing TRPRs may achieve welfare gains, but, as with more conventional barriers to trade, TRPRs tend to cause welfare losses in other countries.[7] They thus effectively render benefits to the implementing country at the expense of others. This phenomenon has been manifested in more traditional barriers to trade which are commonly referred to as "beggar thy neighbor" policies.

TRPRs are intended to cause firms to pursue practices that would otherwise not be chosen in the open market. For example, local content requirements are intended to cause firms to locate production facilities locally. The central consideration in determining where to locate production facilities in a free market setting is comparative advantage.[8] Profit maximizing firms will choose to locate their production facilities where they can be operated most efficiently and where the firms can purchase components on the most advantageous terms, which is generally from the most efficient producer of the components. Indigenous firms able to sell components to foreign investors because of local content requirements are usually not the most efficient producers of that good. Thus, inefficient production is maintained even though more efficient facilities could be established elsewhere. If the market were allowed to allocate its resources to those sectors where production is most efficient, firms would benefit from greater efficiency through higher profits and consumers would benefit from better, cheaper products. Furthermore, the economy of the host country may be adversely affected as higher prices and subsidization costs are incurred in order to accelerate development in a sector that may have little chance of achieving a true competitive advantage.

Export performance requirements also cause firms to locate more production facilities locally than they otherwise would. This results from the need to achieve the export levels TRPRs impose. For instance, all other considerations being equal, a firm might produce X amount for the local market and Y amount for export based on the demand in the respective markets. If the TRPR calls for Y + Z exports and Z is greater than or equal to zero, which will generally be the case as export performance requirements are artificial export floors by definition, firms must locate additional production facilities locally in order to meet the minimum export levels.[9] Thus, export performance requirements result in welfare costs, due to misallocation of productive resources, similar to those caused by local content requirements.

When a firm does not adequately increase production to meet both domestic demand and an export performance requirement, the inadequate production has an effect similar to the effect an export subsidy has on a domestic economy. The producer must shift sales to international markets, which decreases domestic supply and accordingly causes domestic prices to rise. Even where a firm does increase production sufficiently, too many productive resources are channelled into exports at the expense of other sectors of the economy producing goods for the domestic market, as happens when export subsidies are conferred.[10] Furthermore, because a firm may be forced to export at a certain level, it must capture a sufficient share of the international market through such means as undercutting market prices, thereby causing harm to foreign commercial interests. This last effect is also analogous to the effect export subsidies or dumping have on international trade.

Several rationales have been advanced to support the implementation of TRPRs. One view is that TRPRs are an appropriate means to promote and protect a local industry during its infancy.[11] Once the industry is established, the argument is made, it should be able to compete in the world marketplace. Accordingly, the costs of trade distortions caused by TRPRs are viewed as only temporary, and are a limited price to pay in order to allow a country to establish a competitive industry. The weakness in the infant industry rationale is that it leaves the task of selecting the industries to be promoted and protected through the use of TRPRs to national governments.[12] The government selects which industries will eventually become competitive, presumably selecting the sectors in which the country enjoys a comparative advantage. This entails government tampering with the free market allocation of resources, and net welfare gains can only be obtained if the right sectors are chosen.[13]

TRPRs also can be viewed as a tool for preventing pricing abuses. Dealings between local subsidiaries and foreign parent companies are often not arms-length transactions. The cost of imports purchased from the parent company and used by the local subsidiary may be inflated. This reduces the paper profit of the subsidiary, thereby reducing the amount of income taxable by the host government. The imposition of local content requirements may be viewed as a "defense mechanism" against the dangers of transfer pricing abuses. However, more direct regulation of transfer pricing practices, such as the use of world market prices to determine arms-length prices to subsidiaries for tax purposes, would allow host governments to achieve their desired ends without inducing the trade distortions caused by TRPRs. If no such market exists, other commercial standards can be applied in evaluating for tax purposes the prices that foreign-owned subsidiaries must pay for inputs purchased from the parent company. For example, one can presume that arms-length prices have been applied in cases where the incidence of taxation is roughly comparable in the host country and the country where the parent is located.[14]

TRPRs may also be used in order to foster technology transfer. Local content requirements may encourage domestic manufacturers placed in the position of supplying production inputs to foreign-owned subsidiaries to adopt high, internationally accepted production standards.[15] Foreign-owned subsidiaries would presumably assist local producers in meeting the standards of the international marketplace. On the other hand, TRPRs have the effect of protecting local industry. Foreign-owned subsidiaries are forced to purchase inputs locally and the local manufacturers do not have to fear that foreign-owned subsidiaries will take their business elsewhere.

The technology transfer rationale also underlies the view that TRPRs are an effective means of allowing a country to develop a comparative advantage in a particular sector of its economy. Countries implementing TRPRs may not initially enjoy a comparative advantage in the production of the goods in question; however, once the foreign investor imports the technology required to meet the given TRPR, that country may in fact possess a comparative advantage. In other words, the country may possess a "latent" comparative advantage, having the needed factor endowments and simply requiring the necessary technology to exploit them. This raises the same issues that the infant industry argument raises, since governments are put in the position of selecting the sectors in which the country can become competitive, once given the needed technology. Finally, the need to eliminate balance of payments deficits, by stimulating exports and limiting imports through TRPRs, is a standard justification for the use of TRPRs. The use of performance requirements is not, however, the optimal means to solve balance of payments problems. Deflationary monetary or fiscal policies or exchange-rate depreciation are superior alternatives since they can be used to achieve the same result without distorting international trade.

The economic consequences of TRPRs are, in the long run, negative. Although TRPRs may be used by national governments to control and promote economic development, TRPRs generally place the various actors in the international economic system as a group in a worse position than without the use of TRPRs. To the extent this negative impact of TRPRs extends to the countries using·them, the use of other policy tools that do not have such a distorting effect on trade is preferable. In the final analysis, the economic distortions caused by TRPRs are the same in nature as the more conventional barriers to trade.

Political Issues

Strong political arguments have been raised both for and against the use of TRPRs. Countries that use them argue that they are an important domestic economic policy tool, and that to apply international legal standards to these practices would fail to recognize the necessity and political sensitivity of these measures.[16] The perceived need for the use of TRPRs is based, in part, on the long-standing distrust among many host countries of the most common foreign investor, the multinational corporation.[17] By serving their own interests in the course of establishing and operating foreign investments, multinational corporations are thought to act counter to the best interests of the host country. Peformance requirements are viewed by the host governments as a means of requiring multinationals to serve national goals. Otherwise, important sectors of the economy would be controlled or influenced by decision-makers with no responsibility to the host country. In order to preserve the government's control over the national economy and its development, it is thought necessary to channel the behavior of foreign investors by using performance requirements.

The concern over uncontrolled foreign direct investment and the resulting loss of sovereignty by national governments to the managers of the investing firms is understandable. However, performance requirements are inimical to free market economics and the promotion of international trade which is based on the free market. If they are implemented by host governments without objection, TRPRs will gain international legitimacy as a policy tool. Due to the economic welfare costs of TRPRs, this would be against the best interests of the international community as a whole. Moreover, there are two specific responses to the concerns expressed by countries using TRPRs. First, the use of performance requirements may cause economic inefficiencies in the host country, thereby thwarting the ends which the government pursues in adopting them. Second, the concept of free trade is simply irreconcilable with government controls in the form of TRPRs. The need to relinquish some measure of national sovereignty must be accepted if free trade is to be promoted. To argue that performance requirements are needed to preserve national sovereignty is tantamount to arguing that national sovereignty can only be preserved if a national government gives no quarter in its use of regulatory measures which affect the domestic economy. Export subsidies, import quotas, and tariffs are all tools of domestic economic policy. However, they have been banned or brought under international discipline through the GATT-MTN system in the interest of advancing free trade. Since TRPRs restrict international trade to the same extent, they should be subject to similar international control. The reduction of policy options for governments must simply be an acknowledged cost of international free trade. An argument that may be raised by less developed countries (LDCs) utilizing TRPRs is that performance requirements are needed to redirect more benefits of the international economic system toward LDCs. Without TRPRs, investing firms simply use LDCs as markets for their products unless a true comparative advantage exists in any of these countries; at most, these firms may assemble products locally, using only unskilled labor, without locating a substantial proportion of the manufacturing, or high technology, facilities in those countries.[18] Under these circumstances, the LDCs arguably will not be able to develop their industries to the point that they can become economically competitive with the developed countries. Local content requirements aimed at import substitution, and requiring firms to locate increased proportions of their manufacturing facilities in host LDCs[19] will shift jobs and capital to LDCs that otherwise would have gone to developed countries.

Performance requirements are not, however, a satisfactory tool for promoting a new international economic order. First, TRPRs tie a developing country into a whole set of trade restrictive measures, *e.g.*, quotas and licensing, that are needed to make the system work effectively. Second, TRPRs are unsatisfactory because of their net welfare cost to the international economic community. Third, performance requirements are only effective for those LDCs that are already economically prosperous relative to other LDCs. Mexico, for instance, among the wealthiest of the LDCs, has an extensive and very successful system of TRPRs.[20] The wealthier LDCs can offer lucrative markets, more educated workers, and more developed economic infrastructures than the less wealthy LDCs, enabling them to attract foreign investors willing to comply with TRPRs. The poorest LDCs, on the other hand, have a great deal of difficulty attracting foreign investment and are not in a position to make demands on foreign investors.[21] The use of TRPRs will accelerate the process of industrialization for a few LDCs, while stagnating the development of most. It therefore provides limited advantages and does little to create a more equitable economic system. It should be noted, however, that this argument against the use of TRPRs loses a great deal of its persuasiveness given the failure of developed countries to provide adequate and effective development aid. Under these circumstances, performance requirements can be defended as a second best means of assisting some developing countries in the absence of greater generosity by the developed countries.

The political arguments made against the use of TRPRs are those which have often been made for free trade.[22] The free flow of trade and capital promotes economic interdependence, and this, in turn, causes international political stability. Countries that rely on each other economically are less likely to allow their disagreements to result in armed conflict and more likely to develop international institutions that will facilitate diplomatic dispute resolution.[23] Further, a more interdependent world is more stable economically and less susceptible to global economic collapse of the sort experienced in the late 1920s. The result of such a collapse would likely be political instability and violence on the national and international levels. Of course, TRPRs will not, by themselves lead to such political instability. However, they are an impediment to international trade, and therefore, a threat to the political stability encouraged by free trade.

TRADE-RELATED PERFORMANCE REQUIREMENTS UNDER THE GATT-MTN SYSTEM

The most persuasive reason for the abolition of TRPRs is that they violate a variety of international agreements, most notably the General Agreement on Tariffs and Trade and the MTN Subsidies Code. While most TRPRs were not contemplated when these agreements were entered into, they violate both the spirit and the letter of the agreements because they have the same or similar effects as the measures in use at the time of the agreements which were made illegal.

General Agreement on Tariffs and Trade

Although no single article of GATT is applicable to all forms of TRPRs, all TRPRs arguably violate one article or another. Some TRPRs clearly run afoul of specific provisions while the case against other forms is weaker, given a strict construction of treaty obligations. Nonetheless, where obligations do not appear, on their face, to prohibit certain TRPRs, the general intent and context of the GATT-MTN system should be considered. The system is intended to foster free trade, while TRPRs are protectionist measures. The presumption should, therefore, be against considering any TRPR valid under GATT. Of course, these provisions are only applicable to those countries that are signatories to GATT.

Application of GATT Rules to TRPRs

GATT Tariff Concessions and Nullification and Impairment.   In one sense, GATT is nothing more than a multilateral tariff agreement, with a set of rules designed to protect the value of tariff concessions.[24] Against this background, TRPRs may properly be challenged as having the effect of providing protection above and beyond that provided for in a country's tariff schedule. Hence, they violate the provisions of Article II, paragraph 1, which stipulate that imports shall receive no less favorable treatment than that provided for in each GATT member's schedule.

This principle can be illustrated quite simply by considering the effect of a local content requirement. Assume that a country has a GATT tariff concession under which the duty on automobile engines is bound at 10 percent. At the same time, the country has a local content requirement that specifies that cars produced in the country must contain at least 75 percent local content. To comply with this requirement, a company decides to substitute locally produced engines for engines imported from the United States. If the engines produced locally would not have been purchased absent the local content requirement, the requirement has the effect of protecting local production of auto engines beyond that specified in the GATT bound tariff on that item.

GATT panels carried this principle one step further in their interpretations of Article XXIII.[25] Under that article, GATT members can complain against any measure applied by another GATT member, whether or not it conflicts with the provisions of GATT, if such measure has the effect of "nullifying" or "impairing" any benefit accruing directly or indirectly to the complaining party under GATT.[26] In one of the earliest GATT panel decisions, it was concluded that the benefits of tariff concessions would be impaired if it could be shown that the competitive relationship between the domestic product and the imported product was upset by government action, the effect of which could not have been reasonably anticipated at the time the concession was negotiated.[27] A local content requirement has the effect of upsetting this competitive relationship and accordingly can be viewed as a nullification or impairment of GATT tariff concessions.[28]

An extension of this logic can be applied to export requirements. The analogue to the principle that countries may not impose on imports treatment more onerous than their tariffs is that a country is entitled to the protection its tariff provide—which is the rationale for allowing countries to impose countervailing and antidumping duties to prevent foreign subsidies and unfairly low priced sales from undercutting the protection afforded by tariffs. Export requirements have the same effect as subsidies because they stimulate exports beyond what the market would dictate. Export accordingly can be viewed as a nullification or impairment of the benefits the United States is entitled to under GATT—the protective effect of its own tariffs. The result of an export requirement is to deny that benefit, and the United States is entitled to seek removal of the practices or may be entitled to take offsetting measures.

National Treatment. Article III, entitled "National Treatment on Internal Taxation and Regulation," bans all local content requirements.[29] This article requires that imported goods be taxed and regulated in the same manner as domestically produced goods. Essentially it is a rule of nondiscrimination. This basic principle is stated in paragraph 1:

> The contracting parties recognize that internal charges, and laws, regulations and requirements affecting the internal sale, offering for sale, purchase, transportation, distribution or use of products, and internal quantitative regulations requiring the mixture, processing or use of products in specified amount or proportions, should not be applied to imported or domestic products so as to afford protection to domestic production.

Local content requirements are "internal quantitative regulations" which require foreign investors to include a certain proportion of locally produced content in their products. These TRPRs protect domestic production by causing the foreign investor either to purchase needed components from existing local producers or to establish additional local production facilities. Therefore, local content requirements "should not be applied" under a strict construction of Article III. Indeed, the GATT draftsmen specifically intended to prohibit local content requirements in Article III: "Mixing [local content] requirements received extensive consideration by the draftsmen. For example, a requirement might be imposed that margarine contain at least 20 percent domestically produced margarine or butter. This would violate the GATT obligation.[30]

Paragraph 5 of article III bans local content requirements in even more forceful terms than does paragraph 1. It disallows quantitative regulations "relating to the . . . use of products in specified . . . proportions which" require that the specified "proportion of any product . . . must be supplied from domestic sources. The wording is a virtual definition of local content requirements, and simply reinforces the paragraph 1 ban.[31]

Paragraph 4, which establishes a rule of equal treatment in the application of domestic laws, has a more limited applicability to local content requirements than do paragraphs 1 and 5, but it applies to certain export promotion performance requirements as well. Paragraph 4 forbids all local content requirements that are tied to market access *i.e.*, the firm is denied access to the country's market unless it is willing to produce a certain proportion of its product's content locally; it also prohibits all export performance requirements tying the required level of exports to the firm's level of imports. Paragraph 4 requires that rules governing "internal sale, offer for sale, purchase, transportation, distribution or use" be no less favorable for imports than products of national origin. The export requirements described above are rules governing the internal "use" of imports since the level of imports that the firm can use is limited by the level of its exports. The effect is thus discriminatory against imports.

Paragraph 2 forbids "internal taxes or other charges (against imported goods) of any kind in excess of those applied, directly or indirectly, to like domestic products." Paragraph 2 thus outlaws the use of taxes or special charges levied against firms that do not comply with local content requirements; by charging higher tax rates, or other fees, to investments not meeting local content requirements, a country is indirectly charging imported goods which a manufacturer chooses to use instead of local goods.

In sum, all forms of local content requirements are banned under article III. Paragraphs 1 and 5, and in some instances paragraph 4, forbid local content requirements. Export performance requirements that are tied to the level of a firm's imports are prohibited under paragraph 4 as well.

General Elimination of Quantitative Restrictions.   One of the most significant contributions of GATT has been the effort to eliminate quantitative restrictions on imports, leaving tariffs as the only permissible trade barrier. Article XI, entitled "General Elimination of Quantitative Restrictions," prohibits restrictions other than duties, taxes, or other charges, whether made effective through quotas, licenses, "or other measures" applied to imports.

Local content requirements function as quantitative restrictions on imports. If a firm sells X worth of its product locally and if ⅓ of the value of the goods it sells locally must be produced locally, the firm can import only ⅔ X worth of the components for that good. Without this restriction the firm would be able to import any proportion of X that efficiency and consumer demand dictate. Even though X itself will be determined by the market, this simply means that the import restriction will be determined by a domestic market criterion. This is no more permissible than a conventional import quota adjusted according to some domestic market criterion. For instance, if a country set a quota on the import of a given product and then adjusted the quota in accord with the level of domestic sales of that product in order to preserve the market share of domestic producers, the quota would violate Article XI. Local content requirements have the same effect on individual foreign firms and therefore violate one of the most significant GATT provisions.

A similar argument can be made that the GATT ban on quantitative restrictions applies to export performance requirements, although the argument is not as compelling. The wording which applies to quantitative restrictions on imports in paragraph 1 also applies to "prohibitions or restrictions" on the "exportation or sale for exportation of any product. . . ." Export performance requirements can be viewed as restricting an investing firm's export decisions by imposing a minimum level of exports, whether that level be fixed or indexed. However, given common usage of the word "prohibition," the language used in Article XI was probably intended to prohibit export ceilings and not to impose minimum export levels. Export performance requirements which are not linked to any prohibited government subsidy are, therefore, less susceptible to challenge under GATT provisions.[32] Nevertheless, the pernicious effects of export performance requirements, which are in some ways analogous to export subsidies, should make them the target of future multilateral trade negotiations.

GATT provides a broad exception to the ban on quantitative restrictions where they are implemented for balance of payment reasons.[33] An extensive discussion of the lengthy and detailed provisions which constitute this exception would not be useful here. A brief review, however, is in order. Article XII provides that quantitative import restrictions can be used in order to safeguard a country's external financial position and balance of payments. The article further provides that such restrictions shall not exceed those necessary:

> (i) to forestall the imminent threat of, or to stop, a serious decline in its monetary reserves, or (ii) in the case of a contracting party with very low monetary reserves, to achieve a reasonable rate of increase in its reserves.

Any contracting party imposing a quota under this exception is also required "to avoid unnecessary damage to the commercial or economic interests of any other contracting party" and the unreasonable prevention of imports "which would impair regular channels of trade."[34] Furthermore, GATT members imposing balance of payments quotas must undertake, to "avoid an uneconomic employment of productive resources." Given these obligations, the long-term use of TRPRs cannot be justified under the balance of payments exception. TRPRs cause long-term diversion of capital and jobs from other contracting parties, effects which do not accompany more traditional means of combating balance of payments deficits. Because the long-term harm to other contracting parties can be avoided and is thus unnecessary, Article XII should not be seen as a broad exception allowing quantitative restrictions which would otherwise violate Article XI.[35]

TRPRs commit firms to export at or above some level, or to import at or below a given level. This imposes a rigidity on trade relations which Article XI was intended to ban. The longstanding U.S. policy towards such restrictions reflects strong concern over their restrictive effects. At the first GATT preparatory session in 1947, the U.S. delegation stated that "[of] the forms of restrictionism ever devised by the mind of man, Quantitative Restriction is the worst."[36]

Subsidies. Investment incentives or other subsidies linked to export performance requirements on "nonprimary products,"[37] resulting "in the sale of such product for export at a price lower than the comparable price charged for the like product to buyers in the domestic market," are prohibited under paragraph 4 of Article XVI.[38] The standard for determining the legality of subsidies linked to export performance requirements for primary products is different. They are not allowed where they result in "more than an equitable share of world export trade" for the subsidizing nation. Government-supplied benefits linked to export performance requirements generally set a firm's exports at levels higher than the level that the firm would choose under free market conditions. Paragraph 3 defines an export subsidy as one "which operates to *increase the export*" of the primary product in question. A 1960 GATT panel concluded that the phrase "increased exports" was intended "to include the concept of maintaining exports at a level higher than would otherwise exist in the absence of the subsidy.[39] Thus, artificially high export levels induced by government-supplied incentives would be characterized as being caused by an export subsidy subject to the provisions of paragraph 3. At least one authority feels that the definition of subsidy in paragraph 3 applies to primary products in paragraph 4 as well.[40] Government-supplied benefits used to induce compliance with export performance requirements are thus prohibited by GATT Article XVI.

State Trading Enterprises. Article XVII, entitled "State Trading Enterprises," provides that state enterprises or firms receiving "exclusive or special privileges" from the state must be permitted to make purchases and sales involving imports or exports in a manner: (a) consistent with the "general principles of nondiscriminatory treatment" contained in GATT, and (b) made solely in accordance with commercial considerations.[41] Paragraph 1(c) of this article applies these principles not only to the controls on "state enterprises," but to any firm under the jurisdiction of the host government.[42]

Firms bound by local content requirements must limit their imports or inputs for their products and use more local inputs. This violates the national treatment principle of nondiscrimination contained in Article III. Furthermore, the local content requirements are limitations imposed for national economic policy rather than for purely commercial considerations. Export performance requirements linked to import levels violate the same principles. Due to limitations imposed by export markets, the firm may not be able to raise exports to desired levels and, therefore, have to curtail imports.

There are several strong counterarguments based upon comments made in GATT preparatory meetings[43] and a strict interpretation of Article XVII,[44] that Article XVII only requires adherence to the most-favored-nation principle tempered by commercial considerations. First, it may be argued that, because subparagraph (1)(a) refers to purchases or sales involving "imports or exports," the nondiscrimination principle was intended to be limited to the issue of discrimination among imports or exports of different foreign governments, *i.e.*, the most-favored-nation principle. In response, however, it should be noted that Article III, which contains the national treatment principle of nondiscrimination, refers to nondiscrimination "involving imports or exports." The similar language in both articles suggests that the limited view of Article XVII is not the proper interpretation.

A second argument in support of a limited view is that the nature of state enterprises is such that expecting them to comply with national treatment principles is illogical. State enterprises are established to achieve national policy goals and they must act according to the dictates of these goals, not the forces of the free market. The inclusion of Article XVII in GATT to provide rules under which state enterprises may operate is itself an indication that enterprises of this sort are permissible.

The application of the most-favored-nation principle to state enterprises, however, indicates an intent to limit the types of behavior through which state enterprises achieve national policy goals. Application of the national treatment principle is merely an extension of this concept. State enterprises may continue to exist, and therefore serve national policy goals, as long as they do not violate these principles or other applicable GATT rules. They may be used, for instance, to advance the level of technology in a country by conducting research and development and by producing and marketing high technology goods.

Finally, an argument supporting a limited interpretation of Article XVII can be found in an Interpretative Note added to clarify the application of the most-favored-nation principle. This provision could indicate the intent of the draftsmen that the principle of nondiscrimination referred to in the article was the most-favored-nation principle. However, the Note does not indicate that the inclusion of the national treatment principle was meant to be precluded; in fact, the wording of the Note may also be applied to the national treatment principle.[45]

Several additional points should be considered in evaluating this issue. First, subparagraph 1 (a) refers to "the general principles of non-discriminatory treatment." This plural reference indicates that more than the most-favored-nation principle was incorporated. All GATT principles of nondiscriminatory treatment, such as the national treatment principle, should be included under this wording. Second, if the national treatment principle of Article III is not incorporated into Article XVII, Article III could be circumvented through the use of state enterprises, or private enterprises which are granted exclusive or special privileges to implement a wide variety of policies that discriminate against imported goods. Domestic producers could be granted an exclusive right to market domestically so that foreign producers could only export to the domestic market by selling to these domestic firms. In return, the domestic firms could be required to discriminate against foreign producers in the same ways as would be prohibited under Article III if done by the government directly.[46]

Given the danger of undermining Article III, one of the most essential of the GATT provisions, any ambiguity should be resolved in favor of construing Article XVII to require national treatment. Local content requirements and export performance requirements linked to import levels are, therefore, prohibited by the national treatment principle in Article XVII.

Article XXIII as a Means of Recourse

Article XXIII, entitled "Nullification or Impairment," provides a dispute settlement mechanism through which contracting parties imposing TRPRs can be challenged for violating GATT obligations. Under this provision the contracting parties, acting in a judicial capacity, hear the arguments that a benefit under the GATT is being "nullified or impaired," and make recommendations to the parties or give a ruling "as appropriate." If the circumstances are "serious enough," the contracting parties may authorize a specific form of retaliation. The party or parties bringing the action may suspend the application of "concessions or other obligations" under GATT to the party's or parties' impairment.

Because any government measure that violates one of the GATT provisions discussed above constitutes a *prima facie* nullification or impairment of a GATT benefit,[47] TRPRs can be challenged through the dispute settlement mechanism. Once an infringement of a provision is shown, it is incumbent upon the government imposing a TRPR to bring forth evidence showing that nullification or impairment has not occurred. Where the accused country fails to produce substantive evidence or arguments to the contrary, the Contracting Parties must determine whether the circumstances are serious enough to justify authorization of remedial actions.

Prima facie nullification or impairment may also be found where quantitative restrictions, such as those relating to TRPRs, are challenged. Of course, even where quantitative restrictions are shown to exist, a balance-of-payments justification can be made. Nonetheless, it has been argued that even where a quantitative restriction is legal under GATT because of a balance-of-payments justification, there is *prima facie* nullification and impairment.[48] In addition, since the balance-of-payments exception should not apply whre TRPRs are used, TRPRs should be *prima facie* nullification or impairment.

All TRPRs may be seen as *prima facie* nullification or impairment of at least one GATT provision. Thus, where one contracting party brings an Article XXIII action against another for implementing a TRPR, the burden is upon the latter party to show that its TRPR does not cause nullification or impairment of a benefit accruing under the particular GATT provisions violated by the imposition of that TRPR. Whether the contracting parties then recommend that the TRPR be discontinued, or go further and authorize suspension of a concession or other obligation, should depend on the economic impact of the TRPR.

Subsidies Code

Under the Subsidies Code, all export performance requirements linked to investment incentives or other subsidies for nonprimary products are banned outright.[49] The rule on "certain primary products" remains fundamentally the same as under GATT Article XVI. However, Article 10(2) sharpens the definition of "equitable share of world trade," making it easier to apply.[50]

The requirement that export prices for nonprimary products be shown to be below the home market price of the like product in order to show a violation of Article XVI of the GATT relating to subsidies appears to have been dropped.[51] While this was not done explicitly, the Code imposes a flat ban on "export subsidies" and includes in the illustrative list in the attached annex practices considered to be "export subsidies" without reference to a price differential. The illustrative list also defines an export subsidy as "[t]he provision of governments of direct subsidies to a firm or an industry contingent upon export performance."

In recognition of the importance of subsidies to economic development programs of developing countries, the ban on export subsidies on nonprimary products does not apply to LDCs. However, these countries are obligated not to use export subsidies in a manner that causes "serious prejudice to the trade or production of another signatory." Since "serious prejudice" is not specifically defined, it is not clear how effectively this obligation can be invoked against export performance requirements linked to government-supplied benefits in LDCs.

Article 14(5) states that an LDC signatory should "endeavor to enter into a commitment to reduce or eliminate export subsidies when the use of such export subsidies is inconsistent with its competitive and development needs." U.S. negotiators intended that this provision apply specifically to the more advanced LDCs. These LDCs are arguably most likely to induce export performance by supplying benefits, such as investment incentives, since the poorer LDCs cannot afford to do so. The United States indicated in the negotiations that it would require a commitment to phase out export subsidies or it would not extend the benefits of the more stringent injury test in countervailing duty cases to the country in question. The United States has subsequently undertaken negotiations to obtain agreements designed in part to phase out export performance requirements linked to government-supplied benefits.

Where the terms of the Subsidies Code are violated, part VI of the Code provides for a dispute settlement mechanism. If the parties involved fail to settle a dispute through consultations, a report is prepared by a panel for a committee comprised of all signatories to the Code. This committee, acting in an adjudicatory capacity, makes recommendations based on the report; if these are not followed it may authorize "appropriate countermeasures."[52] Because of the adverse impact of TRPRs on the world economic order, the committee should recommend abolition where export performance requirements linked to government-supplied benefits are found, and authorize countermeasures where this recommendation is not followed.

TRADE-RELATED PERFORMANCE REQUIREMENTS UNDER U.S. LAW

Two avenues are available under U.S. law to challenge TRPRs implemented by other countries. They are the countervailing duty provisions and section 301 of the Trade Agreements Act of 1979 (Trade Agreements Act). The countervailing duty provisions are limited in scope and will only apply to TRPRs where government-supplied benefits are used to induce compliance.[53] Section 301, on the other hand, is extremely broad in scope and does not provide for detailed procedures and specific legal standards similar to those in countervailing duty actions.[54] Rather, the section 301 procedure is informal and is geared strongly to international agreements and dispute settlement procedures, including those of the GATT-MTN system.

Countervailing Duty Proceedings

Goods imported into the United States that are produced in facilities subject to any TRPR linked to a government-supplied benefit are subject to countervailing duties where those goods threaten to cause or in fact do cause "material injury" to a domestic industry.[55] Because proof of the government-supplied benefit and "material injury" is sufficient, a countervailing duty proceeding could be used to counter the methods used by the host country to coerce or simply encourage compliance with TRPRs, rather than against the TRPR itself.

The countervailing duty provisions apply to subsidies provided "directly or indirectly . . . with respect to the manufacture, production, or exportation of a class or kind of merchandise imported into the United States. . . ." Government-supplied benefits linked to local content requirements are provided "with respect to" manufacture or production because local content requirements, like all performance requirements, apply to production facilities by definition. Government-supplied benefits linked to export performance requirements are also provided "with respect to" exportation. Furthermore, these benefits are included by reference in the Trade Agreement Act's definition of subsidy. The Act states that the term "subsidy" includes, but is not limited to, "[a]ny export subsidy described in Annex A to the [Subsidies Code] relating to an illustrative list of export subsidies." As discussed above, item (a) on this list refers specifically to government-supplied benefits linked to export performance requirements.

The Trade Agreement Act's legislative history shows that subsidies conferred by other countries as part of their domestic economic policy were intended to be actionable. Both the House and Senate reports use subsidies offered in conjunction with regional development plans as an example in defining the concept of "net subsidy": "[I]f a firm were given a tax deduction for moving to a disadvantaged area, the value of the subsidy is the tax deduction available."[56] The selection of such subsidies to serve as the example indicates that virtually all forms of subsidies, including those related to TRPRs, are covered by the Act.

The courts, in reviewing countervailing duty determinations, have also concluded that any benefit conferred upon a firm for whatever purpose is a subsidy under the countervailing duty provisions. Although this case law was developed under the countervailing duty provisions preceding the Trade Agreements Act, the definition of subsidy under the current provisions explicitly incorporates every practice included in the previous definition. The House of Representatives report on the Trade Agreements Act states "[t]he meaning of 'subsidy' under this title retains the meaning which practice and the courts have ascribed to the term 'bounty or grant'. . . ." In *Nicholas & Co. v. United States*,[57] the Supreme Court gave a very broad reading to the term "bounty or grant," stating: "If the word 'bounty' has a limited sense the word 'grant' has not. A word of broader significance than 'grant' could not have been used. Like its synonyms 'give' and 'bestow,' it expresses a concession, the conferring of something by one person upon another."

Recent case law regarding the granting of subsidies for domestic policy reasons was developed in the "float glass cases."[58] In *ASG Industries Inc. v. United States*, countervailing duty actions were brought by U.S. manufacturers against imports of float glass from various European countries. The European float glass manufacturers had benefited from regional development programs and had received such benefits as low-interest loans and investment incentives in the form of cash grants. On appeal of the unsuccessful administrative proceedings, the courts found "bounties or grants" subject to countervailing duties.

In a different administrative proceeding, countervailing duties were imposed on Michelin tire imports from Canada on the grounds that the Canadian Michelin plant had benefited from subsidies under a regional development plan.[59] Prior to this decision, it had been administrative practice to apply countervailing duties only against subsidies intended as artificial export stimulants.[60] This practice resulted from the view that action taken against production subsidies designed to develop regional industries might be seen as interference in domestic affairs.[61] The current rule, as defined in the legislative history of the Trade Agreements Act, the *Michelin* decision, and the "float glass cases," provides an additional tool which can be used by private parties against government-supplied benefits linked to TRPRs. If such a subsidy is shown and "material injury" is established, a countervailing duty should be levied on the imports regardless of the purpose of the government-supplied benefit.

Section 301 Proceedings

Section 301 of the Trade Agreements Act[62] allows private parties to request presidential action "to enforce the rights of the United States under any trade agreement . . . "[63] and to initiate international legal proceedings and consultations. Section 301 proceedings are an appropriate means for parties aggrieved by violations of the GATT-MTN obligations discussed above to gain access to a forum and to initiate action in the form of consultations and dispute settlement procedures against the TRPRs.

Under section 301, a private party may petition the U.S. Trade Representative to initiate an investigation of a violation of U.S. rights under a trade agreement. The Trade Representative has discretion to deny this petition.[64] If the petition is granted, however, notice of the investigation must be published in the Federal Register and an opportunity for a public hearing must be provided. This affords interested parties the opportunity to express views regarding the TRPR involved and the way in which it violates GATT or Subsidies Code provisions. If a practice is found to be inconsistent with international obligations or unjustifiably or unreasonably burdensome to U.S. commerce, the Trade Representative must commence consultations with the country in question. In this way, a dispute over a TRPR may be raised directly with the offending country. If no mutually acceptable resolution, presumably involving withdrawal of the TRPR, is agreed upon with the other country during the consultation period, the U.S. Trade Representative must initiate dispute settlement proceedings if such proceedings are provided for in the negotiated agreement.[65] This would involve the Subsidies Code dispute settlement mechanism and/or GATT Article XXIII, depending on the type of TRPR complained against.

The Trade Representative must also prepare recommendations for action by the President based upon the findings of its investigation.[66] The President may "respond to any act, policy, or practice of a foreign country or instrumentality that is inconsistent with the provisions of, or otherwise denies benefits under, any trade agreement. . . ." The President may take retaliatory action by withdrawing concessions made to the foreign country in a trade agreement and may impose duties or other import restrictions on the products of the country in question. Thus, the President has extremely broad latitude to act against countries implementing TRPRs.

ALTERNATIVE U.S. STRATEGIES TO LIMIT THE USE OF TRPRs

The continuing proliferation of TRPRs and the ineffectiveness of U.S. efforts to mitigate their adverse effects on U.S. trade interests have prompted the suggestion that an improved legislative framework is needed to deal with the problem.[67] Indeed, several legislative proposals are currently pending before Congress.[68] This section will consider possible U.S. strategies for addressing the issue of TRPRs, including the legislative alternatives being considered.

International Negotiations

The most effective solution to the problems posed by TRPRs would be the formulation of a multilateral agreement, either through the GATT-MTN system or separately,[69] that would specifically prohibit or limit the use of TRPRs. This approach has the advantage of dealing in an explicit or comprehensive manner with TRPRs and could include countries not currently members of GATT. The United States has been seeking such an agreement,[70] but there is little evidence that these efforts will soon reach fruition unless the United States acquires additional leverage to force the pace.[71]

Work toward an international consensus on the need to limit TRPRs has been initiated by the United States in a variety of international forums. For example, the United States has prompted the Organization for Economic Cooperation and Development to agree to examine the impact of TRPRs on international trade. The United States also raised the issue in the GATT Consultative Group of 18 and persuaded the Secretariat to examine the issue in light of relevant GATT articles; in its review, however, the GATT Secretariat avoided taking a position on the relevance of particular GATT articles, preferring to leave that issue open to a case-by-case review.[72] In the Development Committee, a group sponsored jointly by the World Bank and the International Monetary Fund, a major study has been initiated to examine the impact of investment incentives and performance requirements on investment and trade patterns. This study is to be based on a selected group of industry-country case studies.

The fact that these initiatives are only designed to discuss the issue of the formulation of new rules directed specifically at TRPRs suggests that many countries do not share the U.S. view that TRPRs pose a real challenge to existing international trade rules. Indeed, these countries may perceive that their self-interests are best served by retaining the flexibility to impose TRPRs. If this is the case, actions to enforce U.S. rights under existing agreements may be the most effective alternative.

Changes in Section 301

As discussed above, section 301 provides a means of recourse for domestic parties against TRPRs implemented abroad. However, section 301 proceedings have never been initiated against any TRPR even though there is now significant U.S. opposition to their use and a sound case can be made under section 301 that TRPRs violate U.S. rights under international agreements.[73] Several possible reasons for this failure to file section 301 complaints may exist. U.S. companies have a natural tendency to take international markets as they find them.[74] Where performance requirements exist, a business judgment must be made either to accommodate the investment to the requirement or to invest elsewhere. Once an investment is made there is little incentive to challenge TRPRs for fear of retaliation or, perhaps more importantly, to avoid making the way any easier for a potential competitor to enter the local market. Furthermore, private parties may not perceive section 301 as a meaningful alternative to dealing with TRPRs. A number of changes could be made to change this perception and to make section 301 an even more effective remedy.

Legislation to promote the use of section 301 against TRPRs should contain three primary elements. First, Congress should express its sense that section 301 should be used more aggressively to counter the use of TRPRs abroad. In particular, the administration should be encouraged to use its authority to initiate cases against TRPRs to avoid the threat of retaliation against any private parties. Private parties might thus also be encouraged by such a statement because it would be more difficult for the administration to refuse to press the case. Second, section 301 should be amended to refer specifically to TRPRs. This, together with the first change, would publicize to private parties that section 301 is an appropriate response to TRPRs. It would also make private parties more confident of success before incurring the expense of bringing a section 301 action, thereby making such actions more likely. Third, the President should be authorized to fashion investment-related retaliation against countries implementing TRPRs. This, in combination with the existing section 301 authority to impose sanctions on trade and services, would allow the President to tailor measures to fit the offending measures where countries refuse to negotiate an agreement limiting the use of TRPRs.

The same legislation should contain three provisions to make section 301 more effective. First, the U.S. Trade Representative should be given the authority to make a final decision as to the appropriate U.S. action to be taken, including possible retaliation.[75] Decisions could be referred to the President for review to take effect 20 days thereafter, unless the President decided to override the Trade Representative. Focusing responsibility on the Trade Representative would significantly enhance his negotiating leverage and probably lead to more consistent, less politicized decisions. Second, the Trade Representative should be authorized to appoint special experts from other agencies or from U.S. industry in order to provide expertise in individual cases. This would significantly improve the fact-finding aspects of the section 301 process, a critical element in a successful international dispute settlement process. Third, the Trade Representative's decision-making process should be made slightly more formal. The Trade Representative should be required to publish a preliminary determination within a stated period of accepting a petition for investigation[76] before reaching a final determination. This preliminary determination procedure would give the USTR an opportunity to use an affirmative preliminary determination for bargaining leverage, thereby promoting early settlements and possibly avoiding the need to proceed to a final determination and formal consultations with the government concerned.[77] A preliminary determination would also serve to focus the investigation, providing an opportunity to discard issues on which the case against the foreign government is weak.

Generalized System of Preferences

The Generalized System of Preferences (GSP) is a program under which less developed countries can export certain qualified goods to the United States duty free.[78] The criteria for determining which countries and which goods from these countries qualify for GSP benefits do not take into account the adherence of developing countries to international agreements generally, and in particular their use of trade-distorting performance requirements.[79] Several proposals, including a bill introduced by Senators Heinz and Moynihan, seek to ensure that the use of TRPRs is taken into account in determining GSP eligibility. This would bring additional pressure to bear on countries which would be designated as eligible for GSP benefits but for their use of TRPRs.

International Financial Institutions

The international financial institutions exercise significant influence on developing countries' economic policies. Furthermore, as a major contributor, the United States has considerable influence on the lending policies of these institutions. It is appropriate, therefore, for the United States to urge these institutions to review carefully the use of TRPRs in their financing decisions. Countries that use TRPRs as economic policy tools should be urged to change their policies as a condition for obtaining financing. Furthermore, the U.S. executive directors of these institutions should be directed by legislation to vote against loans to countries that impose TRPRs. By making it more difficult to receive loans from these institutions, negotiations may lead to concessions in some cases and an overall reduction in the use of TRPRs.[80]

Other Proposals

A number of other proposals addressing the TRPR issue have been made. In one case, legislation has been enacted that would limit the Overseas Private Investment Corporation's authority to insure or guarantee any investment subject to performance requirements that would tend to reduce significantly the positive benefits of such investments to the U.S. trade balance.[81] A key issue with respect to this legislation is the impact that it will have on U.S. investment and the possibility that it will put U.S. investors at a disadvantage relative to their foreign competitors who receive similar guarantees without any consideration of the impact of a TRPR. This suggests the need for a multilateral agreement among investment guarantee agencies not to support investments in such circumstances.

Other proposals have suggested the need for improved private rights of action. Some proposals adopt the increasingly popular reciprocity approach. In other words, a private party would have a statutory right to obtain restrictions on foreign investors that "mirror" the restrictions faced in a foreign country. Such action has been suggested to deal with the restrictions imposed by the Canadian government on U.S. energy investments in Canada, but this proposal does not appear to have gained wide support, in part because it tends to grant a sense of legitimacy to national policies intended to restrict the outflow of capital and because it would deny the United States a potentially valuable source of investment capital. Suggestions have also been made to improve the rights of parties seeking redress against TRPRs under the antidumping and countervailing duty laws. These proposals would make it easier to invoke those laws against TRPRs by creating certain presumptions. For example, a subsidy could be defined to include TRPRs, and a minimum subsidy amount, perhaps 10 percent, would be presumed to exist, unless the respondent could show otherwise. One could also presume injury to exist whenever any TRPR is proven, thereby shifting the burden of proving lack of injury to the respondent. Finally, in cases in which subsidies are granted to gain acquiescence to export requirements, one could allocate the entire subsidy to the net additional exports and impose a countervailing duty equal to the amount so allocated.[82] The higher the amount of countervailing duty, the more unlikely that the additional units can be sold for export. Each of these proposals has certain drawbacks, most notably that they could have adverse effects on third parties who are not associated with the use of TRPRs. For this reason, they are clearly not preferable to the elimination or limitation of TRPRs through the enforcement of existing international agreements and through new multilateral negotiations. Consequently, statutory changes should be made as part of a broad effort to bring pressure to bear against the use of TRPRs. This effort should incorporate both the enactment of new measures and the initiation of actions in domestic and international forums.

CANADA'S FOREIGN INVESTMENT REVIEW ACT: A BRIEF CASE STUDY

The Canadian Foreign Investment Review Act (FIRA)[83] provides an excellent example of government control over foreign investment in the form of TRPRs. In broad outline, all foreign investments must be approved by the government after consideration of specific statutory criteria, which include local sourcing and export promotion. Generally, foreign investors agree to certain performance requirements, called undertakings, formulated to satisfy the statutory criteria, prior to the investment's approval. The TRPRs under the Act are typical in that their terms are not generally made public, which makes useful analysis of the effects of the TRPRs difficult or impossible. Nevertheless, available information is adequate to reveal that they run afoul of the obligations contained in GATT and the Subsidies Code, and that remedies are available under both GATT Article XXIII and U.S. law.

FIRA was enacted by the Canadian Parliament out of concern that "Canadian industry, trade and commerce has become acquired by persons other than Canadians and the effect thereof on the ability of Canadians to maintain effective control over their economic environment [has been impaired]. . . ." The desire to prevent infringement of national sovereignty is also the rationale for imposing performance requirements under the Act. FIRA established the Foreign Investment Review Agency and stipulated that it should only approve those foreign investments that are, or are likely to be, of "significant benefit" to Canada. The Act lists the factors to be considered in this decision. These include "the effect on . . . the utilization of parts, components and services produced in Canada, and on exports from Canada."

Potential foreign investors must file proposals with the Review Agency. The Compliance Branch of the Review Agency makes a preliminary determination of whether the proposal is reviewable under the Act. If the basic criteria are satisfied, the proposal is advanced to the Assessment Branch which evaluates it in terms of the domestic economic policy factors stated in the Act. During this stage, further information regarding the planned investment may be obtained through direct contacts between the Agency and the potential investor. This in essence constitutes a negotiation process in which more favorable undertakings can be obtained from the firm. Upon completion of this process, the Assessment Branch prepares a report for the Minister of Industry, Trade, and Commerce who, in turn, recommends to the Cabinet whether or not to approve the investment.

The Review Agency's Compliance Branch regularly monitors the implementation of undertakings by investors and where an investment fails to comply, the Minister of Industry, Trade, and Commerce may initiate legal proceedings under the Act to compel compliance. The Canadian government claims a high degree of compliance. The FIRA Annual Report for 1979–80 states: "Most investors by far are fulfilling their commitments. In a few cases changed economic circumstances make it necessary to renegotiate undertakings and to obtain new undertakings to replace original ones." This compliance system indicates the mandatory character of Canadian TRPRs, although there is flexibility in formulating the terms that firms must meet. The case is currently before a panel of experts formed under Article XXIII of GATT.

Two specific examples demonstrate the means by which the Canadian government imposes performance requirements under the Act to achieve domestic economic goals. In 1979, Phillips Cables Limited, a U.S. firm, acquired Northern Telecom, a Canadian firm. Phillips Cables' first proposal to the Review Agency for the acquisition, however, was turned down; only after the firm substantially modified its proposal was it approved. Phillips undertook to double its exports and to replace, with goods produced in Canada, approximately $1 million in goods that Northern Telecom had been importing annually. When Amer Sports International Inc. purchased Novasport Ltd. it committed itself to certain levels of export performance and local sourcing. The Canadian government cited these among the principal reasons for approving the investment.[84]

Both private and U.S. government action can be taken to counteract the TRPRs imposed by FIRA. Indeed, the United States has begun the process of challenging the Canadian practices under FIRA as a violation of applicable GATT rules. Furthermore, given the GATT violations involved in the Canadian practices,[85] an affected U.S. party could initiate a section 301 action. For example, one party could be a former supplier of Northern Telecom whose sales were among the $1 million in eliminated imports. This supplier could petition the U.S. Trade Representative, arguing that these TRPRs violate GATT. If the U.S. Trade Representative accepted the petition, consultations would commence with Canada in an effort to have the TRPRs removed. If this were unsuccessful, the President, besides commencing an Article XXIII action, has the option of choosing from a broad array of retaliatory sanctions against Canada, although this last possibility is unlikely, due to the political importance of maintaining friendly relations with Canada. The best opportunity for success lies in the less hostile process of GATT consultations.

CONCLUSION

Trade-related performance requirements should be opposed for legal and policy reasons. However, a blind confrontational strategy toward TRPRs without sensitivity to the outlooks of the governments implementing them would be neither productive nor desirable. Diplomatic efforts that focus on alternative means for the removal of TRPRs through which countries can achieve their policy goals without the same trade-distorting effects may be the most effective. In the case of LDCs, for instance, increased aid to facilitate economic infrastructure development might be offered in exchange for the abolition of TRPRs. Such aid would make LDCs more attractive to foreign investors as sites for manufacturing facilities. Although aid may, for domestic political reasons, be costly for the United States to provide, such costs may be necessary to gain the removal of TRPRs.

Regional development plans provide another means by which host-country development goals can be achieved without resort to TRPRs. The United States could negotiate such plans with the understanding that a redevelopment plan would be agreed to only if TRPRs were not used by the host country. This approach to negotiations could avoid a situation such as the Michelin Tire case, where the plant in question was in a location from which Michelin could easily penetrate the U.S. market.[86] The benefits provided to Michelin in effect subsidized exports to the United States, producing the same effect as an export performance requirement. While the regional development goals involved in the Michelin case, and the use of subsidies to achieve them, were not objectionable in themselves, the regional development aid in that case became an export subsidy. Negotiations over regional development plans accordingly should seek to avoid similar situations.

The preceding examples are offered only to indicate that domestic policy concerns can be accommodated in negotiations over the elimination or reduction of TRPRs. It is as important to possess leverage as it is to make concessions and present a reasoned case. International and domestic legal remedies which apply to TRPRs can provide such leverage. The best use of these provisions may be to raise the possibility of legal action in negotiations.

Domestic parties should bring countervailing duty and section 301 proceedings against foreign TRPRs. Such actions could be used to advantage by U.S. negotiators. Recent negotiations between U.S. and European Community officials to avert the bringing of countervailing duty cases by U.S. steel companies demonstrates this point—the Europeans only expressed a willingness to compromise when their actions were threatened. However, sufficient concessions were not forthcoming and the companies proceeded with their actions.[87] Threats of countervailing duty and section 301 actions could be used in a similar manner with respect to TRPRs and, failing adequate concessions in their use, such petitions should be filed. The threat of sanctions may deter the use of TRPRs and cause some countries unilaterally to dismantle all or part of their TRPR programs.

The abolition of TRPRs should also be pursued through the dispute settlement mechanisms of GATT and the Subsidies Code, if necessary. As a first step, the possibility of such actions should provide valuable bargaining leverage in negotiations. The U.S. Trade Representative should vigorously pursue its diplomatic initiatives against the use of TRPRs.[88] The ultimate goal of these negotiations should be a Multilateral Trade Agreement dealing specifically with TRPRs. It may require the give and take of multilateral negotiations to gain concessions from many countries. However, it should be recognized that in entering these negotiations the United States is merely seeking adherence to existing norms embodied in the GATT-MTN system. The institutions and dispute settlement mechanisms of the system should ultimately be flexible enough to deal with new efforts, such as the imposition of TRPRs, to circumvent the established rules. New negotiations should focus on ways to utilize existing mechanisms to the greatest extent possible and make the applicability of the existing norms to TRPRs more explicit.

NOTES

1. INDUSTRY AND TRADE ADMINISTRATION, U.S. DEP'T. OF COMMERCE, INCENTIVES AND PERFORMANCE REQUIREMENTS FOR FOREIGN DIRECT INVESTMENTS IN SELECTED COUNTRIES, 1 (Staff Economic Report 1978); The Labor-Industry Coalition for International Trade, Performance Requirements, viii, 2 (1981).

2. Both neighbors of the United States have instituted TRPRs. The Canadian system is discussed in this chapter. The Mexican Auto Decree, Decree for the Development of the Automotive Industry, Diario Official (June 20, 1977), provides an excellent example of a TRPR and how one functions.

The Decree requires compensation for all foreign exchange expenditures by 110 percent if the firm fails to meet minimum local content requirements. C. Ford, Past Developments and Future Trends in Mexican Automotive Policy: Implications for United States-Mexican Trade Relations (Apr. 1980). Thus, for every dollar's worth of production inputs and furnished products imported to Mexico by an automotive manufacturer, that manufacturer must export one dollar's worth of its products, or $1.10 worth if the manufacturer does not satisfy minimum local content requirements.

Minimum local content requirements are 50 percent for passenger cars and 65 percent for commercial vehicles. Recommended levels are 75 percent for cars and 85 percent for commercial vehicles. The Decree and other complex regulations stipulate how these proportions are to be calculated and how much of the local content must be obtained from Mexican-owned suppliers. See Department of Patrimony and Industrial Development, Directive Establishing the Regulations for the Application of the Decree for Development of the Automotive Industry, Diario Official (Oct. 19, 1977).

The Mexican government uses a variety of investment incentives in promoting the domestic automobile industry which are only available to firms in compliance with the Decree. For example, imports of spare parts not produced in Mexico receive a 75 percent duty reduction, or a 25 percent reduction if they are available locally. Mexico Sweetens the Pot for Automotive, Fishing and In-Bond Industries, BUS. LATIN AMERICA, Mar. 7, 1979, at 25. Also, various regional incentives are available for new facilities constructed in priority areas or away from highly congested regions. Mexico's Auto Parts Plan Lays Out Incentives/Goals to Spur Sector's Advance, BUS. LATIN AMERICA Feb. 6, 1980, at 43.

3. *See generally* R. Caves & A. Jones, World Trade and Payments 189, 332–34 (2d ed. 1977).

4. The GATT is an international agreement and is the principal instrument for the regulation of world trade. General Agreements on Tariffs and Trade, *opened for signature*, Oct. 30, 1947, 61 Stat. A3, T.I.A.S. No. 1700, 55 U.N.T.S. 187. The GATT has been modified in several respects since 1947. The current version is contained in 4 General Agreement on Tariffs and Trade, Basic Instruments and Selected Documents (1969).

5. Agreement on Interpretation of Articles VI, XVI, and XXIII of the General Agreements on Tariffs and Trade, *done* Apr. 12, 1979, MTN/NTM/W 236 [hereinafter cited as Subsidies Code], *reprinted in* Agreements Reached in the Tokyo Round of the Multilateral Trade Negotiation, H.R. Doc. 153, 96th Cong., 1st Sess., pt. 1 (1979). The use of TRPRs also contradicts the basic policies of the GATT-MTN System. *See* Jackson, *The Birth of the GATT-MTN System: A Constitutional Appraisal*, 12 Law & Pol'y Int'l Bus. 21 (1980), which first analyzed the GATT-MTN system in terms of its underlying policies.

6. The Trade Agreements Act of 1979, Pub. L. No. 96–39, 93 Stat. 144, Title I, 93 Stat. 150 (to be codified in scattered sections of 19 U.S.C.), provides recourse against TRPRs. The countervailing duties provisions, contained in title I of the Act, apply where a benefit is provided by a host country to an investing company that subsequently imports goods into the United States. Tariff Act of 1930 § 701 *as amended by* Trade Agreements Act, *supra*, § 901, 19 U.S.C. § 2411 (Supp. III 1979). Title IX of the Act, which amended section 301 of the Trade Act of 1974, may also be applied to counteract TRPRs. Trade Act of 1974, § 301, *as amended by* Trade Agreements Act, *supra*, § 901, 19 U.S.C. § 2411 (Supp. III 1979). Domestic parties can initiate section 301 and countervailing duties proceedings to obtain relief against TRPRs. Tariff Act of 1930, § 702, *as added by* Trade Agreements Act, *supra*, § 901, 19 U.S.C. § 1671a (Supp. III 1979); Trade Act of 1974, § 302, *as amended by,* Trade Agreements Act, *supra*, § 901, 19 U.S.C. § 2412 (Supp. III 1979).

7. The absence of adequate data makes empirical analysis of the nature and magnitude of resultant welfare losses difficult if not impossible. *See* Narasimham, Performance Criteria Stipulated by Host Countries, (Jan. 8, 1980) (unpublished paper of the Joint Ministerial Committee of the Boards of Governors of the [World] Bank and the [International Monetary] Fund on the Transfer of Real Resources to Developing Countries, IMF Task Force on Private Foreign Investment).

8. Even if there were no government intervention to encourage or regulate foreign investment, however, firms would not always choose to locate production facilities in countries with a comparative advantage. There are many other market distortions to consider, such as imperfect information and political risk. Furthermore, there may be a variety of considerations unique to individual firms, such as the advantages of locating certain new facilities in close proximity to the firm's existing facilities. *See* C. Kindleberger, International Economics 87–105 (3d ed. 1963); Caves & Jones, *supra* note 3, at 25–29. In fact, performance requirements have been rationalized as necessary to encourage technology transfers and acceleration of development of potential comparative advantages.

9. A firm's only alternative is to curtail domestic sales in order to satisfy the export requirement.

10. R. Baldwin, Nontariff Distortions of International Trade 46 (1970).

11. Bergsten, Host Country Policies: Performance Requirements 11, 13 (Jan 25, 1980) (unpublished paper for the Joint Ministerial Committee of the Boards of Governors of the [World] Bank and the [International Monetary] Fund on the Transfer of Real Resources to Developing Countries, Task Force on Private Foreign Investment).

12. Therefore, the counterargument, premised on the difficulty of determining specific sectors of a national economy in which a nation has the potential of becoming competitive, is that it would be better for "market forces to determine allocation of resources than for this to be attempted through a centralized, bureaucratic process." *Id.*

Another counterargument is that such protective measures could have the effect of actually preventing the transition from a noncompetitive to a competitive status. This result might occur if the local industry were to be shielded from the "stimulatory discipline" of having to compete with efficient firms.

13. Application of TRPRs to industries possessing "latent" comparative advantages has led to exploitation of those advantages and contributed to a more rapid economic development of the nation.

14. For a review of this issue, see TRANSFER PRICING AND MULTINATIONAL ENTERPRISES, OECD (1979).

15. The argument has been made that export obligations help to ensure that domestic manufacturers will meet international standards regulating quality as well as costs. For this reason, some export performance requirements establish not only quantitative goals, but also qualitative goals, such as setting a minimum amount of high technology and processed products to be exported which in turn requires the foreign subsidiary's domestic suppliers to manufacture products conforming with those goals.

16. Some parties in the United States have urged that controls be placed on foreign investment in this country in order to maintain independence in economic and political policy objectives. *Hearings on the Operations of Federal Agencies in Monitoring, Reporting on, and Analyzing Foreign Investments in the United States Before the Subcomm. on Commerce, Consumer and Monetary Affairs of the House Comm. on Government Operations,* 96th Cong., 1st Sess., pt. 3, 17–18 (statement of Benjamin J. Cohen, Associate Professor of International Economic Relations, Tufts Univ.).

17. Because multinational corporations generally take a global outlook in making their operational decisions, it is argued that they are less concerned about any particular subsidiary in a foreign country. *See, e.g.,* KINDLEBERGER, *supra* note 8, at 410, who argues that multinationals employ a "gambling theory" whereby only a percentage of overseas profits are reinvested in foreign-located subsidiaries, thus ensuring minimum loss should the foreign investment fail.

18. An example of this tendency is the drug and pharmaceutical industry in several developing countries. The foreign investor in this particular sector often stipulates that raw material procurement and value addition occur in their own countries.

19. For example, the drug industry is required by some LDCs not to limit their investments to importing bulk drugs and packaging them, but also to produce the basic and intermediate drugs in the host country. This type of performance requirement is intended to bring technology into the LDCs, as opposed to the mere packaging procedure.

20. The Mexican government estimates that the Mexico Auto Decree will have the effect of raising exports of Mexican auto parts from $650 million in 1979 to over $5 billion by 1985.

21. For example, because of their accumulation of necessary information links, experience in production, and reliable, on-time delivery, the Republic of Korea and Taiwan account for a large majority of LDC clothing exports even though other LDCs that are trying to export clothing have lower wage structures. World Bank, Staff Working Paper No. 314, The Changing Composition of Developing Country Exports 25 (1979).

22. The underlying premise of the argument is that capital resources will be efficiently allocated in the international economy as long as the market is allowed to operate freely. LIBRARY OF CONGRESS; CONGRESSIONAL RESEARCH SERVICE, ISSUE BRIEF No. IB78091, FOREIGN INVESTMENT IN U.S. INDUSTRY 13 (1979). Foreign exchange of investments in a free trade environment generally produces a "win-win" situation economically for the sending and receiving countries. Ellis, *United States Multinational Corporations: The Impact of Foreign Direct Investment on United States Foreign Relations,* 11 SAN DIEGO L. REV. 1, 3 (1973).

23. This result is more likely to occur when foreigners are allowed to place businesses freely in other countries, because the foreigners' interest no longer will be independent from

those of the host country. Because the success or failure of foreign investment is bound up with the host country's economy as a whole, it is less likely that the foreign investor will act in a manner contrary to interests of the host country. *See, e.g.*, U.S. DEP'T OF COMMERCE, I REPORT TO THE CONGRESS ON FOREIGN DIRECT INVESTMENT IN THE UNITED STATES 236 (1976), where an administrative agency concludes that foreign disruption of the host country's economy is improbable when foreigners invest for profit-maximizing reasons.

24. *See* J. JACKSON, WORLD TRADE AND THE LAW OF GATT 29, § 1.7 (1969).

25. For an insightful analysis of the GATT Panel process and important GATT Panel decisions, see R. HUDEC, THE GATT LEGAL SYSTEM AND WORLD TRADE DIPLOMACY (1975); Hudec, *GATT Dispute Settlement After the Tokyo Round: An Unfinished Business*, 13 CORNELL INT'L. L. J. 145 (1980).

26. For a thorough treatment of the GATT nullification and impairment doctrine, see Hudec, *Retaliation Against "Unreasonable" Foreign Trade Practices: The New Section 301 and GATT Nullification and Impairment*, 59 MINN. L. REV. 461–64 (1975).

27. The case involved the termination by Australia of a subsidy relating to sodium nitrate fertilizers imported from Chile. GATT Doc. C.P.3/61 (1949).

28. Of course, the United States would have to show that at the time the concessions were negotiated, it could not have anticipated that the foreign government would use TRPRs, but this will not be difficult for many products on which the concessions were originally made many years prior to the proliferation of TRPRs.

29. Paragraph 1 states that no internal quantitative regulations requiring the mixture, processing or use of products in specific amounts so as to afford protection to domestic production should be allowed.

30. JACKSON, *supra* note 24, at 289.

31. For example, in examining a United States complaint that an EEC regulation requiring producers and importers of certain goods to purchase minimum levels of local skimmed milk violated GATT, a GATT panel included in its analysis a discussion of the interaction of paragraphs 1 and 5 of article III. GATT, Doc. No. L/4599 paras. 4.5–4.9 (Dec. 2, 1977).

32. Export performance requirements which are not linked to government subsidies violate Article II.

33. See JACKSON, *supra* note 24, at 673–716 for an in-depth discussion of balance of payments problems and the GATT.

34. The right to impose restrictions under Article XII, however, is limited in paragraph 3.

35. Article XVIII allows contracting parties, whose economies can only support low standards of living and are in the early stages of development, to temporarily deviate from the other provisions of the agreement. Article XVIII also recognizes that economics that come within the terms of paragraph 4(a) of that article will tend to experience balance of payments difficulties because of their rapid process of development and efforts to expand their internal markets as well as from instability in their terms of trade. However, the same types of criteria which make the use of TRPRs inappropriate under the general exception provided by Article XII also apply to the special rule for LDCs contained in Article XVIII. For example, the criteria listed under Article XVIII, para. 9, are the same as those listed under Article XII, para. 5. Furthermore,

> Paragraphs 10 and 11 [of Article XVIII] reproduce in substance the provisions of sub-paragraph 2(b) and of paragraph 3 of article XII. These provisions have, however, been rearranged and the thought contained in the first sentence of sub-paragraph 3(d) of Article XII has been omitted as it was already expressed in the first two paragraphs of Section B.

Government Assistance to Economic Development, Reports Relating to the Review of the Agreement, GATT, BASIC INSTRUMENTS AND SELECTED DOCUMENTS, 183 (3d. Supp. 1955).

36. U.N. Doc. EPCT/A/PV.22 (1947) at 16, *supra* note 87, at 309.

37. "Primary products" are defined in the Interpretive Notes to the GATTas being "any product of farm, forest or fishery or any mineral, in its natural form or which has undergone such processing as is customarily required to prepare it for marketing in substantial volume in international trade." "Nonprimary products" are all those products not falling within this definition.

38. This criterion is generally known as the bilevel pricing requirement.

39. GATT, Basic Instruments and Selected Documents, 191 (9th Supp. 1961).

40. Jackson, *supra* note 24, at 396–97.

41. The pertinent GATT provision defines "commercial considerations" to include, "price, quality, availability, marketability, transportation and other conditions of purchase of sale. . . ."

42. Sub-paragraph 1(c) states the coverage of the Article XVII principle:

No contracting party shall prevent any enterprise (whether or not [a state] enterprise described in sub-paragraph (a) of this paragraph) under its jurisdiction from acting in accordance with the principles of sub-paragraphs (a) and (b) of this paragraph.

Thus sub-paragraph (c) appears to broaden the scope of Article XVII to all enterprises under the jurisdiction of the state.

43. ESCOR, Preparatory Committee of the International Conference on Trade and Employment, Committee II, Drafting Sub-Committee on State Trading, Discussion of Addendum to Draft Report of Rapporteur (4th mtg.), U.N. Doc. E/PC/T/C.II/52 (19raphy46) at 2–3 (statement of Mr. Tung of China); ESCOR, Preparatory Committee of the International Conference on Trade and Employment, Verbatim Report of the Fifth Meeting of Committee II on Oct. 30, 1946, U.N. Doc. E/PC/T/C.II/PV/5 (1946 at 35–37 (statement of Mr. Hawkins of the United States). Preparatory Committee of the International Conference on Trade and Employment, Verbatim Report of the Fourteenth Meeting of Commission A on Jun. 19, 1947, U.N. Doc. E/PC/T/A/PV/14 (1947) at 24 (statement of Mr. Webb of New Zealand).

In the Havana Chapter, Article 31 provided for procedures through which protective measures applied by state enterprises could be reduced by negotiation. If Article 29, sub-paragraph 1(a) (which is almost identical to Article XVII) were read to require national treatment, the purpose of Article 31 would be virtually eliminated. While the latter provision was not included in the GATT, paragraph 3 of Article XVII requires that contracting parties "recognize the importance of negotiations." The Contracting Parties would not have added this provision in 1955, if they had considered national treatment required by paragraph 1.

However, the addition of (the more vague) paragraph 3 may simply reflect a recognition that obtaining compliance with national treatment by state enterprises would be extremely difficult. Therefore, ongoing negotiations would be required to limit or reduce the barriers to trade which they might create, in spite of this provision. The term "recognize" indicates a knowledge of the difficulties likely to be created by state enterprises, rather than an intent to acknowledge their discriminatory practices.

44. This argument is presented in Jackson, *supra* note 24, at 345–48.

45. The Interpretive Note states:

It was the understanding of the Sub-Committee that the charging by a state enterprise of different prices for its sales of a product in different markets is not precluded by the provisions of the Article, provided that such different prices are charged for commercial reasons to meet conditions of supply and demand in export markets.

ESCOR, Second Session of the Preparatory Committee of the United Nations Conference on Trade and Employment, report to Commission A by Sub-Committee on Articles 31 & 32, U.N. Doc. E/PC/T/160 (1947) at 5–6. This Note can be interpreted as a clarification of the MFN principle with respect to paragraph 1(a) of Article XVII in that it does not require that the same prices exist for all foreign markets. Rather, commercial considerations, presumably applied on an MFN basis, are to determine price. However, the Note can also be interpreted as a clarification of the national treatment principle in that "different markets" might be read to include the domestic market and that prices charged for exports may differ from those for domestic sales only if the reasons are truly commercial as in the interaction of supply and demand.

46. The national treatment principle of Article III protects foreign producers only in respect to "laws, regulations and requirements" affecting sale, distribution, purchase, transportation and use. Article VII applies to state enterprises and any private enterprise that is granted, "formally or in effect, exclusive or special privileges. . . ."

47. GATT panel discussing Article XXIII procedures stated:

In cases where there is a clear infringement of the provisions of the General Agreement, or in other words, where measures are applied in conflict with the provisions of GATT and are not permitted under the terms of the relevant protocol under which the GATT is applied by the contracting party, the action, *prima facie*, constitutes a case of nullification or impairment and would *ipso facto* require consideration of whether the circumstances are serious enough to justify the authorization of suspension of concessions or obligations.

Uruguayan Recourse of Article XXIII, GENERAL AGREEMENTS ON TARIFFS AND TRADE, BASIC INSTRUMENTS AND SELECTED DOCUMENTS 100, para. 15 (11th Supp. 1963), GATT Doc. L/1923.

48. *See* JACKSON, *supra* note 24, at 182–83.

49. The Code declares that "[s]ignatories shall not grant export subsidies on products other than certain primary products."

50. In defining the phrase, the Code declares that:

(a) "more than an equitable share of world trade" shall include any case in which the effect of an export subsidy granted by a signatory is to displace the exports of another signatory bearing in mind the developments on world markets;
(b) with regard to new markets traditional patterns of supply of the product concerned to the world market, region, or country, in which the new market is situated shall be taken into account in determining "equitable share of world export trade. . . ."

51. Rivers & Greenwald, *Negotiations of a Code on Subsidies and Countervailing Measures: Bridging Fundamental Policy Differences*. 11 LAW & POL'Y INT'L BUS. 1447, 1475–76 (1979).

52. Appropriate countermeasures include "withdrawal of GATT concessions or obligations."

53. The provisions are applicable when subsidies are granted with respect to the "manufacture, production, or exportation" of merchandise imported into the United States.

54. In the section 301 setting, the President is authorized to take action to respond to any act, policy or practice of a foreign country that "is unjustifiable, unreasonable, or discriminatory and burdens or restricts United States commerce. . . ." 19 U.S.C. § 2411(a)(2) (Supp. III 1979).

55. The goods will also be subject to countervailing duties where the establishment of an industry in the United States is materially retarded. Where the offending country is not a signatory to the Subsidies Code, "material injury" need not be shown in order for a countervailing duty to be imposed.

56. HOUSE COMM. ON WAYS AND MEANS, TRADE AGREEMENTS ACT OF 1979, REPORT TO ACCOMPANY H.R. 4537, H.R. REP. No. 96-317, 96th Cong., 1st Sess. 74 (1979); *cf.* SEN., COMM. ON FINANCE, TRADE AGREEMENTS ACT OF 1979, REPORT ON H.R. 4537, (1979).

57. 249 U.S. 34 (1919).

58. ASG Indus. v. United States, 610 F. 2d 770 (C.C.P.A. 1979) (West German subsidies to float glass exports violative of Tariff Act); ASG Indus. v. United States, 495 F. Supp. 904 (Cust. Ct. 1980) (Belgian regional relocation aid considered grant or bounty); ASG Indus. v. United States, 467 F. Supp. 1200 (Cust. Ct. 1979) (Italian regional relocation aid considered grant or bounty).

59. X-Radial Steel Belted Tires From Canada, T.D. 73-10, 7 CUST. BULL. (Jan. 19, 1973), 38 Fed. Reg. 1018 (1973) *appeal docketed sub. nom.* Michelin Tire Corp. v. United States, 75-9 (Cust. Ct. 1979). *See* Recent Decision, *The Michelin Decision: A Possible New Direction for U.S. Countervailing Duty Law,* 6 LAW & POL'Y INT'L BUS. 237 (1974) (arguing that the *Michelin* case was wrongly decided).

60. King, *Countervailing Duties—An Old Remedy With New Appeal,* 24 BUS. LAW. 1179, 1181 (1969).

61. *See* Feller, *Mutiny Against the Bounty: An Examination of Subsidies, Border Tax Adjustments, and the Resurgence of the Countervailing Duty Law,* 1 LAW & POL'Y INT'L BUS. 17, 26-27 (1969).

62. 19 U.S.C. §§ 2411-2416 (Supp. III 1979). *See generally* de Kieffer, *GATT Dispute Settlements: A New Beginning in International and U.S. Trade Law,* 2 Nw. J. INT'L L. & BUS. 317, 327-33 (1980) for a clear and concise discussion of the section 301 enforcement process in respect to GATT dispute settlements.

63. The President is also given power to act where he determines that it is appropriate to "respond to any act, policy, or practice of a foreign country or instrumentality that—

(A) is inconsistent with the provisions of, or otherwise denies benefits to the United States under any trade agreements, or
(B) is unjustifiable, unreasonable, or discriminatory and burdens or restricts United States commerce. . . ."

64. If the petition is denied, the Trade Representative must inform the petitioner of the reasons for denial and must publish notice of the determination with a summary of the reasons in the Federal Register.

65. In preparing for both dispute settlement proceedings and consultations, the Trade Representative must seek advice and information from the petitioner and other private sector representatives.

66. Before the Trade Representative can recommend action to the President, however, he must provide the opportunity for the presentation of views (including a public hearing if requested by an interested person) and must obtain advice from appropriate private sector advisory representatives. The Trade Representative may request the views of the International Trade Commission. If the Trade Representative determines that expeditious action is necessary, compliance with these requirements may be deferred until after making the recommendations to the President.

67. *See Oversight Hearings on Trade Related Performance Requirements Before the Subcomm. on International Economic Policy of the Senate Comm. On Foreign Relations,* 97th Cong., 1st Sess. (1981) (statement of Gary C. Hufbauer); *Oversight Hearings on U.S. Trade Policy Be-*

fore the Subcomm. on Trade of the House Comm. on Ways and Means, 97th Cong., 1st Sess. (1981) (statement of Howard D. Samuel, President, Industrial Union Department, AFL-CIO, and Lawrence C. McQuade, Senior Vice-President, W. R. Grace and Company, on behalf of the Labor-Industry Coalition for International Trade).

68. *See* S. 2071, 97th Cong., 2d Sess., 128 Cong. Rec. S426 (daily ed. Feb. 4, 1982) (statement of Sen. Heinz); S. 2067. 97th Cong., 2d Sess., 128 CONG. REC. S423 (daily ed. Feb. 4, 1982) (statement of Sen. Symms); H.R. 4407, 97th Cong., 1st Sess., 127 CONG. REC. H5997 (daily ed. Aug. 4, 1981) (statement of Rep. Schulze).

69. *Compare* Goldberg & Kindleberger, *Toward a GATT for Investment: A Proposal for Supervision of the International Corporation*, 2 LAW & POL'Y INT'L BUS. 295, 321–23 (1970) (suggesting resolution of the problem by formation of a General Agreement for the International Corporation similar to the GATT *with* C. F. BERGSTEN, T. HORST & T. MORAN, AMERICAN MULTINATIONALS AND AMERICAN INTERESTS 487–92 (1978) (proposing a number of specific recommended policy measures for home and host countries).

70. *See generally,* C. F. BERGSTEN, THE INTERNATIONAL ECONOMIC POLICY OF THE UNITED STATES 3–11 (1980).

71. *See Oversight Hearings on U.S. Policy Toward International Investment Before the Subcomm. on International Economic Policy of the Senate Comm. on Foreign Relations*, 97th Cong., 1st Sess. (1981) (statement of C. F. Bergsten, Senior Associate, Carnegie Endowment for International Peace).

72. Investment Performance Requirements: A Note by the Secretariat, GATT Doc. CG. 18/W64 (Oct. 15, 1981).

73. However, the U.S. Trade Representative has acted on its own to challenge the practices of Canada, described below in the [missing copy] as a violation of the GATT, but without initiating a case under section 301.

74. For an interesting description of the views of the U.S. automobile manufacturers to TRPRs, *see Oversight Hearings on U.S. Policy Toward Foreign Trade-Related Performance Requirements Before the Subcomm. on International Economic Policy of the Senate Comm. on Foreign Relations*, 97th Cong., 1st Sess. (1981) (statement of the Motor Vehicle Manufacturers Association of the United States, Inc.) (industry suggesting that there are long-term efficiency-enhancing effects of TRPRs despite short-term trade distortions).

75. Under current law, the Trade Representative recommends action to the President. Only the President is authorized to take punitive action. This procedure would be similar to that applicable to certain decisions of the Civil Aeronautics Board regarding issuance of foreign air carrier permits. 49 U.S.C. § 1461 (1976 & Supp. III 1979).

76. Under current law, no determination as to punitive action is made until the President is actually required to decide on retaliation, which permits a foreign country to refuse to negotiate on the expectation that the President will find that the foreign practice is not even actionable under 19 U.S.C. § 2411(a).

77. Comparable provisions for preliminary determinations have been included in the countervailing duty and antidumping laws. Tariff Act of 1930, § 703, *as added by* Trade Agreements Act, § 101, 19 U.S.C. § 1671b (Supp. III 1979); *id.* § 733, *as added by* Trade Agreements Act, § 101, 19 U.S.C. § 1673b (Supp. III 1979).

78. Trade Act of 1974 § 501, 19 U.S.C. § 2461 (1976).

79. In determining which countries are to receive beneficiary developing country status, the President is required to consider whether the country wants to be so designated, the level of economic development of the country, what treatment is afforded the country by other major developed countries, and the extent to which the country has assured the United States of access to its markets and community resources.

80. A World Bank Staff committee to which the TRPR issue was remanded, has proposed a major study of the issue, but no action has been taken.

81. Overseas Private Investment Corporation Act of 1981, Pub. L. No. 97–65, 95 Stat. 1021 (1981); *see* Note, *The 1981 OPIC Amendments and Reagan's "Newer Directions" in Third World Development Policy* 14 LAW & POL'Y INT'L BUS. 181 (1982).

82. Assume, for example, that a company agrees to increase exports from 100 to 150 units in return for a $150 million subsidy. Under current rules, the amount of the subsidy (and hence the countervailing duty) is $1 per unit. Under the allocation rule, the countervailing duty would be assessed only on fifty units but in an amount equal to $3 per unit.

83. Act of Dec. 12, 1973 (Foreign Investment Review Act), ch. 46, 1973–74 Can. Stat. 619, *amended by* ch. 52, 1976–77 Can. Stat. 1193.

84. In accepting the Amer Sports proposal, the Canadian government noted the beneficial impact expected in terms of increased capital investment, employment, exports, import replacement. Canadian sourcing and increased productivity and industrial efficiency.

85. The local content requirements arguably violate GATT articles III, XI, and XVII, while the export performance requirements violate Articles XI and XVII.

86. Michelin chose a location in Nova Scotia after being offered a substantial grant and a low interest loan for locating its facility in that region of Canada. The plant subsequently exported a substantial majority of its production to the United States. X-Radial Steel Belted Tires from Canada, T.D. 73-10, 7 CUST. BULL. 11 (Jan. 10, 1973), 38 Fed. Reg. 1018 (1973).

87. Several of the largest steel producers in the United States—U.S. Steel, Bethlehem, Republic, Jones & Laughlin, National, Inland, and Cyclops filed the antidumping and countervailing duty petitions. The petitions filed with the Commerce Department and the International Trade Commission are directed against producers in Belgium, France, Italy, Luxembourg, the Netherlands, the United Kingdom, West Germany, Brazil, South Africa, Spain and Romania. U.S. IMPORT WEEKLY (BNA) (Jan. 13, 1982) at 337.

88. Mr. William Brock, the United States Trade Representative, indicated concern over TRPRs at a recent meeting of Trade Ministers from the United States, the Common Market, Japan and Canada. Mr. Brock put forth the idea that, in order to strengthen and broaden GATT, the next round of GATT talks should include the issues of services and investment, including a look into the problems associated with the use of performance requirements. *Trade Talk Topics are Determined*, N.Y. Times, Jan. 18, 1982, at D1, col. 6.

6

Mexican
Regulation of
the Computer
Industry
Mark P. Jacobsen

INTRODUCTION

In September 1981, the Mexican government announced a policy designed to promote the development of its computer industry. This program, known as the Computer Decree, offers investors in the computer sector a number of incentives, which include energy subsidies and tax credits. To receive these incentives, however, investors must comply with a number of requirements, including performance requirements, such as local content and export promotion rules. The United States government should be concerned about these requirements because they tend to hurt the United States computer industry overall and generally distort the international flow of trade and investment.[1]

This chapter is a detailed case study of the imposition of performance requirements by Mexico on the computer industry. The Computer Decree may well be an example of the "hardest case" incidence of performance requirements for the United States to deal with because unfavorable and complex circumstances complicate the formulation of a U.S. response to the Computer Decree. If the difficult issues of Mexico's performance requirements can be solved, however, a multilateral approach to investment issues in general might be possible. Thus, the case of the Mexican Computer Decree should be considered carefully before any multilateral negotiations on similar international investment issues begin with other countries.

A substantially similar version of this article originally appeared as *Mexico's Computer Decree: The Problem of Performance Requirements and a U.S. Response*, in 14 Law & Pol'y Int'l Bus. 1159 (1982). Used with permission of *Law and Policy in International Business*.

This chapter first examines the background of the Computer Decree, which can be understood only in the context of Mexico's economic problems and the national development programs that Mexico has implemented to remedy these problems. It then analyzes the Computer Decree and its detailed provisions. Next, the chapter discusses the particular difficulties of fashioning a U.S. response to the Computer Decree. Finally, the chapter examines the responses available to the United States, including retaliation. In conclusion, the chapter suggests a more forward-looking response to performance requirements in general and the Computer Decree in particular.

BACKGROUND

The Problem

Between 1940 and 1970, the Mexican economy grew at an astounding rate,[2] averaging a 6.5 percent increase each year.[3] This rapid economic growth, however, created problems. The policies of the Mexican government tended to make the distribution of income more and more unequal. Neither Mexico's taxation system nor its expenditure policies prevented it from leading almost all other Latin American countries in terms of income inequality. Also, the rapid growth accelerated external trade deficits and foreign debt. The level of foreign investment in the Mexican economy had political consequences as well because multinational corporations were gaining control of particular branches of industry. For example, although foreign investors in 1970 controlled only 27 percent of the Mexican manufacturing industry, they controlled 79 percent of the electrical machinery industry and 84 percent of the rubber industry. Moreover, the multinational corporations increasingly were ousting national competition rather than opening new areas of industry.

In the early 1970s, it was believed that Mexico's trade and investment policies, particularly its "import substitution" policy, actually exacerbated these economic and political problems.[4] The import substitution policy, which used import permits to encourage foreign companies to construct plants in Mexico rather than to import from abroad to serve the Mexican market, did not help the balance-of-payments problem because it failed to encourage exports. The policy might have even increased imports by creating an incentive for the protected industries to import machinery. In addition, this policy encouraged only those industries that manufactured consumer products; it did not sufficiently encourage development of Mexico's raw materials. Finally, it promoted a domestic industry that was generally inefficient and therefore unable to compete in the world markets.

The Prescription

Given these economic and political problems, the Mexican government established the in-bond assembly program, the Foreign Investment Law, the laws affecting transfer of technology, and the Industrial Development Plan. The Computer Decree had its origins within the context of these national development programs.

Beginning in 1965, the Mexican government permitted 100 percent foreign ownership of in-bond companies which process duty-free imported materials for reexport to the United States or other countries.[5] This program was developed to operate in conjunction with U.S. tariff provisions that assess a duty on imported products on the value added to those products outside of the United States.[6] The purpose of the in-bond program was both to reduce Mexican unemployment along the U.S.–Mexican border[7] and to help U.S. manufactured products compete with U.S. imports.

The Mexican government considers foreign investment in Mexico to be a privilege. In 1973, Mexico enacted the Law for the Promotion of Mexican Investment and the Regulation of Foreign Investment. In general, this law prohibits foreign investment of more than 49 percent of a Mexican company's total equity. In some industries, such as petrochemicals and transportation, the 1973 law limits investment exclusively to the Mexican state or Mexican corporations that exclude foreign ownership by charter. Although the law permits exceptions to the 49 percent rule, the Mexican government, which must approve the exceptions, rarely grants them.

The Mexican government implemented two laws to counter the abuses that resulted from the use of licensing agreements with foreign firms. Passed in 1973, the Law on the Registration of the Transfer of Technology and the Use and Exploitation of Patents and Trademarks requires the registration of all such licensing agreements and absolutely prohibits registration of certain agreements, such as those that involve the transfer of technology already available in Mexico. In 1982 the Mexican government further stiffened this law. Passed in 1976, the Industrial Property Code shortens a patent's validity to ten years and specifies certain classes of inventions for which patents would no longer be granted. In addition, the law prohibits the use of trademarks, which originate outside of Mexico, on products produced in Mexico unless they are used jointly with a purely Mexican registered trademark.

The Industrial Development Plan, begun in 1979, for the first time established a coordinated set of fiscal and other incentives to develop the economy through 1990.[8] In its introduction, the Industrial Development Plan recognizes the motivating factors behind its preparation: the need to cope with an immediate economic crisis and the new petroleum industry. One of the Development Plan's principal objectives has been to reduce unemployment and underemployment. It encourages investments in certain priority zones, such as medium-sized cities, particularly along the border and coastal areas. Most of these cities are along the national gas distribution system and were selected to facilitate exports of manufactured products. The Development Plan designates priority industries. Some 70 priority sectors were selected and divided into two categories. The first category includes primarily the agricultural and capital goods industries. Among many other industries, the computer industry is included in the second category. For each of these priority industries, the Development Plan establishes goals for the annual growth rate.

The Development Plan offers a series of incentives. Its tax credits take into consideration the priority zones and industries. The Development Plan grants credits against federal taxes to Mexicans who invest in fixed assets in industrial firms, increase employment or establish additional work shifts, or purchase machinery and equipment made in Mexico. These credits range from 10 percent to 25 percent. The Development Plan also establishes special fuel subsidies for Mexican companies that set up new plants or significantly expand existing ones in Zone 1. These subsidies range from 10 percent to 30 percent. In addition, the Development Plan calls for a 14 percent annual growth in public outlays for infrastructure and an expansion of government-run industries, and continues the use of tariff policies and import controls as basic incentives for Mexican industry.

An Evaluation

Because the Computer Decree is a component of these programs, the success of these other programs, or their lack of it, may predict whether the Computer Decree can obtain its objectives. Any evaluation of these programs, however, must be somewhat tentative because the most ambitious program, the Industrial Development Plan, has been in effect only since 1979.

First, these national development programs seemingly have not adversely affected the level of foreign direct investment in Mexico. Between 1970 and 1979, U.S. foreign direct investment grew from $1.9 billion to $4.6 billion, averaging a 10.5 percent increase annually.[9] Although foreign direct investment slowed somewhat between 1976 and 1978, U.S. foreign direct investment rose from $4.6 billion in 1979 to $5.9 billion in 1980. Significantly, this 28 percent increase happened after Mexico implemented the Industrial Development Plan. Actions in 1982, of course, slowed significantly the growth of foreign direct investment in Mexico. On September 1, 1982, then-President Portillo nationalized the private banks and imposed foreign exchange controls, which have hampered Mexico's ability to attract foreign investment funds. These actions, not the Industrial Development Plan, primarily will be responsible for any further decreases in foreign direct investment.

Second, the effect of these national development programs on Mexico's international trade is difficult to assess. On the one hand, between 1977 and 1980, U.S. exports to Mexico almost tripled, and U.S. imports from Mexico increased more than 2.5 times. On the other hand, Mexico's trade deficit increased significantly in 1981. The Mexican policy of trade liberalization, in effect since 1977, probably resulted in increased trade between the United States and Mexico. Mexico, for example, had replaced much of its import licensing program with tariff rates. In 1981, however, the increasing trade deficits led the Mexican government to reverse its policy of trade liberalization by reimposing import licensing requirements and by increasing tariffs. This reversal probably was due to Mexico's worsening balance-of-payments problems as a result of declining oil prices on the world market.

Third, after these programs were implemented, but before President Lopez Portillo's actions were taken in September 1982, the number of jobs created and the amount of wage increases had surpassed the goals set by the Lopez Portillo administration. As of December 1982, however, inflation had reached almost 100 percent, the peso had lost more than three-quarters of its value against the U.S. dollar, the country's GNP was stagnant, and the unemployment rate had increased to almost 15 percent. Since both external factors, such as the weakening world oil market, and internal factors, such as the country's high growth policy, contributed to Mexico's worsened economic plight, the overall effect of the national economic programs remains unclear.

THE COMPUTER DECREE

The Mexican Bureau of Industries promulgated the Development Plan for the Manufacturing of Electronic Computer Systems, Their Main Modules and Peripheral Equipment (Computer Decree) in September 1981.[10] The Computer Decree was issued in response to the growing number of imports of computer products, which increased from 1979 to 1980 by 175 percent. Imports into Mexico came primarily from the United States, amounting to over 70 percent of the total imports.[11]

The Computer Decree describes five goals, which it hopes to attain under its development program. First, Mexico wants to expand and consolidate its computer sector in order to supply 70 percent of the national need in five years, which is probably its most ambitious goal because Mexico has virtually no domestic production of computers. Second, the program expects to promote exports quickly by defining productivity levels that ensure effective import substitution and competition. Third, Mexico wants to diversify investment in the computer sector, and fourth, to promote national technological development. Finally, the Computer Decree intends to contribute to the technical training of Mexico's human resources.

Computer Decree Incentives

To encourage participation in the development program set forth in the Computer Decree, Mexico employs a number of investment incentives. The first incentive is a 20 percent tax credit for investing in or expanding a computer industry. In addition, a 20 percent tax credit is given for the amount of new jobs generated by an investment or the creation of new shifts. This provision generally parallels the 20 percent tax credit in the Industrial Development Plan. The provision in the Computer Decree, however, does signal a change in the strategy of the Industrial Development Plan because it originally included the computer sector in a category of industries that would receive only a 10–15 percent tax credit. A second incentive in the Computer Decree, which also is paralleled in the Industrial Development Plan, is preferential prices (up to 30 percent) for energy products. The program also gives a 15 percent tax credit to buyers who purchase nationally manufactured computer equipment and to computer manufacturers who purchase nationally manufactured components. The Industrial Development Plan has a similar provision but allows only a five percent tax credit.

A major incentive in the Computer Decree is its tariff protection provision. It grants tariff protection for a minimum of three years, which will be removed "when the development of the sector so requires." The amount of protection depends upon the type of computer equipment imported. The Computer Decree divides the computer industry into five sectors: microcomputers, minicomputers, macrocomputers, peripheral equipment, and components.[12] Under this provision, microcomputers receive a 30 percent customs tariff; minicomputers, macrocomputers, and components receive a 15 percent tariff.

One provision of the Computer Decree is listed with the other incentives, but it includes many characteristics of a sanction. The provision allocates import quotas on manufacturers and distributors so that imports will represent "a minimal part of the national supply" of computer products in five years. The provision is divided into two parts. The first part allocates between manufacturers and distributors what percentage of computer imports each may receive during the first three years of the program. In the first year, manufacturers and distributors each receive 50 percent of the imports. During the next two years, the manufacturers' percentage increases to 70 percent and the distributors' percentage decreases to 30 percent. Import quotas for macrocomputers, however, are calculated individually, provided there is no national production. This import quota system was to go into effect in 1982. The Mexican government, however, enacted import quotas for the last half of 1981 to reduce the deficit in its foreign trade balance. The total market value of the assigned quotas was only 36 percent of the total for 1980. Thus, import quotas enacted in the last half of 1981 severely restricted computer imports into Mexico.

The second part of the import quota provision determines 1) for manufacturers, the permitted ratio of imports to the amount produced in the plant; and 2) for distributors, the permitted ratio of imports to Mexican units distributed. In the first two years of the program, manufacturers may import an amount equal to four times what they produce. By the fifth year, however, manufacturers may import only as much as they produce. In the first two years of the program, distributors may distribute three times as many imported products as Mexican units. In the second two years, the ratio is two times. After this period, distributors must continually distribute a greater proportion of Mexican computer units.

Preferential treatment in government procurement is another incentive provided by the Computer Decree. This is a major incentive because the public sector, including all government-owned enterprises, buys over 45 percent of the computers and related equipment sold each year in Mexico. Other incentives in this program include: preferential interest rates and financing, tax incentives for the creation of technological companies and laboratories, and government promotion of agreements between manufacturers and research institutions.

Computer Decree Requirements

To receive the benefits of the Computer Decree incentives, computer companies must comply with a number of other requirements. First, new companies must locate in the priority zones, established by the Industrial

Development Plan. Existing companies can receive the benefits only if they are located in Zones I or II. Second, in accordance with the 1973 Foreign Investment Law, new companies must have a minimum 51 percent of national capital. The Computer Decree, though, allows established companies with majority foreign capital to receive the benefits of the program only if they manufacture mini- or macrocomputer systems. This provision suggests that Mexico is targeting the microcomputer industry for national development; however, past experience with the 51 percent rule suggests that the intention of this provision may be thwarted by foreign companies' elaborate attempts to "get around" the law.[13]

The two most important, yet controversial, provisions of the Computer Decree are the local content and export requirements. The local content requirement continues Mexico's import substitution policy, discussed previously, and the export promotion requirement represents an alternative development strategy that Mexico first began to use in the late 1960s. Under the local content provision, each computer system must contain "a minimum total incorporation of Mexican made production." The degree of incorporation of Mexican made production is calculated according to a complex formula and depends upon the type of computer system. Microcomputers must have at least 35 percent local content in the first year, which increases to 45 percent by the third year. Minicomputers must have at least 25 percent local content in the first year, and by the third year, 35 percent. The degree of local incorporation for peripheral equipment ranges from 20 percent to 90 percent. Macrocomputers have no local content requirements.

Under the Computer Decree's export requirement, "companies promise to compensate their payments abroad with exports." The development program does this by establishing a minimum export-import ratio for each year and for each type of computer system. The export-import ratio for microcomputer manufacturers runs for five years but does not begin until the second year. In the second year, the ratio is 25 percent; that is, for every four units imported, the manufacturer must export one unit. By the fifth year, the ratio increases to 70 percent. For minicomputer manufacturers, the export-import ratio runs for four years, starting at 30 percent and increasing to 70 percent. The export-import ratio for manufacturers of peripheral equipment also runs for four years, beginning at 25 percent and increasing to 70 percent. As with the local content requirements, no export requirements exist for manufacturers of macrocomputers.

The use of both local content and export requirements in the Computer Decree clearly indicates that Mexico has abandoned its sole reliance on import substitution policies. Nevertheless, several commentators recently have criticized Mexico for its use of export promotion policies, particularly in light of the 1977 Auto Decree experience.[14]

To receive the benefits of this national development program, companies must comply with several more requirements set forth in the Computer Decree. In the area of technology and royalties, companies must promise "to manufacture products in the country that have the most advanced technology available in the field . . . [and] . . . to have access to advances of the manufacturer's research and development centers abroad." Probably to correct the Mexican private sector's modest contribution to scientific and technical research, the Computer Decree requires companies to make an annual contribution for research and development. The Decree specifies an exact amount for manufacturers of microcomputers (6 percent of the value of total sales) and minicomputers (5 percent of the value of total sales). This provision also requires companies to comply with the transfer of technology laws for the use of royalties, patents, and trademarks. Other requirements in the Computer Decree extract promises by the companies to generate the necessary jobs and to contribute to the workers' technical training; to abide by standards of quality and to furnish maintenance services; and to maintain or increase their levels of efficiency and productivity. These requirements are vague and ambiguous, and give Mexico additional leverage with the companies.

A final provision of the Computer Decree concerns export toll manufacturers under the in-bond assembly program. This provision permits 100 percent foreign ownership. but seems to prohibit such ownership for manufacturers of microcomputers. In addition, companies under the in-bond assembly program are subject to several requirements. First, these companies must export at least 75 percent of their production and must sell no more than 25 percent of their production within the country. Second, these companies must substitute importations and must export three pesos worth of product for each peso worth imported. These requirements should not affect the in-bond assembly program's principal benefits: favorable duty treatment and lower costs of production.

The Decree's Status and the U.S. Response

Although the Computer Decree has not been published in Mexico's Official Gazette, it is official policy and legally in effect. In 1981, Presidents Reagan and Portillo established the Joint Commission on Commerce and Trade to improve cooperation and to resolve trade issues between Mexico and the United States. The Commission established sector working groups, including ones for automobiles, petrochemicals, and electronics. The Sector Study Group on Electronics, which is studying computers as part of its mandate, met several times in 1982.[15] Although no significant progress was made during these meetings, the Mexican government, at the request of the U.S. government, agreed to delay formal publication of the implementing regulations for the Computer Decree. The Mexican government, however, refused to reduce the present quotas on computers to the levels existing prior to the announcement of the Computer Decree.

Several provisions of the Computer Decree, particularly the local content and export requirements, offend the free trade and investment policy of the United States. Although Mexico is not a member of the General Agreement on Tariffs and Trade (GATT), these provisions probably violate the GATT and the agreements negotiated at the 1979 Multilateral Trade Negotiations. Because other commentators have capably analyzed the general problem of performance requirements,[16] this chapter will not concentrate on the broader issues. Instead, this chapter will examine the particular and unique problems of preparing a U.S. response to performance requirements imposed by the Computer Decree, a response that is constrained by two factors.

Constraining Factors

About 25 principal companies, in addition to approximately 20 smaller companies supply the Mexican computer market. Of the 25 principal companies, however, eight control 96 percent of the market; IBM alone controls 44 percent of the market. The response of these companies to the Computer Decree, and its performance requirements, has been very quiet. In fact, these 45 companies have signed individual agreements and are registered under the program. This industry acquiescence is explainable. First, although generally opposed to performance requirements, the U.S. computer firms already doing business in Mexico have demonstrated a willingness to negotiate individual deals with the Mexican government.[17] Moreover, the Computer Decree allows for negotiation; performance requirements generally are administered with great flexibility. Second, many companies have not complained openly about the Computer Decree probably because they fear retribution. The agreements already negotiated probably are less than secure and subject to change at any moment. Because these agreements are tenuous, most companies would not want to be identified publicly with any criticism of the government.[18] Third, the Computer Decree, standing alone, may not be so bad for the individual computer firm. For example, the Decree offers tax credits, energy subsidies, and tariff protection. The benefits of these incentives may counterbalance the negative effects of the obligatory requirements.[19] In addition, to the extent that the Computer Decree discourages investment, the few companies that make the investment will dominate a very profitable, protected market. Finally, the Computer Decree probably hurts most those companies, especially the smaller ones, not yet doing business in Mexico. Because these firms do not have an established interest in the Mexican computer market, there is little incentive for these companies to complain about the new performance requirements. The new rules will be just one of many factors that these companies will consider if, and when, they decide to invest in Mexico.

Thus, the United States cannot rely on pressure from the private sector, either on the Mexican government or on U.S. policymakers, to address the problem of performance requirements in Mexico. A U.S. response to the Computer Decree, therefore, must be initiated by the U.S. government itself. The problem with depending on such an initiative, however, is that U.S. policymakers often have advocated a policy of government neutralism in foreign investment decisions. The U.S. government believes that it should not intervene in private-sector decision making. Moreover, U.S. trade laws, such as the antidumping and countervailing duty statutes, rely heavily on industry petition to initiate government action. Although this policy of government neutralism may be changing, its continuance would be detrimental to U.S. interests in the international trade and investment area.

Performance requirements distort the international flow of trade and capital. Although performance requirements may benefit the host country, they do so at the expense of other countries. Performance requirements can cause firms to pursue practices that they would otherwise not choose in the open market. For example, the Computer Decree's local content requirement may cause firms to purchase computer components from local manufacturers who may not be the most efficient producers of that product. The Computer Decree's export requirements may also cause firms to locate manufacturing plants locally, in spite of open market considerations, in order to produce the amount needed for export.

In addition to these international consequences, performance requirements imposed by other countries may be partly responsible for the adverse trends in U.S. imports and exports. The LICIT study on performance requirements has noted that U.S. exports to countries that have imposed "import-limiting" performance requirements have grown at a slower pace than exports to other countries.[20] Moreover, imports from countries applying "export-expanding" performance requirements have grown at a faster rate than imports from all countries.[21] Both the international consequences and the domestic implications of performance requirements, therefore, call for a government-initiated response to Mexico's Computer Decree.

The Mexican Computer Decree probably violates provisions of both the GATT[22] and the Subsidies Code.[23] Several provisions of the GATT prohibit the use of performance requirements.[24] The Computer Decree's local content requirements, which range from 20 percent to 90 percent, for example, are an "internal quantitative regulation requiring the . . . use of products in specified amounts" and thus seem to violate article III(1).

Unfortunately, Mexico is not a member of GATT and is not a signatory to the Subsidies Code, and thus the United States cannot use the dispute resolution provisions in these agreements to address the performance requirements established by the Computer Decree.[25] On March 18, 1980, the Mexican government postponed indefinitely its GATT membership. As a result, the U.S. government cannot challenge in the GATT Mexico's restrictive investment policies.

THE REMEDY

As the foregoing discussion suggests, the response of the United States to the Computer Decree is constrained by two factors: industry acquiescence and Mexico's nonparticipation in international agreements. Thus, the U.S. response must be a bilateral or unilateral action, initiated by the government. Although there are some risks, the United States should respond to the Mexican Computer Decree because the Decree's performance requirements distort the international flow of trade and capital and they directly affect U.S. imports and exports adversely.

Formulating a response to Mexico's investment policies will be difficult because any discussions or actions will touch upon deeply entrenched national beliefs. Although the Mexican government recognizes the importance of U.S. investments, it nonetheless believes the government must maintain strict controls over foreign investors. This belief directly counters the U.S. government's view that the viability of existing U.S. investments and the strength of a continued U.S. presence in that market depend significantly on the Mexican government's willingness to liberalize the investment climate. Given this stark divergence of views, the U.S. government must proceed carefully so as not to worsen a difficult situation.

The present economic crisis confronting the Mexican government may work to the advantage of the U.S. government in its efforts to liberalize the investment climate. Government-imposed restrictions may be loosened to attract new investment or to help foster current investment. At this point, however, it is too early to determine what effect this crisis and the change in administrations in Mexico will have on Mexican investment policies.

Notwithstanding the risks of alienating the Mexican government, the U.S. government must take initiatives designed to promote U.S. interests. The various options available to the U.S. government are reviewed below.

If a country is not a signatory to the Subsidies Code, an action cannot be brought against the country under title VII of the 1979 Trade Agreements Act. Instead, an action can be brought under amended section 303 of the Tariff Act of 1930.[26] Under the 1979 amended version, an investigation may be initiated either by the Secretary of the Treasury or by an "interested party" petition. Because of industry acquiescence to the Computer Decree, however, the Secretary of Treasury should initiate the investigation against Mexico. Unlike title VII of the 1979 Trade Agreements Act, amended section 303 of the 1930 Tariff Act does not require a showing of material injury to the industry. Mexico's nonparticipation in the Subsidies Code, therefore, works to the advantage of the United States because material injury of the healthy U.S. computer industry might be difficult to prove.

The principal issue under section 303 is whether a country has paid or bestowed, "directly or indirectly, any bounty or grant upon the manufacture or production or export" of a product. Several U.S. court decisions have defined "bounty or grant." In *G. S. Nicholas* v. *United States*,[27] for example, the Supreme Court held that Britain's payment of three to five pence for each gallon to distillers on export of their product was a bounty or grant requiring a countervailing duty. The Court defined "bounty or grant" broadly, stating: "If the word 'bounty' has a limited sense, the word 'grant' has not. A word of broader significance than 'grant' could not have been used. Like its synonyms 'give' and 'bestow', it expresses a concession—the conferring of something by one person upon another." The latest Supreme Court decision on this matter, *Zenith Radio Corp.* v. *United States*,[28] held that the nonexcessive remission of an indirect tax was not a bounty or grant under the 1930 Tariff Act.

Several of the "incentive" provisions in Mexico's Computer Decree, coupled with its export promotion requirements, probably are bounties or grants under the definitions given in these decisions. Mexico's preferential prices for energy products and preferential interest rates probably are "concessions" under the *G. S. Nicholas* definition. Moreover, the various Computer Decree tax credits for investment in capital, new jobs, or research are bounties or grants because they are not remissions of *indirect* taxes under *Zenith Radio*. Each of these incentives are bounties or grants because Mexico grants them only if the computer firms meet certain export requirements. After a "bounty or grant" is established, section 303 requires the assessment of "a duty equal to the net amount of such bounty or grant."

An action also could be brought against the Mexican Computer Decree under section 301 of the Trade Act of 1974.[29] A section 301 action may begin by petition to the U.S. Trade Representative (USTR). If an interested person, such as a domestic computer firm, filed a petition, the USTR would have to decide whether to begin an investigation within 45 days. If an affirmative determination is made, the USTR must immediately request consultations with the foreign country. In the case of the Computer Decree, a request for negotiations may upgrade the current consultations, giving them more force than the current discussions by the Electronics Sector Study Group. The president can act *sua sponte* under section 301 to begin an investigation. The president should be the moving actor in a section 301 response to the Computer Decree because of industry acquiescence.

Although investment issues are not yet included specifically in the jurisdiction of section 301, the president could retaliate against Mexico's Computer Decree because it probably is an export subsidy on a good. Under section 301, the Computer Decree could be considered an "unreasonable or discriminatory" act. The Senate Report to the amended section 301, in fact, states explicitly that foreign export subsidies are covered under section 301.[30] Moreover, the language of section 301 was meant to be broad and inclusive. Possessing extensive powers under section 301, the president may take "all appropriate and feasible action," including the imposition of duties or other import restrictions on the products of Mexico.

Under recently enacted legislation, the Overseas Private Investment Corporation (OPIC) has been enjoined "to refuse to insure, reinsure, or finance any investment subject to performance requirements which could reduce substantially the positive trade benefits likely to accrue to the United States from the investment."[31] OPIC, therefore, might refuse to insure investments subject to the Computer Decree. Proving that the Computer Decree reduces substantially positive trade benefits should not be difficult. For example, the import quotas that Mexico enacted in the last half of 1981 severely restricted computer imports into Mexico.

Under the Generalized System of Preferences (GSP) program, less developed countries can export some goods to the United States duty free. Because the GSP statute currently does not provide specific criteria for determining which countries and which goods are eligible for GSP treatment, the USTR has broad discretion in making these decisions.[32] As a response to the Computer Decree, therefore, the United States could deny GSP treatment to some or all of Mexico's exports. Because the United States is a significant trading partner of Mexico, this retaliatory action might affect Mexico considerably.

The problem with any unilateral approach, however, is that retaliation often invites further retaliation. Counteractions could damage the current world trading system and adversely affect the U.S. economy and foreign policy. What the United States needs instead is a more forward-looking policy, that minimally would include the following actions.

First, the United States should expand the negotiation of bilateral investment treaties to include other countries, including Mexico. West European nations and developing countries routinely conclude bilateral investment treaties. Those treaties provide broad rights of establishment, national treatment, and most favored nation treatment for foreign investors.[33] The model U.S. treaty, in fact, specifically prohibits performance requirements, providing that "[n]either Party shall impose performance requirements as a condition for the establishment, expansion or maintenance of investments owned by nationals or companies of the other Party." The United States could use bilateral investment treaties as a mechanism to phase out gradually the incidences of performance requirements abroad. If negotiation of a Bilaterial Investment Treaty (or even a limited investment treaty for border industries) with Mexico proves impossible, the U.S. government should consider instead negotiation of a positive statement on investment. Although such a statement would lack the force and effect of a binding treaty, it nonetheless should lead to a better mutual understanding of each country's differences on investment issues.

Second, the United States should pressure Mexico, and other developing countries, to join the GATT and then to sign the various multilateral codes. A multilateral approach in the long run is the best solution to international investment problems, such as performance requirements. In the case of Mexico, the United States has leverage in several areas and could encourage either bilateral or multilateral consideration of investment issues. The threat of a countervailing duty or section 301 action might encourage Mexico to seek a broad-based solution. Similarly, negotiation of U.S. immigration policy could be linked to Mexico's participation in bilateral or multilateral investment solutions. Because the United States has not yet negotiated a tax treaty with Mexico, its negotiation also might be used as leverage to promote U.S. investment goals. The U.S. government also could use as leverage the international rescue package offered Mexico, under which Mexico will receive assistance as it attempts to decrease its $80 billion foreign debt. Given U.S. banks' dependency on Mexico's financial health, however, the U.S. government must be careful not to extract too many concessions at the cost of Mexico's economic health. Moreover, as noted previously, investment issues touch upon long-standing deeply felt national beliefs.

Finally, the United States government should continue to bring "test cases" against countries that impose performance requirements. (The United States has brought such a case in the GATT against Canada.)[34] The countries chosen, like Canada, preferably should be signatories to the Subsidies Code. The actions, therefore, could be brought under the dispute settlement provisions of the Code and, if necessary, under the countervailing duty provisions of the 1979 Trade Agreements Act. Such actions would have several benefits. First, they would begin the development of an international law on performance requirements. Although performance requirements are widely used today, the international community has not firmly addressed the international legal validity of performance requirements. A favorable result in the Canadian test case and in other cases might at least curb the growing use of performance requirements. Second, such "test case" actions against signatories to the Subsidies Code should be viewed as more legitimate actions on the part of the United States than a unilateral section 301 action. Third, they should put the world community on notice about the position of the United States on performance requirements. U.S. interests should be advanced if governments believe that the United States is prepared to take specific actions against countries that use performance requirements.

CONCLUSION

Mexico's Computer Decree is only one disturbing example of the growing use of performance requirements by the international community. It is, however, a particularly important problem for U.S. policymakers. The U.S. computer sector is a rapidly expanding industry, and Mexico is the United States' third largest trading partner. Although U.S. policymakers can only really address the problem of Mexico's Computer Decree in the context of a coherent and dynamic foreign policy on performance requirements, 1983 may prove to be an opportune time to create a more positive relationship with Mexico. President Portillo's successor, President Miguel de la Madrid, will be in a good position to create better relations and, with some encouragement from the United States, might give serious attention to the U.S. position on the Computer Decree.

NOTES

1. *See generally* Fonthein & Gadbaw, *Trade-Related Investment Requirements* (chapter 5 of this book); Labor-Industry Coalition for International Trade, Performance Requirements (1981) [hereinafter LICIT Study].

2. One scholar has described this period as "The Mexican Miracle." R. Hansen, The Politics of Mexican Development 41 (1971).

3. Epstein, *Business-Government Relations in Mexico-The Echeverria Challenge to the Existing Development Model*, 12 Case W. Res. J. Int'l L. 525, 526 (1980). *See generally* National Chamber Foundation, Council of the Americas, Impact of Foreign Investment in Mexico (1971).

4. *See* U.S. Dep't of Commerce, Overseas Business Reports: Marketing in Mexico 12 (May 1981); *The New Mexican Industrial Plan*, Int'l Law. 652, 653 (1980).

5. U.S. Int'l Trade Comm., Background Study of the Economies and International Trade Patterns of the Countries of North America, Central America, and the Caribbean 63 (1981) [hereinafter ITC Background Study].

6. U.S. Int'l Trade Comm., Operation of the Trade Agreements Program 155 (1980).

7. Radway, *Doing Business in Mexico: A Practical Legal Analysis*, Int'l Law. 361, 369 (1980).

8. Secreteria de Petrimonio Y Fomento Industrial, Industrial Development Plan 1979-1982-1990 (1979).

9. *See* ITC Background Study, *supra* note 5, at 38.

10. Development Program for the Manufacturing of Electronic Computer Systems, Their Main Modules and Peripheral Equipment, Mexico, Fed. Dist. The Computer Decree is divided into three parts: titles, sections, and addenda. The titles set forth the broad policy outlines and purposes of the Computer Decree. The sections set forth the rules governing each type of computer product. The addenda list mathematical formulas for companies to use to determine the standards the Mexican government will use in implementing the Computer Decree.

11. Int'l Trade Admin., U.S. Dep't of Commerce, Computer and Peripheral Equipment: Mexico (1981).

12. Microcomputers have a word length of between 4 and 16 bits, a maximum central memory capacity of 64K, and a U.S. sales price of between $300 and $20,000. Minicomputers have a word length of between 16 and 32 bits, a central memory capacity of between 64K and 4MB, and a U.S. sales price of between $15,000 and $200,000. Macrocomputers have a word length greater than 32 bits, a memory capacity of greater than 4MB, and a U.S. sales price in excess of $200,000. Peripheral equipment includes printers, video units, and tape and disc units.

13. For a discussion of how foreign-owned companies have circumvented the restrictions on majority ownership imposed by the 1973 Foreign Investment Law, *see* Wall St. J., Feb. 16, 1982, at 12, col. 3.

14. The experience of the auto industry provides a good example of the course taken by the Mexican government in developing and implementing export promotion requirements. *See* Bennett & Sharpe, *Transnational Corporations and the Political Economy of Export Promotion: The Case of the Mexican Automobile Industry*, 33 Int'l. Org. 177 (1979). *See generally* James, *Mexico: America's Newest Problem*, 3 Wash. Q. 87 (1980).

15. The objectives of the Sector Study Group on Computers include: (1) examining issues of concern to the computer industry in both countries; (2) identifying areas in which cooperative efforts can better promote the growth and development of both countries' computer industries and the freer flow of trade and investment; and (3) making recommendations to the Bilateral Trade Commission.

16. *See generally* Fontheim and Gadbaw, *supra* note 1; LICIT Study, *supra* note 1.

17. *See U.S. Policy Toward International Investment: Hearings before Subcomm. on International Economic Policy of the Senate Comm. on Foreign Relations*, 97th Cong., 1st Sess. 27 (1981) (statement of Alan W. Wolff).

18. *Id.* at 24 (prepared statement of Rowland H. Thomas, American Electronics Ass'n).

19. As Fontheim and Gadbaw indicate, firms generally acquiesce to performance requirements rather than relocate production facilities in another country. First, withdrawing may be more expensive than remaining in the country and complying with the requirements. Second, the host-country may require firms to locate production facilities in the country as a prerequisite to gaining access to the domestic market. Third, the host-country may have a natural competitive advantage. Finally, the host-country may provide benefits that outweigh the costs of compliance. *See generally* Fontheim & Gadbaw, *supra* note 1.

20. Seventeen major host-countries impose "import-limiting" performance requirements. Whereas U.S. exports, in the aggregate, increased at an annual average rate of 25.8 percent between 1973 and 1979, U.S. exports increased by only 22.6 percent during the same period in these countries.

21. Nine major host countries impose "export-expanding" performance requirements. U.S. imports from non-OPEC countries grew at an average annual rate of 25.6 percent between 1973 and 1979. Imports from the five non-OPEC countries in the above group, however, grew at an average annual rate of 36.9 percent during this period.

22. General Agreement on Tariffs and Trade, *open for signature*, Oct. 30, 1947, 61 Stat. A3, T.I.A.S. No. 1700, 55 U.N.T.S. 187. The current version of the agreement is contained in 4 General Agreement on Tariffs and Trade, Basic Instruments and Selected Documents (1969).

23. Agreement on Interpretation of Articles VI, XVI, and XXIII of the General Agreement on Tariffs and Trade, *done* Apr. 12, 1979, MTN/NTM/W 236, *reprinted in* Agreements Reached in the Tokyo Round of the Multilateral Trade Negotiations, H.R. Doc. 153, 96th Cong., 1st Sess. pt. 1 (1979).

24. *See generally* J. Jackson, World Trade and the Law of the GATT (1969).

25. Mexico has not joined the GATT for several reasons. First, many Mexicans believe that GATT membership would impose too many restrictions on Mexico's trade policy, which is designed to promote industrial development. Second, former President Portillo believed that Mexico's new oil wealth would attract new foreign direct investment and would increase international trade without membership in the GATT. Finally, because the U.S. government was eager to have Mexico join, many Mexicans perceived GATT membership as benefiting the United States more than Mexico. *See generally* Purcell, *Mexico-U.S. Relations: Big Initiative Can Cause Big Problems*, 60 For. Affairs 379 (1982).

26. Tariff Act of 1930, ch. 497, § 303, 46 Stat. 590, 687, *amended by* Trade Act of 1974, § 331(a), 88 Stat. 1978, 2049 (1975), and Trade Agreements Act of 1979, § 103, 93 Stat. 144, 190 (codified at 19 U.S.C. § 1303).

27. 249 U.S. 34 (1919).

28. 437 U.S. 443 (1978).

29. 19 U.S.C. §§ 2411–2416 (Supp. III 1979).

30. S. Rep. No. 249, 96th Cong., 1st Sess. 236–37 (1979).

31. 22 U.S.C.A. § 2191 (West. Supp. 1982).

32. 19 U.S.C. § 2561 (1976).

33. *See generally* Coughlin, *The U.S. Bilateral Investment Treaty: An Answer to Performance Requirements?* (chapter 7 of this book).

34. *See* Turner, *Canadian Regulation of Foreign Direct Investment* (Chapter 2 of this volume).

7

The U.S. Bilateral Investment Treaty: An Answer to Performance Requirements?
William E. Coughlin

INTRODUCTION

United States investment abroad has increased over $227 billion, yet no formal international system of regulating foreign direct investment has taken root and expanded in like manner. As developing and developed countries alike vie for increasingly scarce investment capital, U.S. and other investors will be confronted more frequently by incentives designed to lure them into host-countries and by restrictions designed to limit their activities once they have entered those markets. These host-government devices, some of which are known as performance requirements, are a particular cause for concern in the United States because the U.S. service sector is taking on a greater role in national output and because investment in traditional manufacturing facilities is moving abroad.

The dilemma now facing the United States government is how to protect U.S. foreign direct investment from the distorting effects of performance requirements at the least political cost and in the absence of an international regulatory mechanism. While this topic has been high on the foreign trade and investment agenda, the most interested U.S. government agencies, the Office of the United States Trade Representative (USTR) and the Departments of State and Commerce, as well as the Congress, have not had much success with the multilateral and unilateral approaches to the problem. The recently proposed Bilateral Investment Treaty (BIT),[1] however, offers some hope for greater, albeit limited, success.

This chapter describes the origins of the BIT, the U.S. model BIT's key provisions, and the two BITs that recently have been negotiated and signed with Egypt and Panama. Then, it briefly catalogues the types and effects of performance requirements and assesses multilateral and unilateral attempts at meeting performance requirements. After analyzing the advantages and disadvantages of bilaterally regulating performance requirements by means of the BIT, this chapter concludes that, although BITs are far from perfect, the U.S. government should actively attempt to negotiate BITs as a means of protecting U.S. foreign direct investment.

THE U.S. BILATERAL INVESTMENT TREATY

In order to capitalize on and reinforce the comparatively favorable international investment climate that still prevails, early in 1982 the USTR proposed negotiating BITs with a limited number of developing countries.[2] The Model BIT's roots can be traced to the roughly forty Treaties of Friendship, Commerce and Navigation (FCN) currently in force, some of which find their origins in the early nineteenth century. The scope and purpose of these treaties were quite broad, ranging from the diplomatic to the legal to the economic, and encompassing the protection of individual liberties, promotion of trade, establishment of consular rights, regulation of customs, access to local courts, and protection against expropriation.[3]

While some commentators argue that the inherent flexibility of such expansive treatment, representing a body of internationally accepted principles upon which further agreement can be built, lends itself to the protection of U.S. investment abroad,[4] the FCN provisions that deal with investment lack the detail and focus which characterize the U.S. Model BIT, the recently signed U.S. BITs, and bilateral treaties negotiated between other developed countries and developing countries. For example, the FCNs make no mention at all of performance requirements. Much detail and a specific investment orientation are probably requisites to meaningful protection of U.S. foreign direct investment.

Although the U.S. government probably would applaud the eventual establishment of a "GATT for Investment,"[5] for purely international political reasons it is, at best, a distant prospect. Consequently, the USTR has taken a "triple-barreled" approach to investment protection: 1) it hoped for multilateral discussion of performance requirements at the Ministerial meeting of the General Agreement on Tariffs and Trade (GATT) in November 1982, as well as in the Organization for Economic Cooperation and Development (OECD); 2) it has considered various unilateral responses to the problem; and 3) it has continued to seek negotiations to conclude several BITs.

For the present, the bilateral treaty approach holds the most promise, even though the model BIT's key provisions present certain problems. While the preamble sets forth generally accepted principles, including nondiscrimination, the treaty text is somewhat confused and controversial. For example, the definition of "company of a Party" is overly restrictive, including in its criteria a showing of a "substantial interest" of nationals in the enterprise. Likewise, while the definition of investment is designed to be broad, its enumeration of specific examples of covered investments may work inadvertently to exclude nonenumerated types of investment.

Article II guarantees the application of the "most favorable" form of protection as between national treatment and most favored nation (MFN) status to investments, both in their establishment and in their operation. Although useful, it has not been uniformly accepted in treaties negotiated by other developed countries, and was changed to "more favorable" in the treaty with Panama. Moreover, the state trading clause provides, somewhat unrealistically, that such entities shall not be accorded special advantage by parent-governments.

Adequate, prompt, and effective compensation is mandated for losses due either to expropriation or, in some cases, to insurrection. Expropriation includes partial or full, direct or indirect, takings. Governments are precluded from expropriating property that is protected by a preexisting "contractual stability" agreement, a principle of doubtful international legal validity, at least among countries that interpret sovereignty expansively. The transfer article assures unburdened movement of money in and out of the Parties, except for minimal formalities such as reporting requirements. In the event a disagreement results from one or both Parties' actions, the Parties agree to consult and to exchange information, including business information, as long as confidentialities are not compromised.

The model treaty sets forth a two-level dispute settlement mechanism. Both government versus investor and government versus government conflicts are resolved by either conciliation or binding arbitration. Government versus investor disputes are to be settled in accordance with the rules of the International Centre for the Settlement of Investment Disputes (ICSID) or its Additional Facility. The investor is not obliged to exhaust local remedies and, during the settlement proceedings, reference to home country insurance is forbidden.

Finally, the most controversial provision contains a prohibition against performance requirements. A uniquely U.S. provision, it reads:

> Neither Party shall impose performance requirements as a condition of
> establishment, expansion, or maintenance of investments owned by na-

tionals or companies of the other Party, which require or enforce commitments to export goods produced, or which specify that goods or services must be purchased locally, or which impose any other similar requirements.[6]

U.S. Trade Representative William Brock and Egyptian Minister of Investment and International Cooperation Wagih Shindy signed the first U.S. BIT on September 29, 1982, in Washington, D.C.[7] The U.S.-Egyptian treaty tracks the U.S. model in many respects, such as definition of terms, most favored nation and national treatment, dispute settlement, and compensation in the event of expropriation. Free transfer of capital and earnings is limited only by Egyptian balance of payments considerations. However, the U.S. government was able to extract only a "best efforts" clause with respect to performance requirements, which reads:

> In the context of its national economic policies and objectives, each Party shall seek to avoid the imposition of performance requirements on the investments by nationals and companies of the other Party.

The Egyptians proved to be tough negotiators, probably because they already have concluded roughly 15 of these treaties with other developed countries. Although the Egyptians have been disappointed by the small amount of investment generated by these other treaties, they expect this new BIT to expand U.S. investment in Egypt beyond its 1981 level of a little more than $1 billion, notwithstanding the weaker performance requirements provision.

The United States concluded its second BIT on October 27, 1982, with Ambassador Brock and Panamanian Ambassador to the United States Aquilino Boyd signing for each Party in Washington, D.C.[8] It, too, follows the U.S. model in all of its key provisions, including dispute settlement, which had been expected to be a serious obstacle due to Panama's adherence to the Calvo Doctrine. This doctrine, subscribed to by many Latin American countries, requires in part that investment disputes be resolved by local courts rather than by foreign or international tribunals. To avoid a conflict with the doctrine, Panama agreed to submit disputes to ISCID's Additional Facility. Although Panama is not an ICSID member, it cooperates with the Additional Facility and has been reported to be considering full ICSID membership.[9]

As for performance requirements, the U.S. negotiators were more successful in this second attempt. Panama agreed to a clause prohibiting their use, which states:

> Neither Party shall impose performance requirements as a condition for the establishment of investment owned by nationals or companies of the

other Party, which require or enforce commitments to export goods produced, or which specify that goods or services must be purchased locally, or which impose any other similar requirements.

Again, the language is not as "iron clad" as in the model. For example, no reference is made to performance requirements as a condition for expansion or maintenance of existing foreign investments. Nonetheless, the provision appears significantly more protective than its Egyptian counterpart.[10]

Like the Egyptian treaty, the Panamanian BIT has not yet been submitted for Senate ratification. The State Department will not transmit the BIT to the U.S. Senate before substantial progress is made on three outstanding investment disputes between U.S. investors and the Panamanian government that involve expropriations. In addition, as suggested by Ambassador Boyd in his remarks at the signing ceremony, the treaty is expected to encounter some political resistance in Panama. Unless a special legislative session is called in early 1983, which is unlikely, it will not be debated until October 1983. Thus, although this treaty contains greater restrictions on the use of performance requirements, significant obstacles stand in the way of its ultimately coming into force.

Several other countries have expressed an interest in opening negotiations with the United States. They include the People's Republic of China, Morocco, Burundi, Cameroon, Gabon, Antigua and Barbuda, Barbados, El Salvador, Guatemala, Jamaica, Costa Rica, Zaire, Zimbabwe, Honduras, Saudi Arabia, and Singapore. All U.S. embassies have received copies of the model BIT. Of those countries that have shown an interest, it is unclear how many are serious about seeing negotiations through to their conclusion.[11] However, this wide distribution of the model text does put other countries on notice that the United States opposes the imposition of performance requirements and intends to prevent the passage of time from *de facto* legitimizing existing restrictive practices.

PERFORMANCE REQUIREMENTS

The Commerce Department defines performance requirements as "any requirement placed upon a foreign controlled enterprise by a host nation."[12] They include imposed floors on local content and value-added; job quotas (quantitative and qualitative); export quotas; export-mix enhancement; size, sector, and industry specifications; specified sites; and equity ownership restrictions. Performance requirements were the primary focus of the USTR efforts on the larger issue of trade-related investment restrictions in Geneva in November 1982. Although there was no success in that GATT forum, performance requirements remain a high priority since, as one expert noted in recent testimony, they are "clearly the most important, and most rapidly growing, problem in the area of international investment today."[13]

Despite all the attention that has been directed toward performance requirements, very little is actually known about their effect on trade and investment flows. Indeed, in the studies completed to date, there exists only a generalized intuitive feeling that performance requirements create distortions. No definitive economic research documenting these distorting effects has yet been published.[14] All of these studies, however, advance persuasive hypotheses that reasonably demonstrate that welfare losses occur as the result of the imposition of performance requirements.

Ironically, whether these hypotheses are confirmed by economic reality is largely irrelevant as long as performance requirements are portrayed by the United States as such objectionable host government devices. Recent USTR pronouncements suggest that the U.S. government intends to keep the spotlight focused brightly on them.[15] Since it has already publicized the issue so highly, the U.S. government is left with little choice but to attack performance requirements diligently, hopefully with minimum additional international political cost, if it is to maintain credibility. An assessment of the alternatives available for the accomplishment of that task follows.

CONTROLLING PERFORMANCE REQUIREMENTS: ALTERNATIVE APPROACHES

Multilateral

At first blush, the international organization that would seem the most suitable candidate to regulate performance requirements is the GATT, although its jurisdiction over this matter is far from clear. Indeed, the high-level Ministerial meeting in Geneva that took place in late November 1982, had seemed the ideal occasion, at least in the eyes of U.S. officials, to highlight the worldwide proliferation of performance requirements. However, even from the start of the preparations for the meeting's agenda, it became clear that the United States' trading partners were not interested in treating the issue. As it turned out, the ministers did not discuss performance requirements.

There has been some debate as to whether performance requirements fall within the jurisdiction of the GATT. On the one hand, the proponents of jurisdiction argue that the requirements violate article III (national treatment), article XI (prohibition on quantitative restrictions), article XX-

III (nullification and impairment of rights), article XVI (subsidies), and the Multilateral Trade Negotiations (MTN) Code on Subsidies, as well as other GATT provisions and precedents.[16] On the other hand, opponents argue that GATT jurisdiction does not extend beyond barriers that explicitly restrict international trade in goods; investment restrictions are utterly irrelevant. Performance requirements designed to affect production are aimed primarily at influencing the use of investment capital, so any residual effect on trade is not sufficient to trigger GATT jurisdiction. Moreover, they argue, the GATT prohibition on export restrictions only forbids quantitative ceilings, therefore, export requirements, which encourage exports, do not fall within its ambit.[17]

Events in Geneva last November rendered the outcome of this debate largely academic. The GATT is basically a political entity that succeeds only on the basis of consensus. As a practical political reality, its member nations flatly rejected U.S. attempts to bring performance requirements within its purview. Consequently, it is not reasonable to expect a change in the member nations' view of GATT jurisdiction, absent a change in their attitude toward performance requirements.[18]

USTR officials cling to the view that other multilateral forums remain where U.S. views regarding performance requirements can be aired, such as the Paris-based OECD, which is comprised exclusively of the world's developed countries. As these same officials will admit, however, the OECD is also a political institution whose pronouncements are not binding, and many of its members are the very same countries which rebuffed the U.S. government's overtures on performance requirements at the GATT Ministerial.

Overall, the multilateral approach to the assault on performance requirements holds little promise for the United States in the current international political and economic climate.

Unilateral

Also available to U.S. policymakers is the unilateral approach. Its greatest appeal is the wide range of options it offers. The problem, however, is identifying one that will succeed.

A unilateral approach might take several forms, including section 301 (enforcement of U.S. trade rights) actions;[19] denial of Generalized System of Preferences (GSP) status, which accords duty-free treatment to imports from less developed countries; decreased U.S. funding of multilateral organizations; and denial of Overseas Private Investment Corporation (OPIC) insurance protection for prospective investments in countries which impose performance requirements,[20] as well as other country- and industry-specific political and economic retaliatory acts, such as delayed tax treaty ratification, reciprocity legislation, and auto local content requirements. The Assistant USTR for Investment Policy expressly left open the unilateral option in response to the rebuke of the U.S. proposal at the GATT Ministerial.[21]

The common thread running through these and other unilateral acts is that they only result from the failure to agree with relevant trading partners on the regulation of performance requirements. While the threat of unilateral action may be productive, its actual use is self-defeating since it reduces international economic activity. It may even provoke further hostile action by the targeted country or countries or, in the case of an OPIC denial, may prompt a search for alternative investors or insurers. At best, actual use might placate temporarily domestic critics of a perceived weakness in U.S. trade policy. However, even they may experience a change of heart when it becomes clear that the United States has much more to lose than any other nation.

Bilateral

Although it is not without disadvantages, the bilateral approach to the regulation of performance requirements, as embodied in the BIT, is the most realistic of the three approaches. This option has been used most extensively by other developed countries for the general protection and encouragement of their foreign direct investment. However, only the U.S. treaty deals with performance requirements.

By way of comparison, the existing BITs negotiated between OECD members and less developed countries (LDCs) are much less specific, demanding, and "legalistic" than their U.S. analogue. While other developed countries, too, are interested in capitalizing on the present, comparatively favorable investment climate via the BIT, they see its added utility in the multilateral organization and negotiation contexts as documentary evidence of host government attitudes toward foreign direct investment. Whether these agreements have contributed materially to the protection of OECD investments is unknown. Whatever the case, capital exporting nations continue to negotiate them at a rapid pace, pushing the existing number of such agreements to over 200.[22]

The OECD treaties differ from the U.S. model in several significant ways. First, they generally do not employ the "laundry-list" approach to defining investment. For example, some define it simply as "every kind of asset." Second, the definition of "company of a Party" may or may not include a "substantial interest" requirement, that is, mere incorporation under the laws of one or the other Party suffices. Third, they allow screening of investments and, as noted earlier, none makes any mention of performance requirements. Completely free transfer of capital is not guaranteed. Either most favored nation combined with national treatment, or one or the other is the standard of treatment.

In addition, they often contain "saving clauses" for customs unions and provide for a single level of dispute settlement (between governments) or a unified dispute settlement mechanism (for both governments and investors). Furthermore, they include explicit subrogation clauses for protection of the home government insurer (and occasionally provide for guaranteed, rather than most favored nation or national treatment, recovery for losses due to war or insurrection). Finally, several conclude with astonishing "pork-barrel" protocols, in which special allowances and protections are accorded to various interests.

In some respects, such as in the free transfer of capital and customs union clauses, the Egyptian and Panamanian U.S. BITs are more like the other developed country treaties than the U.S. model. This suggests that the U.S. version is capable of greater adaptation to political realities in the actual negotiations than its legalistic tone would suggest is otherwise possible.

Like other developed nations' BITs, the utility of the U.S. BIT is limited because the treaty is aimed primarily at developing countries. Moreover, since the model treaty was not drafted with nonmarket economies in mind, the proposed treaty with the People's Republic of China will require revisions to make it applicable. The inclusion of a prohibition on performance requirements may further limit its potential targets to the poorer LDCs because the newly industrializing countries (NICs) such as Brazil, Taiwan, and Mexico, which until now have been attracting vast amounts of foreign investment, do not need a BIT to secure more. Similarly, developed countries are not candidates for the U.S. BIT since they, too, have no incentive to negotiate a treaty, particularly one with a restriction on performance requirements. Nonetheless, U.S. officials occasionally wish out loud that they could open negotiations with Japan or Canada.[23]

Other difficulties stand in the way of the future success of the U.S. BIT, particularly with regard to its prohibition on performance requirements. First, U.S. business has exhibited some ambivalence toward the treaty. U.S. investors who have already entered into contracts that impose performance requirements are not eager to see future competitors operating in the same market free of those restrictions. Existing investors also fear antagonizing host governments by openly lobbying for the BIT's performance requirement prohibition after having already contractually accepted such requirements. Furthermore, prospective investors interested in a particular country or a potential market might be reluctant to support U.S. government efforts aimed at changing the status quo in a way that could be irksome to the host government.[24]

Similarly, U.S. organized labor, which had joined with industry to form the Labor-Industry Coalition for International Trade (LICIT) in opposition to performance requirements imposed by foreign governments, finds itself in the somewhat awkward position of currently supporting a potential U.S. performance requirement: local content legislation directed at foreign automobile producers. In contrast, the industry component of LICIT still generally supports the elimination of all performance requirements. Both LICIT partners, however, apparently remain united in opposition to export requirements. Indeed, notwithstanding the investor who may be hesitant to endorse the BIT's prohibition on performance requirements for individual reasons, U.S. Chamber of Commerce and National Association of Manufacturers representatives have stated that they were impressed with the business-government cooperation that resulted in successful completion of a treaty with Egypt.[25]

Of course, there remain many other obstacles to signing more BITs, both as to the treaty in general and the performance requirements clause in particular. With respect to performance requirements, a major problem may be of the U.S. Government's own making. Surprisingly, State Department and USTR officials indicated informally that the Ministerial rebuff did not persuade them to respond by expanding the list of BIT target countries or by adding emphasis to the treaty's requirements prohibition. Other problems generally threatening the success of the treaty include:

- the U.S. model's lengthy and demanding provisions which, while negotiable, may be deterring overtures by potential treaty partners;
- the lack of coordination among interested U.S. agencies, both as to the approach to be taken (unilateral versus bilateral versus multilateral) and as to the allocation of responsibility for the negotiations;
- unexpected and uncontrollable political events, such as the Falkland Islands crisis, which particularly inflamed many LDCs;
- the absence of clauses specifying clearly the role of domestic laws in government-investor disputes that do *not* involve expropriations;
- the treaty's reliance on ICSID facilities for dispute resolution when certain target countries either are not ICSID members or refuse to adopt ICSID's procedures; and
- since the percentage of LDC exports of manufactured goods attributable to developed country foreign direct investment is declining, LDCs may have less incentive to attract private investment as an "engine for development."[26]

In counterpoise to these disadvantages are the many (and predominating) advantages to the bilateral approach. Aside from avoiding the high profile of multilateral negotiations where failure attracts great publicity, as well as avoiding the hostility which unilateral action can create, a commitment to the bilateral approach vitiates the inconsistency that was implicit in the U.S. negotiating position at the GATT: even while trumpeting the necessity of multilateral regulation, the U.S. government was negotiating on the bilateral level and threatening unilateral action. Also from a negotiating standpoint, the more demanding provisions of the U.S. BIT, such as the free transfer of capital, the guarantee of national treatment, and the limits on expropriation, leave some room for compromise that would enable the requirements clause to escape intact. (Admittedly, this clause could just as easily be the victim of compromise in favor of one of the other provisions.) Furthermore, the problem of the other Party's membership in an international organization, like the GATT, does not arise in the bilateral treaty context, except for ICSID membership, which can sometimes be sidestepped, as in the treaty with Panama.

Moreover, unlike GATT dispute resolution, the BIT permits a private party, rather than only the U.S. government, to initiate directly in an international forum a challenge to the host government's action affecting his investment, much like the private right of action provided by section 301 of the Trade Act of 1974. Indeed, by enumerating rights accorded to the U.S. investor, the treaty complements and gives content to section 301's dual mandate to "enforce U.S. rights under any trade agreement" and to retaliate against any foreign trade practice that is "unjustifiable, unreasonable or discriminatory," whether the current section 301's coverage extends only implicitly to investment, as presently interpreted by the USTR, or whether its protection extends explicitly to investment, as is the purpose of proposed amending legislation introduced in the 97th and 98th Congresses.[27] In short, the BIT assures the investor predictability, for the treaty is a binding and lasting statement of each Party's law and policy on the protection of foreign investment.

The BIT interacts in other positive ways with existing and proposed U.S. law. For example, unlike OPIC bilateral agreements with other nations, the BIT actually has the force of law in both the United States and the host nation. Also, while similar in purpose to existing OPIC agreements, that is, protection of investment, the two agreements are actually very different because the OPIC bilateral applies only when the investor has used OPIC insurance or finance and because OPIC's version has no provision on nondiscrimination. BITs (and particularly the performance requirements clause) with Latin American nations, such as Panama, provide the protection for U.S. investment that the Reagan Administration's Caribbean Basin Initiative, to the extent it survives congressional trimming, is intended to foster. Finally, the BIT's performance requirements clause undermines the effect of foreign automobile local content legislation pending in the U.S. Congress, although the BIT and the local content law are each aimed at different groups of countries.[28] Indeed, it is possible, but not probable, that the interplay of the performance requirements prohibition and the local content legislation may have the ironic effect of inducing foreign car producers to locate their manufacturing facilities in countries that have acceded to the BIT's prohibition clause in order to escape the local content requirement.

Lastly, while the BIT skirts very close to the "beggar thy neighbor" bilateralism that brought economic collapse in the interwar period, it differs significantly, and in a way that actually translates into mutual benefit. Unlike the country- and product-specific agreements of the 1930s that engendered widespread trade reciprocity and retaliation, the BIT is an attempt to decrease international political tension by agreeing on rules that encourage trade and protect investment; it is not an attempt to erect matching trade barriers. Instead, it strikes down the unique barrier that links trade and investment: the performance requirement.

CONCLUSION

If the U.S. government remains intent on removing performance requirements from the international investment arena, it will have to come to an understanding with countries that impose them. Whether for want of a better alternative, or because of its intrinsic merit, the beginning of any consensus at all on performance requirements must be the U.S. BIT. Multilateral regulation, which would have been preferable, has proved politically unattainable. Momentum generated by successful negotiation of more BITs might catapult the issue back, into the GATT or some other multilateral forum. In the meantime, however, without some start at control, performance requirements are likely to proliferate. The U.S. BIT could be the spark that awakens the need for international regulation of foreign direct investment in time to prevent the outbreak of an all-out investment war akin to the disaster of the 1930s.

NOTES

1. (Model) Treaty between the United States of America and _____ concerning the Reciprocal Encouragement and Protection of Investments, *dated* January 20, 1983 (*See* Appendix to this volume). The negotiations with Egypt and Panama were based on earlier but substantially similar, versions of the treaty, dated January 11, 1982 and May 7, 1982.

2. *See* 392 U.S. Export Weekly (BNA) (Jan. 26, 1982) at 438–39.

3. *See* Walker, *Modern Treaties of Friendship, Commerce and Navigation*, 42 Minn. L. Rev. 805 (1952).

4. *See, e.g.*, Walker, *Treaties for the Encouragement and Protection of Foreign Investment*, 5 Am. J. Comp. L. 229 (1956).

5. *See* Goldberg & Kindleberger, *Toward a GATT for Investment: A Proposal for the Supervision of the International Corporation,* 2 Law & Pol'y Int'l Bus. 295 (1970).

6. The earlier models included an additional, limiting clause: "and which potentially or actually have an adverse effect on the trade and/or investments of the nationals or companies of the other Party." This language was deleted in the present version of the draft treaty so that U.S. negotiators could attempt to trade its inclusion in future treaties for further concessions.

7. As of April 1983, the treaty had not been submitted to the Senate for ratification, and it may encounter problems during Senate consideration of it. The treaty is reprinted in 21 Int'l Legal Materials at 927–749 (Sept. 1982).

8. The treaty is reprinted in 21 Int'l Legal Materials at 1227–43 (Nov. 1982).

9. 18 U.S. Export Weekly (BNA) (Nov. 2, 1982) at 170.

10. Some doubt exists because, in the "Agreed Minutes" annexed to the treaty, the Parties expressly recognized Panamanian "incentive laws granting benefits to duly constituted companies which sign contracts with the government in which they agree to meet the requirements established therein."

11. As of mid-April 1983, a treaty had been initiated with Costa Rica and negotiations with Burundi were nearing a conclusion.

12. Int'l Trade Admin., U.S. Dep't of Commerce, The Use of Investment Incentives and Performance Requirements by Foreign Government 7 (1981) (known as the "Benchmark Survey"). The Commerce Department estimated that 14 percent of foreign affiliates of U.S. companies were subject to performance requirements. As between developing and developed countries, 29 percent of U.S. affiliates were subject to performance requirements in the former compared with 6 percent in the latter.

13. *Hearings Before the Senate Comm. on Foreign Relations on S. 993, a Bill to Amend the Foreign Assistance Act of 1961 with Respect to the Activities of the Overseas Private Investment Corporation,* 97th Cong., 1st Sess. 250 (1981) (statement of C. Fred Bergsten).

14. *See* Fontheim & Gadbaw, *Trade-Related Investment Requirements* (chapter 5 of this book); the ITA Survey, *supra* note 12; Labor-Industry Coalition for International Trade (LICIT), Performance Requirements (March 1981). *See generally* C. Bergsten, T. Horst, & T. Moran, American Multinationals and American Interests (1978) (especially chapters 3, 8, 12, 13). A much anticipated review of performance requirements, requested by the president, will be published by the International Trade Commission in 1983.

15. *See, e.g.,* 18 U.S. Export Weekly (BNA) (Dec. 7, 1982) at 404.

16. *See, e.g.,* Fontheim & Gadbaw, *supra* note 14; LICIT Study, *supra* note 14.

17. *See, e.g.,* Bergsten, Horst & Moran, *supra* note 14, at 490. For a discussion of both sides of this jurisdictional issue, *see* Fisher & Steinhardt, *Section 301 of the Trade Act of 1974: Protection for U.S. Exporters of Goods, Services and Capital,* 14 Law & Pol'y Int'l Bus. 569 (1982).

18. In addition, not all nations are GATT members. Thus, even if it were to take up the issue, nonmembers who impose performance requirements would not be bound by GATT determinations.

19. 19 U.S.C. §§ 2411–2416 (Supp. III 1979); *see also* Fisher & Steinhardt, *supra* note 17, for a comprehensive treatment of section 301 actions.

20. OPIC already engages in such a review before approving insurance to see whether the requirements substantially reduce U.S. trade benefits. It is the sole U.S. agency in the foreign trade/investment/aid arena which does so. *See* remarks of S. Linn Williams, OPIC General Counsel, *reported in* 411 U.S. Export Weekly (BNA) (June 8, 1982) at 370–71.

21. *See* 18 U.S. Export Weekly (BNA) (Dec. 7, 1982) at 404.

22. A list of existing bilateral investment treaties, as of October 1, 1982, appears at 21 Int'l Legal Materials 1208–09 (Sept. 1982). The list includes an occasional citation to "U.S." treaties; this is apparently a reference to treaties other than the U.S. BIT, such as FCNs.

23. *See* 18 U.S. Export Weekly (BNA) (March 1, 1983) at 830; 18 U.S. Export Weekly (BNA) (Nov. 11, 1982) at 249.

24. For a discussion of industry acquiescence to Mexican performance requirements, see Jacobsen, *Mexican Regulation of the Computer Industry* (chapter 6 of this book).

25. *See* 18 U.S. Export Weekly (BNA) (Oct. 5, 1982) at 18.

26. *See* Helleiner, *Intrafirm Trade and the Developing Countries*, 6 J. Dev. Econ. 391, 404 (1979).

27. *See generally* Fisher & Steinhardt, *supra* note 17. The legislation also expressly would enlarge the president's retaliatory authority to include investment-oriented sanctions.

28. Enactment of the local content bill would present both legal and political problems for the negotiators of future BITs.

8

Multilateral Regulation of Foreign Direct Investment

George S. Trisciuzzi

INTRODUCTION

Multinational business and investment issues are now international political issues. This reality, already emerging in the late 1970s, will become clearer in the 1980s. Company executives, investors, governments, and unions will be faced with a proliferation of intergovernmental codes of conduct on multinational corporations. The multinational corporation is now perceived by governments and trade unions as a political animal. As such, its behavior, though primarily economic, will be forced to conform to internationally agreed upon political norms.

The aim of this chapter is to trace the contours of transnational investment flows and to analyze the basic issues related to multilateral regulation of those flows. First, the chapter briefly describes recent developments involving foreign direct investment. Second, after generally describing the international investment regulatory structure, the chapter discusses the OECD Guidelines on Multinational Enterprises[1] and the proposed U.N. Code for Transnational Corporations.[2] Finally, the chapter makes recommendations for U.S. policymakers as they seek to promote U.S. interests by protecting U.S. foreign direct investment.

INTERNATIONAL INVESTMENT

Foreign direct investment has played a major role in the international economy since the last half of the nineteenth century. At present, total international direct investment outflows from the 13 most active "inves-

143

tor" Organization of Economic Cooperation and Development (OECD) countries stands at approximately $633.4 billion.[3] U.S. foreign direct investment, the most dominant share, stands at $227.3 billion.[4] U.S. flows can be broken into four principal geographical categories: flows into European Community (EC) countries, Canada, Japan, and developing countries. U.S. investments in the EC countries now total $101.3 billion.[5] There are two primary reasons for this concentration. Traditionally, U.S. investors have been attracted by the relatively stable, hospitable investment climate in the developed countries, which is due particularly to the virtual absence of risk to investment from political turmoil. In addition, the generally booming economies of the developed countries have offered the prospect of higher profitability for investments than in the developing countries. U.S. investments in Canada and Japan total $47 billion and $6.8 billion, respectively.[6] Investment in developing countries now stands at $44.7 billion;[7] this category seems to be the fastest growing component of U.S. foreign direct investment.

The patterns of transnational investment flows, however, are undergoing significant changes. The period since the mid-1970s stands in sharp contrast with the period preceding it in a number of important aspects. A slowdown in the real growth of foreign direct investment flows has occurred. Using only capital flows as a measure, the average annual growth rate of outward foreign direct investment from the top 13 OECD countries during the period 1974 to 1979 was slightly less than the period 1960 to 1963 (11.9 percent versus 12.6 percent).[8] Considering the high inflation in the recent period, there has been a deceleration in real terms. Nonetheless, international direct investment has remained more buoyant than domestic investment, suggesting that multinational enterprises may have been better able to adapt to new and less favorable economic circumstances.

There has been an increase in the foreign share of international direct investment flows. The U.S. share still predominates, but this share of total OECD outflows has fallen. As a percentage of the top 13 OECD country outflows, it has gone from 60 percent in the mid-1960s to about 35 percent in the late 1970s.[9] Particularly noteworthy is the change in U.S.-EC patterns. European movement toward integration and an increasingly overvalued U.S. dollar during the 1950s and 1960s induced considerable U.S. investment in Europe. At the end of the 1970s, the inducement effect of European integration wore off and a decline in the value of the dollar caused a reversal of the trend. More broadly, also, both Europe and Japan have shifted from postwar reconstruction to increasingly active roles in the international economy. With this has come increased foreign investment.

Recently, there also has been a sharpening of differences in the abilities of developing countries to attract investment. The overall average OECD international direct investment flow to developing countries has increased over the last few years in current and real terms. Furthermore, the total share of developing countries as host countries for foreign direct investment of almost all major investing countries has increased since 1974, thus reversing the generally declining trend of earlier periods. This investment, however, has been concentrated in the so-called "newly industrialized" economies such as South Korea, Taiwan, Singapore, Hong Kong, and Brazil, which have emphasized export-led growth.

In the rest of the developing world, except in the oil producing countries, foreign direct investment has tended to stagnate. The basic factors underlying this trend are questionable national economic policies, fear of political instability, and negative policies toward such investment. Increased perception of political risk among investors is a key factor. Unclear and restrictive investment laws and regulations, and the unpredictability of their application, are other important elements, as are the increased use of performance requirements and restrictions on equity holdings.

The characteristics of foreign direct investment are changing as well. There has been an increase in the use of borrowed funds, essentially local currency borrowing, which is now a key source of financing for many firms, especially U.S. enterprises. An increasing number of small- and medium-sized firms are involved in transnational investment activities. Also, the development and internationalization of firms that provide investment support services—such as banks—has grown at a rapid pace since the early 1970s. Finally, enterprises are also diversifying their forms of investment. European state-owned enterprises have become increasingly significant investors in OECD countries and in the developing world. Furthermore, traditional wholly owned subsidiary operations are being replaced by nonequity forms of foreign direct investment, such as management contracts and licensing arrangements.

The final major trend concerns the global capital shortage. The 1980s will be a time of capital scarcity and sharpened competition for foreign funds. As the global economy expands, increasing amounts of capital will be needed to sustain growth. Particularly for developing countries, which, other things being equal, normally should expect the highest growth rates, capital scarcity may well become an even more important constraint on growth than ever before. This constraint is due to increased investor perception of the risks attached to investment in some developing countries and to the real limits on the global amounts of capital available for both domestic and foreign investment.

Numerous and complex interests are bound with transnational investment conditions and trends. International service transactions, for example, play a crucial role in maintaining the U.S. trade balance surplus.[10] There was a surplus approximating $24 billion on such transactions last year.[11] That was more than twice the comparable surplus a decade ago and accounts for over half of 1980's overall service-trade surplus of some $40 billion.[12]

Without the service factor, which tends to be overlooked when foreign trade is mentioned, the current U.S. trade position would be horrendous. Foreign direct investment income constitutes the major factor which keeps the country's overall external account in acceptable and healthy condition. One could say that the U.S. economy is "living-off" its foreign investments. Thus, such investment is not merely a trade-related concern. It constitutes a basis of national strength in political, economic, and inevitably in security terms.

The general global stakes are equally significant. Worldwide foreign direct investment could be approaching one trillion dollars. Global economic well-being is tied to the continued security of such investment to a significant extent. Due to an underlying capital shortage, a slowdown in real growth of investment funds combined with a decreased ability by capital-needy countries to obtain foreign direct investment could lead to new international tensions generated by sharpening competition for foreign capital inflows. This situation will be exacerbated because there is no global consensus regarding regulation and protection of transnational investments. As a result, transnational investment security will become a significant issue in the 1980s.

THE REGULATORY STRUCTURE

Traditionally, transnational investment flows and international business transactions were governed by national laws.[13] "Customary" international law, established through international practice over time, and transaction by transaction "law of the contract" also generated standards and norms. Recently, however, the interest in regulation has manifested itself in intense efforts to extend the international regulatory sphere to commercial and investment activities not previously controlled.[14] These efforts have frequently assumed the forms of bilateral treaties and multilateral conventions.

While many of the bilateral and multilateral agreements in force today affect private corporations, they express that impact in terms of governmental rights. These agreements affect the business opportunities of private persons by regulating intergovernmental transactions or by prescribing government treatment of private parties. There is now, however, a distinct trend toward the development of treaties dealing with private international transactions and decisions, thus bringing contracting governments into fields not previously regulated by international agreement.

This web of treaties and conventions already covers a significant portion of international business activity: civil aviation, treatment of taxes and taxable income, recognition of patent filings or grants, customs cooperation, trademark recognition, vessel loading standards, pollution, and fishing rights. In some cases certain agreements have involved the establishment of international organizations with an independent existence, such as the GATT, which also fulfill a specific regulatory role.

There is little likelihood that multinational enterprises will be subject to the authority of an international regulatory agency in the near future. A great amount of attention, however, is being paid to the establishment of codes of conduct to regulate particular actions of such corporations.[15] These codes have been seen as an alternative means to constitute an international moral authority by agreement among governments and to provide guidelines for multinational business activities.

Four considerations seem to have had the greatest effect on the development of codes of conduct. First, governments increasingly are participating in the direction and regulation of international economic affairs. Some of these actions are stimulated by domestic pressures and domestic regulatory policies, but in other cases international regulation seems to have a life of its own. These governments also are showing greater concern for private international and commercial affairs.

Second, international economic affairs are becoming politicized. This development was perhaps inevitable, given the role that governments are coming to play. They are largely developing political responses to economic problems.

Third, developing country governments have been strong advocates for negotiation of codes of conduct as a means to generalize development efforts on a worldwide scale. Most code proposals deal with subject matter perceived by these governments to be essential to development. Thus, the codes have become a focus of the developing nations in their search for solutions to their economic problems.

Finally, governments increasingly have become aware of the side effects of development, and they desire to avoid the adverse ones. Many code advocates, especially among the developing countries, are basing their arguments on the need to guard against harmful side effects involving urban development, distribution of wealth, and the environment.

These four considerations merge into one transcendent theme: multinational enterprises should be regulated because of their great size and vast power to affect national policies.[16] Most advocates of regulation also suspect that multinational corporations may act as conduits for the policies of a foreign state. Thus, the code proponents' primary objective is to achieve control over multinational corporations in order to safeguard what they perceive to be their nations' basic political and economic interests. Multinational corporations may now control over 60 percent of the world's industrial assets.[17] While certain trends suggest that smaller- and medium-sized firms are entering this investment arena,[18] it is likely that the larger corporations will remain the focus of attention. Likewise, given the deep-rooted nature of the considerations underlying the emergence of the codes, it is not likely that pressure for regulation will diminish significantly despite the apparent, momentary lull in harsh antimultinational corporation rhetoric.

Codes cannot be easily categorized in the traditional terms of international law because they have both private and public aspects. They deal with the rights and duties of private persons but also address standards for the so-called legal behavior of states. Theoretically, codes can serve several broad legal purposes. Perhaps the most important potential benefit would be the harmonization of currently diverse systems of national laws and regulations. For example, harmonization could reduce the high costs borne by multinational corporations in dealing with widely divergent regulatory regimes in different countries. Codes could also have the effect of supplementing national rules of conduct, especially when it is politically difficult for a government to achieve such ends by direct legislation, or could provide models for future national legislation. Thus, codes may provide novel mechanisms for countries to subject private enterprises, which previously had been immune to effective control, to their public policies.

International dialogue on the legal nature of codes of conduct for multinational corporations has centered on the issue of whether the codes should be binding and mandatory or nonbinding and voluntary.[19] Whereas developed countries generally argue that codes should establish broad equitable principles and should be nonbinding, the developing countries usually have demanded specific and binding rules.[20]

Whatever the merits of this debate, codes are likely to have a gradual, binding effect by their application through international political processes. Even codes explicitly declared to be "voluntary," such as the OECD Guidelines, may establish norms of conduct that would probably be observed—perhaps as much as if they were formally "mandatory."[21] On the other hand, codes explicitly not intended to create binding obligations may be considered interpretative of other explicitly binding agreements.

Codes, as a general matter, constitute a new and largely untested approach to the establishment of international law. Codification of standards of conduct for multinational corporations is a concept that is little more than a decade old. Because there has been relatively little experience in the formulation and implementation of codes, it is difficult to predict what the ultimate effects of the recently established and emerging codes will be. Nonetheless, codes have become an important element in the multilateral regulation of foreign direct investment. They are developing rapidly and, at least in terms of subject matter, deal with the major aspects of transnational investments.[22]

THE PRINCIPAL CODES

The OECD Guidelines and the developing United Nations Code are important elements in the emerging code system. The OECD Guidelines reflect the views of the major investor nations,[23] while the U.N. Code will be heavily influenced by the positions of the developing nations.[24] These two codes are the broadest based in terms of the parties involved and the subject matter covered.

The OECD Guidelines

The OECD Guidelines grew out of strong reactions by both developed and developing states to the growth of U.S. enterprises in Europe in the 1960s and 1970s. With about 75 percent of the world's investment taking place among OECD countries, and U.S. investment accounting for about 50 percent of global investment, important political, social, and economic questions arose concerning the role of foreign investment in host countries.[25] A number of governments initiated unilateral action to control foreign direct investment and to ensure that such investment met the needs of the host-country.

Initially, the U.S. government sought to extend the principle of national treatment of foreign direct investment. The goal was to achieve an acceptable multilateral standard for treatment of foreign direct investment, coupled with a systematic monitoring of government compliance with the standard. Other OECD countries, however, insisted that a code of conduct had to balance many multilateral measures addressing government responsibilities.

U.S. reluctance to establish a code of conduct was overcome by appreciation of the benefits that could flow by an expression of standards of good practice. Thus, what began as an effort to deal with government treatment of foreign direct investment became a balanced package of complementary and interconnected instruments dealing with all aspects of international direct investment relationships.

The adoption of the Guidelines coincided with significant changes in the underlying nature of international investment relations. First, the OECD economies were entering a period of economic slowdown. Second, multinational enterprises were no longer an "American" problem. European and Japanese firms were becoming significant actors. Third, the fundamental nature of multinational enterprises was changing. State-owned enterprises, such as Renault and British Leyland, had become increasingly significant among OECD countries. Their presence changed the view that multinational enterprises are primarily profit-maximizing entities and significantly affected such basic concepts as national treatment. Fourth, the "traditional" wholly owned subsidiary form was being replaced increasingly by operations such as joint ventures, management contracts, and licensing arrangements. Finally, the growing power of trade unions, in particular European-based international trade union secretariats, became more significant. Politically influential union pressures in the direction of codetermination and collective bargaining at the international level became serious issues.

The Guidelines are a series of provisions annexed to the Declaration of June 21, 1976, on International Investment and Multinational Enterprises by governments of OECD member countries. The Declaration recommends the annexed Guidelines to the member states and emphasizes that they are based on applying the concept of national treatment in dealing with international investment incentives and disincentives, intergovernment consultation procedures, and review of the Guidelines. The introductory language urges that member states consult concerning issues arising under the Guidelines, including cases when multinational enterprises are made subject to conflicting requirements by member states. Of particular importance, the introductory language notes that "observance of the guidelines is voluntary and not legally enforceable."[26]

Several key issues have emerged relating to the Guidelines since their enactment. On June 21, 1979, the same 23 OECD countries that established the Declaration and Guidelines adopted a report prepared by the OECD Committee on International Investment and Multinational Enterprises (CIME) on those instruments and subsequent Decisions regarding them. The Review emphasized two aspects of the OECD investment instruments—their stability and their credibility. Stability was ensured, in that the Guidelines will remain in force in nearly the same form as initially established until 1984, and credibility was enhanced, in that a workable dispute resolution process was agreed upon.

The explanatory comments in the Review Report discussed several key issues regarding the Guidelines that had risen in various cases that had been presented to the CIME between 1976 and 1979. The principal issues involved were the responsibility of parent corporations for subsidiary obligations, closure of a profitable subsidiary, rights of employees, unfair influence in employer-employee negotiations, and worker access to decision makers.

The first issue has become increasingly important as U.S. corporations seek to disinvest in Europe in response to changing economic conditions. Such disinvestment often raises questions about termination payments to separated employees. Furthermore, there may be extralegal issues raised as a result of conflicts with applicable government employment policies. The Badger case is the classic situation in this regard. The Badger Company, Inc., had decided to close its unprofitable Belgian subsidiary and refused to pay its debts, including those to cover staff terminations. In legal terms, the parent was entitled so to act. The trade unions, however, believed that a multinational company should not be allowed to avoid its social obligations to the Belgian community. The unions took a number of political countermeasures, including requests to the OECD to require that the Guidelines be respected. Discussions at the OECD level followed, resulting in agreement by Badger to negotiate a settlement with the staff. The company agreed to indemnify the individual employees for their dismissal, a move which represented an historical precedent regarding respect for the OECD Guidelines.

The second issue was raised by the British-American Tobacco Company (BATCO) case. The case demonstrated that historical profitability (the workers' perspective) and future profitability (the company's perspective) are not the same. The controversy pointed out another problem as well. While companies should exploit their competitive advantage in domestic and local markets, the requirements of specialization and sound commercial practice constrain total integration. The BATCO conclusion, which barred closure, is especially important in light of these factors and the trend toward disinvestment in Europe.

The right of employees to be represented by unions has caused most of the adverse reaction to the 1979 Review Report from the business community. While certain statements therein imply a standard of treatment that is governed by national labor laws of each country, others reflect trends in some European countries toward increased worker participation and multinational collective bargaining. OECD governments and trade unions, however, are not unified in their views on these sensitive issues.

Providing information to employees is an area of widely divergent practice among OECD countries. Labor organizations, however, have pressed specially for OECD recognition of trade union access to information on future enterprise plans. The Review Report left the issue to national laws or to the discretion of the enterprise and collective bargaining process in light of the complex concerns—such as business confidentiality, limits of labor and management competence, and national law and practice—which bear on the problem.

The issue of unfair influence in bona fide negotiations was the issue that resulted in the only change made in the Guidelines. The Review process amended the pertinent provisions further to strengthen the proscription on transfer of facilities. There was little controversy among governments over the change.

Finally, the Review Report suggested that the question of access to decision makers is an area where the international character of multinational corporations poses a real problem. It was stated that good faith bargaining could only occur if the company representatives have authority to make decisions on issues under negotiation. Good will of enterprises could remove this irritant, and failure to provide such access could lead to demands for greater information disclosure and international collective bargaining.

One aspect of the 1979 Review Report may have special long-term significance. In a number of cases discussed by the CIME, such as the BATCO case, the question was whether an enterprise operating internationally was entitled to close down its operating subsidiary in a given country even if that subsidiary were profitable. The Guidelines make no attempt to restrict the basic freedom of investors to disinvest, and the Review Report generally reaffirmed this right. There is no question that this right is part of the ownership right that is recognized and respected in the legal systems of all OECD member countries. The Review Report, however, pointed out that the Guidelines establish a number of obligations to respect the host-country's interests. In particular, it stated that a company should consider the degree of integration of its subsidiary into the economic context of the host-country. This position constitutes the first suggestion that multilateral regulation of transnational investment could include control over disinvestment. The OECD Guidelines have been used to counter multinational enterprise policies of this kind. The increased concern with disinvestment, particularly in Europe, and global economic trends, especially the apparent capital shortage, could increase pressure for application of the Guidelines to forestall removal of investments from host countries.

While the U.S. business community generally has expressed support for the instruments,[27] it also has indicated several specific concerns regarding their interpretation and application over the long run, particularly with respect to information disclosure, competition, and employment and industrial relations.

The Guidelines' disclosure provisions could create new obligations beyond those already established by U.S. law. Likewise, the competition provisions may go beyond U.S. law and also may have substantive effects on U.S. multinationals especially through Guideline-induced pressures for stronger antitrust enforcement on both national and international levels. Finally, the employment and industrial relations provisions may open the door to multinational collective bargaining, which is a development to which U.S. business is extremely hostile. Read together, the Badger and BATCO cases suggest that the employment and industrial relations provisions of the Guidelines may provide a primary tool to block or forestall corporations' ability to disinvest in a country. As a result, multinational corporations may find it much more difficult to move investment capital as easily as they might desire.

These business concerns, though circumspect and still muted, reflect the practical implications of the Guidelines. The instruments should not be regarded as toothless and irrelevant formulations. They may, on the contrary, play an increasingly significant role in multilateral regulation of transnational investment.

The Guidelines may have increasingly broad legal, political, and economic significance over time. First, although the OECD Declaration and Guidelines neither create international law nor reflect existing customary international law, they have become a relevant fact under international law by virtue of their nature as official common expressions of national policy. Second, the instruments may have a legitimizing effect with respect to behavior that is consistent with the principles and rules stated in them. Third, the Guidelines may also affect interpretation of existing national business law and contracts relating to international business transactions. The Badger case demonstrated that the instruments are of direct relevance in this regard. Fourth, they may generate the moral suasion that can lead to the creation of new national laws or agreements. Finally, the Guidelines may serve a modeling function in the development of other international codes of conduct and rules on transnational investment.

The U.N. Code on Transnational Corporations

The U.N. Commission on Transnational Corporations has been engaged in work on a proposed code of conduct since 1976. If all goes according to plan, the code of conduct should reach its final form in 1983. It can go into effect as soon as it is approved, either by the U.N. General Assembly or by a special conference.

Preparation of the Code has long been a U.N. priority. The content, form, and nature of such a code, however, are still far from being agreed upon. The Code will be voluntary and therefore will not require government ratifications. It does not follow, however, that a voluntary code will be ineffective. A generally accepted set of standards eventually may have an effect as significant as a more formal agreement.[28]

The overarching difficulty has been in achieving agreement in broad terms on matters of principle. The basic problem of agreement on the Code has been in that it deals with principles, not with specific and identifiable cases. Furthermore, several major principles still remain unsettled. Provisions regarding the Code's preamble, objectives, definitions, jurisdiction, scope, and implementation have not yet been concluded.[29] These gaps give rise to a number of important issues, particularly for the U.S. government.

It has been a major objective of the U.S. government to ensure that the Code includes host government obligations regarding treatment of multinational corporations as well as standards of conduct for corporate behavior. The pertinent provisions of the U.N. Code, however, are for the most part unsettled. Furthermore, the basic subjects of nationalization and compensation have not yet been incorporated into the Code's draft and are addressed only in proposed formulations that have not yet come before the drafting organ as a whole.

Treatment of state-owned enterprises, nondiscriminatory treatment of multinationals, respect for contractual obligations freely entered into, and permissibility of home-country diplomatic protection for multinational corporations also remain incomplete and unresolved. Generally, however, whatever substantive provisions do emerge are likely to be more restrictive of multinational enterprise operations than the OECD Guidelines. The U.N. Code will also include provisions dealing with matters not covered by the Guidelines, such as provisions requiring adherence to socio-cultural objectives and values, respect for human rights and fundamental freedoms, consumer protection, environmental protection, and cessation of multinational enterprise activity in South Africa and Namibia. Those substantive provisions which parallel the OECD Guidelines tend to impose heavier burdens on companies than those of the Guidelines. Finally, the Code goes further than the Guidelines in attempting to prescribe rules for ownership and control, particularly including encouragement of host-country equity participation and employment of host country citizens at decision-making levels.

Clauses in such a Code may pose little threat to the autonomy of multinational enterprises due to their vagueness and formally nonbinding nature. On the other hand, it may be possible that the Code will have considerable substantive effect over time. Furthermore, in light of the general political context in which it has been developed, it is not unreasonable to suggest that the Code would be applied primarily against U.S. multinational corporations.

The U.N. Code also may have a substantial effect on other international codes of conduct. There is already substantial effect at the technical level, where provisions of other codes have been incorporated explicitly or referred to as interpretative guides.[30] Furthermore, as the code of the paramount international organization, it is likely to influence the interpretation of those international codes already in existence and of those being developed by numerous other international bodies. Likewise, the Code could influence national legislation, just as the U.S. Congress had been induced to pass a law against international bribery in anticipation of a U.N. convention on illicit payments.

The U.N. Code would be the capstone of a rapidly expanding structure of international codes of conduct for multinational corporations. These include the ILO Tripartite Declaration, the UNCTAD Code entitled "The Set of Multilaterally Agreed Equitable Principles and Rules for the Control of Restrictive Business Practices,"[31] A Draft International Code of Conduct of Transfer of Technology,[32] and the Andean Investment Code.[33] Other U.N. organizations are developing codes related to multinational enterprises,[34] and negotiations also have been held in the Organization of American States (OAS) for the development of a list of principles or "Guidelines of Conduct" which multinationals should observe when investing in Latin America.[35] Moreover, the European Economic Community has initiated several voluntary codes of conduct for European multinational corporations and is currently developing rules that if enacted by member governments will formally convert expansive readings of sensitive provisions of the voluntary ILO Tripartite Declaration and OECD Guidelines into European law.[36]

Transnational investment flows cannot be immune to substantive effect from such a significant body of standards and rules. The inconsistencies, gaps, and other flaws currently afflicting this new structure of codes do not, and should not, imply irrelevance. In fact, there are clear indications that these codes are already having serious political implications on the international level. These signs raise some disturbing questions regarding multilateral regulation of investment.

International Political Implications

The European Community, in recent years, has been engaging in a clear effort to increase its control over multinational corporations. As further explained elsewhere in this book,[37] the most significant expression of this effort is the so-called "Vredeling Proposal," which would establish binding rules for multinational corporations operating in the Community as to procedures for informing and consulting with their employees. This proposal, even as amended, would create obligations substantially greater than those previously borne by many multinational corporations, particularly closely held U.S. multinationals.

The OECD Guidelines, ILO Tripartite Declaration, and the developing U.N. Code have played a noticeable role in this trend of events. Not only have those instruments been cited in support of the Vredeling proposal, but they also have become a general justification for exercising greater overall control over multinational corporations.[38] The significance of this trend should not be underestimated. The pressures for increased regulation are coming from powerful political interests, the trade unions in particular, and are becoming a major European preoccupation. Furthermore, the fundamental concern underlying these pressures is the apprehension of disinvestment by multinational corporations. Given prevailing economic realities, this phenomenon is bound to continue.

Other effects in the developing world also are discernible. The codes, by their nature, provide developing countries with new methods of attempting to achieve some of their more questionable goals. Codes also are becoming the tactical means to achieve the political ends desired by organized labor, particularly in Europe. These unions, faced with global economic internationalization and trends toward multinational disinvestment are trying to "catch up" with multinational enterprises. Codes are becoming the political counterpart of trade union action, and the labor movement continues to press for implementation procedures and review machinery, with the objective that, little by little, the principles in the codes of greatest interest to labor will become mandatory. Labor organizations also can utilize codes by their incorporation by reference in collective bargaining agreements, thereby giving the codes legal force albeit in a limited, contractual context. The codes also may be invoked when presenting grievances to governments, international labor associations, or the international bodies charged with implementing the codes.

THE U.S. POSITION

U.S. policymakers seem to question the relevance to the United States of efforts to regulate international business transactions and transnational investment flows, particulary those involving codes of conduct. This attitude is inappropriate in light of global economic trends, the vital U.S. interests in protecting U.S. foreign direct investment, and the potential impact that current developments in multilateral regulation could have both in political and legal terms. The United States cannot afford to allow the emergence of norms, practices, and standards that are inconsistent with basic concepts such as national treatment for foreign investments. The basic task, therefore, is to determine which of various courses of action will most effectively promote U.S. interests.

The U.S. government could adopt one of three general attitudes toward negotiation of codes of conduct. The first would call on the United States to embrace the codes and do all in its power to bring them into force as legally binding international agreements.[39] The justification for this position would be that the codes are needed as international business becomes more widespread and complex. Furthermore, it could be argued that the codes express the best of the international community's thinking on the issues and in some cases bring legislation and regulation in line with U.S. laws and practices. Though imperfect, the codes are better than no agreement on the real issues and can be effective regulatory devices.

The second position would be to accept the codes skeptically. Most codes are too ambitious in scope, overly infected by the twin devices of theoretical economics and the political rhetoric of developing countries. Although the codes in general may be inconsistent with U.S. free enterprise ideals, this does not diminish the usefulness of those operative provisions that are reasonable and just. If codes are properly drawn up and implemented with U.S. participation, they may work in practice without harming U.S. interests and perhaps would advance them if they could encourage the stable operation of the transnational investment system.

The third alternative would be to oppose the codes, especially mandatory ones. Some voluntary codes could be reluctantly accepted, but strong efforts would be needed to neutralize undesirable interpretations, revisions, and applications. Binding codes would be seen as intolerable forms of control over private enterprise, imposed by groups of developing countries and labor-dominated developed states for political reasons. Binding codes would inevitably regulate multinational corporations to the detriment of the enterprises themselves and of their home countries.

Each of these three general approaches would establish the broad framework for a comprehensive U.S. policy on multilateral regulation of transnational investment. The correct one in view of U.S. interests probably lies between the second and third options. The first option is patently unreasonable in view of the questionable nature of the existing code system, the political implications already flowing from it, and U.S. economic stakes in protecting investments abroad. The second and third options contain elements that are reasonable in light of all the circumstances. The defensive posture of the third alone would leave the field open to others to develop and attempt to implement codes and norms of international law that could eventually leave U.S. investments abroad at the mercy of predatory host-countries. Continued participation in the international regulatory process, a position inherent in the second option, is essential if only to make it possible to guard against such dangerous trends.

The nature of the challenge to U.S. interests requires a multifaceted and coordinated policy. Attempts should be made at every level to reaffirm international acceptance of basic norms which underlie the security of U.S. investments abroad and to preclude or at least minimize the development and acceptance of countervailing norms. Furthermore, the operation of the existing regulatory system and related international political processes should be monitored constantly to guard against creeping encroachment on broad U.S. interests.

The U.S. government should press strongly international forums against interpretations, reviews, and applications of existing codes that would create new restrictions on the free flow of transnational investments. This would include vigorous advocacy of U.S. interests in the final negotiations of the U.N. Code provisions and active participation in the Code's implementation. Likewise, the U.S. government should move within the OECD structure to restrain the pressures for increasingly expansive interpretation, revision, and application of the Guidelines. Furthermore, it should challenge restrictive policies by OECD member states whenever such policies seem to violate basic concepts of national treatment and freedom of investment.

As a second policy component, the U.S. government should attempt to deal with these issues on a bilateral basis. The United States currently has Friendship, Commerce, and Navigation (FCN) Treaties and tax treaties with many nations. It would seem logical to bring these treaties (or their successors) to bear on the problem of investment protection. However, FCN treaties and tax treaties have little relevance for this particular problem, and it is not clear that U.S. diplomats presently have the leverage to address it by modifying the traditional treaties. The reason U.S. negotiators have so little leverage is that most host-countries are not particularly eager to negotiate such investment treaties in the first place. Countries that follow reasonable pragmatic probusiness policies (such as Singapore or Brazil) are attracting substantial capital inflows already, without binding themselves by treaty.[40] And, countries hostile to U.S. business interests have no reason to negotiate a treaty giving U.S. standards of protection to U.S. firms.

The potential usefulness of bilateral investment treaties, however, should not be underestimated. Such treaties are concluded routinely between West European nations and developing countries. Those treaties are designed to provide broad rights of establishment, national treatment, and most-favored-nation treatment for foreign investors. Often they include dispute settlement procedures to protect investments once made. This potential should be exploited as fully as possible by a comprehensive and energetic treaty program. At the very least it could provide one blanket of security for U.S. investments on a country-to-country basis. Even a moderately successful program could generate countervailing political and legal forces to prevailing trends in multilateral regulation of transnational investment.

There are several existing multilateral arrangements through which the United States also could take special steps in an attempt to protect its foreign direct investment interests. There has been considerable discussion of expansion of the GATT's scope to cover transnational investments. As was made clear at the GATT Ministerial meeting in November 1982, however, GATT members will not react favorably to an explicit, comprehensive proposal to develop and implement a general "GATT for Investment." The GATT approach then must be circumspect and slow. An appropriate first step would be for the United States to continue to propose a GATT work program on certain trade-related aspects of the investment issue, such as performance requirements. It could then be expected that as discussions become more substantive that basic investment issues would come to the fore and member countries would become more comfortable with the idea of dealing with them. The entire process, however, would be slow and certainly insufficient to provide adequate protection for all U.S. investment interests on its own. At most, perhaps a GATT approach could yield a framework covering aspects of investment regulation related to ensuring national treatment of transnational investment flows and standards of dispute settlement consistent with U.S. interests and policy.

A second multilateral approach involving the World Bank could be implemented concurrently with the GATT approach. The focus here would be to establish a multilateral investment insurance system. Such a system, which could provide additional security for U.S. investments abroad, should cover basic political risks to investment such as expropriation, damages due to war and similar events, and exchange transfers. As part of such an insurance plan, the World Bank would establish a set of standards of treatment for foreign investment. Host countries of the prospective insured investors would be required to accept them formally insofar as the specific insured investments would be concerned. These standards would cover rules regarding compensation for expropriation and damages due to war and similar events, capital repatriation, and national treatment in arbitration and dispute settlement contexts.

Taken together, the GATT and World Bank multilateral insurance approaches provide useful and feasible mechanisms for advancing U.S. interests. Each uses well-established institutional frameworks that have traditionally been used to advance U.S. economic interests. The U.S. government's influence in each is substantial. The two basic plans proposed have good prospects for success so long as they are carefully and persistently pursued.

Conventional ongoing diplomatic processes should also be utilized. A constant lobbying approach emphasizing the need to guarantee global investment security directed at other major "investor" and developing countries must become an integral function of U.S. diplomatic policy. Particularly strong efforts are needed in Europe to counteract the trends emerging there. The more clearly that the U.S. government mirrors its concern for transnational investment flows in its day to day diplomatic relations the less likely it is that other governments will feel free to pursue policies adverse to that concern.

Finally, there are a variety of unilateral measures that the United States may take, consistent with its international commitments, designed to offset the effect of restrictive and burdensome investment policies pursued by foreign nations. There are three forms of unilateral measures: a purely public response, a mixed public-private response, and a purely private response. The first seems to offer the best methods of protecting U.S. general investment interests.

A public response would involve retaliation initiated by the U.S. government. Such a response would lie in the discretion of the president, with no private party participating beyond the normal opportunity to petition the government for relief. One avenue available for public response to host-country policies is section 310 of the Trade Act of 1974. Under it, the president can respond to any act, policy, or practice of a foreign country that is inconsistent with a trade agreement or that denies benefits to the United States under any trade agreement, or that is unjustifiable, unreasonable, or discriminatory and burdens or restricts U.S. commerce. Eximbank, Commodity Credit Corporation, and Foreign Military Sales support also might be withheld from countries that encumber U.S. investments abroad. Likewise, U.S. approval or disapproval of World Bank and regional development bank loans could be conditioned in part on the country's adherence to an open investment regime. Finally, new investment in the United States from countries that restrict national treatment or rights of entry might be restricted, on a case by case basis.

A public response, however, will have drawbacks. Such responses will be heavily influenced by political factors that almost invariably militate against taking firm action. Also, private parties injured by host-country policies do not have adequate opportunities to seek direct redress within the public response framework.

A private right of action would inhere in the reciprocity legislation advocated by many U.S. firms. Under such legislation, a "mirror" would be applied to the requirements that a host-country imposes on U.S. investors; similar requirements would then be imposed, at the instigation of a

U.S. petitioner, on firms from that country that invest in the United States. Such legislation has appeared before Congress but to date none has been adopted. Reciprocity legislation would be inconsistent with GATT principles such as most-favored-nation treatment and could generate a backlash abroad that would do considerable harm to broad U.S. investment interests. Generally, it seems that this is not the time to legislate a purely private right of action, with a reciprocity remedy, or some other remedy, as an answer to investment restrictions. Likewise, a mixed public-private right is not yet appropriate until the U.S. government has gained more experience in dealing with such problems. A purely private or a mixed response right would require a complex system of procedural and substantive standards. The U.S. government, however, has had practically no experience in countering investment restrictions. Moreover, investment restrictions are a relatively new type of problem as well. Under such circumstances, it would be best to limit the right of response to host government practices to the U.S. government. Given the delicate political, economic, and legal issues involved, private parties should not have the right to bring an action until some time in the future, if ever, after the government has had an opportunity to assess its own accomplishments or failures. Sudden and draconian actions under section 301, in current or amended form, could intensify the very pressures the United States ought to be neutralizing. Many host governments probably would seize on any excuse to impose restrictions on U.S. investments within their reach. Therefore, section 301 sanctions and similar actions should be applied only after careful consideration of all issues at stake. Foreign governments may be less inclined to impose restrictive rules on U.S. investments if faced with a U.S. government that is apparently willing and able to take contervailing measures.

CONCLUSION

Regulation of foreign direct investment presents serious challenges that will confront the United States and the international community for many years to come. No single approach will provide adequate solutions either at the national or multilateral levels. Certain key issues must be addressed from a nationalist perspective; in such instances the U.S. government should focus on preserving the immediate vitality of its foreign investments. Other concerns, however, transcend national boundaries. U.S. policy must address these matters directly as well, primarily through efforts to promote the long-term viability of foreign direct investment. The economic welfare of the global and national economic systems which are increasingly dependent on foreign direct investment depends much on the ability of the United States to meet these challenges.

NOTES

1. Organization for Economic Cooperation and Development, Guidelines for Multinational Enterprises, *annexed to* Declaration on International Investment and Multinational Enterprises, OECD Doc. C (76) 99 (1976), *reprinted in* 15 Int'l Legal Materials 967 (1976) [hereinafter OECD Guidelines].

2. U.N. Commission on Transnational Corporations, Transnational Corporations: A Code of Conduct, Formulations by the Chairman, U.N. Doc. E/C.10/AC.2/8 (1978) [hereinafter Draft U.N. Code of Conduct for Transnational Corporations]. This draft is no longer up-to-date but no other complete text has been prepared.

3. U.S. Dep't of State, *New Challenges in International Investment* (Current Policy No. 316, Sept. 18, 1981). This figure does not account for outflows from socialist or Third World countries, which would significantly increase the figure.

·   4. Whichard, *U.S. Direct Investment Abroad in 1981*, 62 Survey of Current Bus. 11, 12 (table 1) (Aug. 1982).

5. *Id.*

6. *Id.*

7. *Id.; 22 (table 14).*

8. Scholl, *New Challenges in International Investment*, 61 Survey of Current Bus. 52, 52 (1982).

9. *Id.*

10. Malabre, *Service Transactions Keep Balance of Trade in Surplus Despite the Large Deficit on Goods*, Wall St. J., Feb. 10, 1982, at 54, col. 1.

11. *Id.* at col. 2.

12. *Id.*

13. Horn, *International Rules for Multinational Enterprises: The ICC, OECD, and ILO Initiatives*, 30 Am. U. L. Rev. 937, 937 (1981).

14. R. Waldmann, Regulating International Business through Codes of Conduct 12 (1980).

15. *Id.* at 7.

16. *See* Rubin, *Transnational Corporations and International Codes of Conduct: A Study of the Relationship Between International Legal Cooperation and Economic Development*, 30 Am. U. L. Rev. 907, 907-08 (1981).

17. *Id.* at 907.

18. *See New Challenges in International Investment, supra* note 8.

19. Stanley, *International Codes of Conduct for MNC's: A Skeptical View of the Process*, 30 Am. U. L. Rev. 981, 981 (1981).

20. Fatouros, *On the Implementation of International Codes of Conduct: An Analysis of Future Experience*, 30 Am. U. L. Rev. 941, 950 (1981).

21. Rubin, *supra* note 16, at 917.

22. Verhaegen *International Codes of Conduct for Business: Some Legal Implications*, Belgian American Trade Rev. Jan./Feb. 1981, at 23.

23. *See* Kauzlarich, *The Review of the 1976 OECD Declaration on International Investment and Multinationals*, 30 Am. U. L. Rev. 1009, 1009-13, (1981).

24. *See generally*, Rubin, *supra* note 16, at 911-16.

25. Kauzlarich, *supra* nbote 23, at 1011.

26. OECD Guidelines, *supra* note 1, para. 6. However, the Guidelines further indicate: "[The Guidelines] should help to ensure that the operations of [multinational enterprises] are in harmony with the national policies of the countries where they operate and to strengthen the basis of mutual confidence between enterprises and states." *Id.*

27. *See, e.g.*, United States of America—Business and Industry Advisory Committee on International Investment and Multinational Enterprise [USA-BIAC], *A Review of the Declaration on International Investment and Multinational Enterprises* 10-11 (Nov. 1976) [hereinafter *A Review of the Declaration*]. U.S. business support of the Guidelines generally has been expressed for the following reasons: (1) they contain the basic principles employers seek in a code of conduct; 2) they recognize the primacy of the local law and practice; 3) they differ little from the policies and practices of most progressive companies; 4) they can help improve the images of multinational companies and open up new investment opportunities; 5) they can help reduce the suspicions of host governments and the likelihood of more restrictive legislation; and 6) they are more moderate and workable than those likely to emanate from other sources. USA-BIAC, *A Review of the OECD Guidelines for Multinational Enterprises: Employment and Industrial Relations* 33-34 (May 1978) [hereinafter *Employment Relations*].

28. Rubin, *Transnational Corporations, supra* note 16, at 915.

29. Commission on Transnational Corporations, Report on the Seventh Session (Item 5 of the Provisional Agenda), 5, U.N. Doc. E/C.10/79 (1981).

30. U.N. Conference on Restrictive Business Practices, The Set of Multilaterally Agreed Equitable Principles and Rules for Control of Restrictive Business Practices, U.N. Doc. TD/RBP/CONF 10 (1980), *reprinted in* 19 Int'l Legal Materials 815 (1980).

31. *Id.*

32. U.N. Doc. TD/CODE TOT/25 (1980).

33. The Andean Foreign Investment Code was approved on December 32, 1970. Officially, this agreement is Decision 24 of the Commission (ANCOM's governing body) and is entitled "Common Rules Governing the Treatment of Foreign Capital, Trademarks, Patents, Licenses, and Royalties."

34. Verhaegen, *supra* note 22, at 23. These include the Food and Agriculture Organization (FAO), the United Nations Development Program (UNDP), the World Health Organization (WHO), the United Nations Educational, Scientific, and Cultural Organization (UNESCO), the United Nations Industrial Development Organization (UNIDO), and the United Nations Congress on Prevention of Crime. *Id.*

35. *Id.*

36. *Id.*

37. *See* Schneebaum, *The Company Law Harmonization Program in the European Community* (Chapter 3 of this book).

38. *See, e.g.* [1981-82] European Parliament Working Documents (Eur. Parl. Doc.) (No. 1-169) 16-22 (1981).

39. Waldmann, *supra* note 14, at 77.

40. *Oversight Hearings on Trade Related Performance Requirements Before the Subcomm. on International Economic Policy of the Senate Foreign Relations Comm.*, 97th Cong., 1st Sess. 5 (1981) (statement of Gary C. Hufbauer).

Appendix

Model Bilateral Investment Treaty

TREATY
BETWEEN
THE UNITED STATES OF AMERICA
AND

CONCERNING
THE RECIPROCAL ENCOURAGEMENT AND
PROTECTION OF INVESTMENT

The United States of America and   (each hereinafter referred to as a "Party"),

Desiring to promote greater economic cooperation between them, particularly with respect to investment by nationals and companies of one Party in the territory of the other Party; and

Recognizing that agreement upon the treatment to be accorded such investment will stimulate the flow of private capital and the economic development of both Parties,

Agreeing that discrimination on the basis of nationality by either Party against investment in its territory by nationals or companies of the other Party is not consistent with either a stable framework for investment or a maximum effective utilization of economic resources,

Having resolved to conclude a treaty concerning the encouragement and reciprocal protection of investment, and

Have agreed as follows:

ARTICLE I

DEFINITIONS

For the purposes of this Treaty,

(a) "company" means any kind of juridical entity, including any corporation, company, association, or other organization, that is duly incorporated, constituted, or otherwise duly organized, regardless of whether or not the entity is organized for pecuniary gain, privately or governmentally owned, or organized with limited or unlimited liability.

(b) "company of a Party" means a company duly incorporated, constituted or otherwise duly organized under the applicable laws and regulations of a Party or a political subdivision thereof in which

(i) natural persons who are nationals of such Party, or

(ii) such Party or a political subdivision thereof or their agencies or instrumentalities

have a substantial interest as determined by such Party.

The juridical status of a company of a Party shall be recognized by the other Party and its political subdivisions.

Each Party reserves the right to deny to any of its own companies or to a company of the other Party the advantages of this Treaty, except with respect to recognition of juridical status and access to courts, if nationals of any third country control such company, provided that whenever one Party concludes that the benefits of this Treaty should not be extended to a company of the other Party for this reason, it shall promptly consult with the other Party to seek a mutually satisfactory resolution to this matter.

(c) "investment" means every kind of investment, owned or controlled directly or indirectly, including equity, debt, and service and investment contracts; and includes:

(i) tangible and intangible property, including rights, such as mortgages, liens and pledges;

(ii) a company or shares of stock or other interests in a company or interests in the assets thereof;

(iii) a claim to money or a claim to performance having economic value, and associated with an investment;

(iv) intellectual and industrial property rights, including rights with respect to copyrights, patents, trademarks, trade names, industrial designs, trade secrets and know-how, and goodwill;

(v) licenses and permits issued pursuant to law, including those issued for manufacture and sale of products;

(vi) any right conferred by law or contract, including rights to search for or utilize natural resources, and rights to manufacture, use and sell products; and

(vii) returns which are reinvested.

Any alteration of the form in which assets are invested or reinvested shall not affect their character as investment.

(d) "own or control" means ownership or control that is direct or indirect, including ownership or control exercised through subsidiaries or affiliates, wherever located.

(e) "national" of a Party means a natural person who is a national of a Party under its applicable law.

(f) "return" means an amount derived from or associated with an investment, including profit; dividend; interest; capital gain; royalty payment; management, technical assistance or other fee; and payment in kind.

ARTICLE II

TREATMENT OF INVESTMENT

1. Each Party shall endeavor to maintain a favorable environment for investments in its territory by nationals and companies of the other Party and shall permit such investments to be established and acquired on terms and conditions that accord treatment no less favorable than the treatment it accords in like situations to investments of its own nationals or companies or to nationals and companies of any third country, whichever is the most favorable.

2. Each Party shall accord existing or new investments in its territory of nationals or companies of the other Party, and associated activities,

treatment no less favorable than that which it accords in like situations to investments and associated activities of its own nationals or companies or of nationals or companies of any third country, whichever is the most favorable. Associated activities include:

(a) the establishment, control and maintenance of branches, agencies, offices, factories or other facilities for the conduct of business;

(b) the organization of companies under applicable laws and regulations; the acquisition of companies or interests in companies or in their property; and the management, control, maintenance, use, enjoyment and expansion, and the sale, liquidation, dissolution or other disposition, of companies organized or acquired;

(c) the making, performance, and enforcement of contracts;

(d) the acquisition (whether by purchase, lease or otherwise), ownership and disposition (whether by sale, testament or otherwise), of personal property of all kinds, both tangible and intangible;

(e) the leasing of real property appropriate for the conduct of business;

(f) the acquisition, maintenance and protection of copyrights, patents, trademarks, trade secrets, trade names, licenses and other approvals of products and manufacturing processes, and other industrial property rights; and,

(g) the borrowing of funds, the purchase and issuance of equity shares, and the purchase of foreign exchange for imports.

3. (a) Notwithstanding the preceding provisions of this Article, each Party reserves the right to maintain limited exceptions to the standard of treatment otherwise required if such exceptions fall within one of the sectors or matters listed in the Annex to this Treaty. Each Party agrees to notify the other Party of all such exceptions at the time this Treaty enters into force. Moreover, each Party agrees to notify the other Party of any future exceptions falling within the sectors or matters listed in the Annex, and to maintain the number of such exceptions at a minimum. Other than with respect to ownership of real property, the treatment accorded pursuant to this subparagraph shall not be less favorable than that accorded in like situations to investments and associated activities of nationals or companies of any third country. However, either Party may require that

rights to engage in mining on the public domain shall be dependent on reciprocity.

(b) No exception introduced after the date of entry into force of this treaty shall apply to investments of nationals or companies of the other Party existing in that sector at the time the exception becomes effective.

4. Investment of nationals and companies of either Party shall at all times be accorded fair and equitable treatment and shall enjoy full protection and security in the territory of the other Party. The treatment, protection and security of investment shall be in accordance with applicable national laws, and shall in no case be less than that required by international law. Neither Party shall in any way impair by arbitrary and discriminatory measures the management, operation, maintenance, use, enjoyment, acquisition, expansion, or disposal of investment made by nationals or companies of the other Party. Each Party shall observe any obligation it may have entered into with regard to investment of nationals or companies of the other Party.

5. (a) Subject to the laws relating to the entry and sojourn of aliens, nationals of either Party shall be permitted to enter and to remain in the territory of the other Party for the purpose of establishing, developing, directing, administering or advising on the operation of an investment to which they, or a company of the first Party that employs them, have committed or are in the process of committing a substantial amount of capital or other resources.

(b) Nationals and companies of either Party shall be permitted to engage, within the territory of the other Party, professional, technical and managerial personnel of their choice, regardless of nationality, for the particular purpose of rendering professional, technical and managerial assistance necessary for the planning and operation of investments. Companies which are incorporated, constituted, or otherwise organized under the applicable laws or regulations of one Party, and which are owned or controlled by nationals or companies of the other Party, shall be permitted to engage, within the territory of the first Party, top managerial personnel of their choice regardless of nationality.

6. The Parties recognize that, consistent with Paragraph 1 and 2 of this Article, conditions of competitive equality should be maintained where investments owned or controlled by a Party or its agencies or instrumentalities are in competition, within the territory of such Party, with privately owned or controlled investments of nationals or companies of the other Party. In such situations, the privately owned or controlled investments shall receive treatment which is equivalent with regard to any special economic advantage accorded the governmentally owned or controlled investments.

7. Neither Party shall impose performance requirements as a condition of establishment, expansion or maintenance of investments owned by nationals or companies of the other Party, which require or enforce commitments to export goods produced, or which specify that goods or services must be purchased locally, or which impose any other similar requirements.

8. In order to maintain a favorable environment for investments in its territory by nationals or companies of the other Party, each Party shall provide effective means of asserting claims and enforcing rights with respect to investment agreements, investment authorizations and properties. Each Party shall grant to nationals or companies of the other Party, on terms and conditions no less favorable than those which it grants in like situations to its own nationals or companies or to nationals or companies of any third country, whichever is the most favorable treatment, the right of access to its courts of justice, administrative tribunals and agencies, and all other bodies exercising adjudicatory authority, and the right to employ persons of their choice, who otherwise qualify under applicable laws and regulations of the forum regardless of nationality, for the purpose of asserting claims, and enforcing rights, with respect to their investments.

9. Each Party shall make public all laws, regulations, administrative practices and procedures, and adjudicatory decisions that pertain to or affect investments in its territory of nationals or companies of the other Party.

10. The treatment accorded by a Party to nationals or companies of the other Party under the provisions of Paragraphs 1 and 2 of this Article shall in any State, Territory, possession, or political or administrative subdivision of the Party be the treatment accorded therein to companies incorporated, constituted or otherwise duly organized in other States, Territories, possessions, or political or administrative subdivisions of the Party.

ARTICLE III

COMPENSATION FOR EXPROPRIATION

1. No investment or any part of an investment of a national or a company of either Party shall be expropriated or nationalized by the other Party or subjected to any other measure or series of measures, direct or indirect tantamount to expropriation (including the levying of taxation, the compulsory sale of all or part of an investment, or the impairment or deprivation of its management, control or economic value), all such actions hereinafter referred to as "expropriation", unless the expropriation:

(a) is done for a public purpose;

(b) is accomplished under due process of law;

(c) is not discriminatory;

(d) does not violate any specific provision on contractual stability or expropriation contained in an investment agreement between the national or company concerned and the Party making the expropriation; and

(e) is accompanied by prompt, adequate and effective compensation.

Compensation shall be equivalent to the fair market value of the expropriated investment. The calculation of such compensation shall not reflect any reduction in such fair market value due to either prior public notice or announcement of the expropriatory action, or the occurrence of the events that constituted or resulted in the expropriatory action. Such compensation shall be paid without delay, shall be effectively realizable, shall bear current interest from the date of the expropriation at a rate equivalent to current international rates, and shall be freely transferable at the prevailing market rate of exchange on the date of expropriation.

2. If either Party expropriates the investment of any company duly incorporated, constituted or otherwise duly organized in its territory, and if nationals or companies of the other Party, directly or indirectly, own, hold or have other rights with respect to the equity of such company, then the Party within whose territory the expropriation occurs shall ensure that such nationals or companies of the other Party receive compensation in accordance with the provisions of the preceding paragraph.

3. Subject to the dispute settlement provisions of any applicable agreement, a national or company of either Party that asserts that all or part of its investment in the territory of the other Party has been expropriated shall have a right to prompt review by the appropriate judicial or administrative authorities of such other Party to determine whether any such expropriation has occurred and, if so, whether such expropriation, and any compensation therefor, conforms to the principles of international law as set forth in this Article.

ARTICLE IV

COMPENSATION FOR DAMAGES DUE
TO WAR AND SIMILAR EVENTS

1. Nationals or companies of either Party whose investments in the territory of the other Party suffer

(a) damages due to war or other armed conflict between such other Party and a third country, or

(b) damages due to revolution, state of national emergency, revolt, insurrection, riot or act of terrorism in the territory of such other Party,

shall be accorded treatment no less favorable than that which such other Party accords to its own nationals or companies or to nationals or companies of any third country, whichever is the most favorable treatment, when making restitution, indemnification, compensation or other appropriate settlement with respect to such damages.

2. In the event that such damages result from:

(a) a requisitioning of property by the other Party's forces or authorities, or

(b) destruction of property by the other Party's forces or authorities which was not caused in combat action or was not required by the necessity of the situation,

the national or company shall be accorded restitution or compensation consistent with Article III.

3. The payment of any indemnification, compensation or other appropriate settlement pursuant to this Article shall be freely transferable.

ARTICLE V

TRANSFERS

1. Each Party shall permit all transfers related to an investment in its territory of a national or company of the other Party to be made freely and without delay into and out of its territory. Such transfers include, the following: returns; compensation, payments made arising out of a dispute concerning an investment; payments made under a contract, including amortization of principal and accrued interest payments made pursuant to a loan agreement; amounts to cover expenses relating to the management of the investment; royalties and other payments derived from licenses, franchises or other grants of rights or from administrative or technical assistance agreements, including management fees; proceeds from the sale of all or any part of an investment and from the partial or complete liquidation of the company concerned, including any incremental value; additional contributions to capital necessary or appropriate for the maintenance or development of an investment.

2. To the extent that a national or company of either Party has not made another arrangement with the appropriate authorities of the other Party in whose territory the investment of such national or company is situated, currency transfers made pursuant to Paragraph 1 of this Article shall be permitted in a currency or currencies to be selected by such national or company. Except as provided in Article III, such transfers shall be made at the prevailing market rate of exchange on the date of transfer with respect to spot transactions in the currency or currencies to be transferred.

3. Notwithstanding the preceding paragraphs, either Party may maintain laws and regulations: (a) requiring reports of currency transfer; and (b) imposing income taxes by such means as a withholding tax applicable to dividends or other transfers. Furthermore, either Party may protect the rights of creditors, or ensure the satisfaction of judgments in adjudicatory proceedings, through the equitable, nondiscriminatory and good faith application of its law.

ARTICLE VI

CONSULTATIONS
AND
EXCHANGE OF INFORMATION

1. The Parties agree to consult promptly, on the request of either, to resolve any disputes in connection with the Treaty, or to discuss any matter relating to the interpretation or application of the Treaty, including any

matter relating to the laws, regulations, administrative practices or procedures, adjudicatory decisions, or policies of one Party that pertain to or affect investments of nationals or companies of the other Party.

2. If one Party requests in writing that the other Party supply information in its possession concerning investments in its territory by nationals or companies of the Party making the request, then the other Party shall, consistent with its applicable laws and regulations and with due regard for business confidentiality, endeavor to establish appropriate procedures and arrangements for the provision of any such information.

ARTICLE VII

SETTLEMENT OF INVESTMENT DISPUTES BETWEEN ONE PARTY AND A NATIONAL OR COMPANY OF THE OTHER PARTY

1. For purposes of this Article, an investment dispute is defined as a dispute involving (a) the interpretation or application of an investment agreement between a Party and a national or company of the other Party; (b) the interpretation or application of any investment authorization granted by its foreign investment authority to such national or company; or (c) an alleged breach of any right conferred or created by this Treaty with respect to an investment.

2. In the event of an investment dispute between a Party and a national or company of the other Party with respect to an investment of such national or company in the territory of such Party, the parties to the dispute shall initially seek to resolve the dispute by consultation and negotiation. The parties may, upon the initiative of either of them and as a part of their consultation and negotiation, agree to rely upon non-binding, third-party procedures, such as the fact-finding facility available under the Rules of the Additional Facility ("Additional Facility") of the International Centre for the Settlement of Investment Disputes ("Centre"). If the dispute cannot be resolved through consultation and negotiation, then the dispute shall be submitted for settlement in accordance with the applicable dispute-settlement procedures upon which they have previously agreed. With respect to expropriation by either Party, any dispute-settlement procedures specified in an investment agreement between such Party and such national or company shall remain binding and shall be enforceable in accordance with the terms of the investment agreement and relevant provisions of domestic laws of such Party and treaties and other international agreements regarding enforcement of arbitral awards to which such Party has subscribed.

3. (a) The national or company concerned may choose to consent in writing to the submission of the dispute to the Centre or the Additional Facility, for settlement by conciliation or binding arbitration, at any time after six months from the date upon which the dispute arose, provided:

(i) the dispute has not, for any reason, been submitted by the national or company for resolution in accordance with any applicable dispute settlement procedures previously agreed to by the parties to the dispute; and

(ii) the national or company concerned has not brought the dispute before the courts of justice or administrative tribunals or agencies of competent jurisdiction of the Party that is a party to the dispute.

Once the national or company concerned has so consented, either party to the dispute may institute proceedings before the Center or the Additional Facility. If the parties disagree over whether conciliation or binding arbitration is the more appropriate procedure to be employed, the opinion of the national or company concerned shall prevail.

(b) Each party hereby consents to the submission of an investment dispute to the Centre for settlement by conciliation or binding arbitration.

(c) Conciliation or binding arbitration of such disputes shall be done in accordance with the provisions of the Convention on the Settlement of Investment Disputes Between States and Nationals of other States ("Convention") and the Regulations and Rules of the Center, or if the Convention should, for any reason, be inapplicable, the Rules of the Additional Facility.

4. In any proceeding, judicial, arbitral, or otherwise, concerning an investment dispute between it and a national or company of the other Party, a Party shall not assert, as a defense, counter-claim, right of set-off or otherwise, that the national or company concerned has received or will receive, pursuant to an insurance contract, indemnification or other compensation for all or part of its alleged damages from any source whatsoever, including such other Party and its political subdivisions, agencies and instrumentalities.

5. For the purpose of any proceedings initiated before the Center or the Additional Facility in accordance with this Article, any company duly incorporated, constituted or otherwise duly organized under the applicable laws and regulations of either Party or a political subdivision thereof but that, before the occurrence of the event or events giving rise to the dispute, was owned or controlled by nationals or companies of the other Party, shall be treated as a national or company of such other Party.

6. The provisions of this Article shall not apply to a dispute arising (a) under the export credit, guarantee or insurance programs of the Export-Import Bank of the United States or (b) under other official credit, guarantee or insurance arrangements pursuant to which the Parties have agreed to other means of settling disputes.

ARTICLE VIII

SETTLEMENT OF DISPUTES BETWEEN THE PARTIES CONCERNING INTERPRETATION OR APPLICATION OF THIS TREATY

1. Any dispute between the Parties concerning the interpretation or application of this Treaty should, if possible, be resolved through consultations between representatives of the two Parties, and if this should fail, through other diplomatic channels.

2. If the dispute between the Parties cannot be resolved through the aforesaid means, and unless there is agreement between the Parties to submit the dispute to the International Court of Justice, both Parties hereby agree to submit it upon the request of either Party to an arbitral tribunal for binding decision in accordance with the applicable rules and principles of international law.

3. The Tribunal shall be established for each case as follows. Within two months of receipt of a request for arbitration, each Party shall appoint an arbitrator. The two arbitrators so appointed shall select a third arbitrator as Chairman, who is a national of a third State. The Chairman shall be appointed within two months of the date of appointment of the other two arbitrators.

4. If the required appointments have not been made within the time specified in paragraph 3 of this Article, either of the Parties may, in the absence of any other agreement, request that the President of the International Court of Justice make the required appointments. If the President is a national of one of the Parties or if he is unable to act, the Vice President shall be asked to make the required appointments. If the Vice-President is a national of one of the Parties or if he cannot otherwise perform said duties, the next most senior member of the International Court of Justice who is not a national of one of the Parties and is able to perform said duties shall be asked to make the required appointments.

5. In the event that an arbitrator resigns or is for any reason unable to perform his duties, a replacement shall be appointed within thirty days,

utilizing the same method by which the arbitrator being replaced was appointed. If the replacement is not appointed within the time limit specified above, either Party may invite the President of the International Court of Justice to make the necessary appointment. If the President is a national of either of the Parties or is unable to act for any reason, either Party may invite the Vice President, or if he is also a national of either of the Parties or is unable to act for any reason, the next most senior member of the International Court of Justice who is not a national of one of the Parties and is able to perform said duties, to make the appointment.

6. Unless otherwise agreed to by the Parties, all submissions shall be made and all hearings shall be completed within six months of the date of the selection of the third arbitrator, and the Tribunal shall render its decision within two months of the date of the final submissions or the date of the closing of the hearings, whichever is later.

7. The Tribunal shall decide in all matters by majority vote. Any such decision shall be binding on both Parties. Each Party shall bear the expenses of its own representation in the arbitration proceedings. Expenses incurred by the Chairman, the other arbitrators, and other costs of the proceeding shall be paid for equally by the Parties. The Tribunal may, however, at its discretion, direct that a higher proportion of the costs be paid by one of the Parties. Such a decision shall be binding.

8. The Parties may agree to specific arbitral procedures. In the absence of such agreement, the Model Rules on Arbitral Procedure adopted by the United Nations International Law Commission in 1958 ("Model Rules") and commended to Member States by the United Nations General Assembly in Resolution 1262 (XIII) shall govern. To the extent that procedural questions are not resolved by this Article or the Model Rules, they shall be resolved by the Tribunal.

9. This Article shall not be applicable to a dispute which has been submitted to the Centre or Additional Facility pursuant to Article VII (3). Recourse to the procedures set forth in this Article is not precluded, however, in the event an award rendered in such dispute is not honored by a Party; or an issue exists related to a dispute submitted to the Centre or Additional Facility but not argued or decided in that proceeding.

10. The provisions of this Article shall not apply to a dispute arising (a) under the export credit, guarantee or insurance programs of the Export-Import Bank of the United States, or (b) under other official credit, guarantee or insurance arrangements pursuant to which the Parties have agreed to other means of settling disputes.

ARTICLE IX

PRESERVATION OF RIGHTS

This treaty shall not supersede, prejudice, or otherwise derogate from:

(a) laws and regulations, administrative practices or procedures, or administrative or adjudicatory decisions of either Party;

(b) international legal obligations; or

(c) obligations assumed by either Party; including those contained in an investment agreement or an investment authorization,

whether extant at the time of entry into force of this Treaty or thereafter, that entitle investments, or associated activities, of nationals or companies of the other Party to treatment more favorable than that accorded by this Treaty in like situations.

ARTICLE X

MEASURES NOT PRECLUDED BY THIS TREATY

1. This Treaty shall not preclude the application by either Party of any and all measures necessary for the maintenance of public order, the fulfillment of its obligations with respect to the maintenance or restoration of international peace or security, or the protection of its own essential security interests.

2. This Treaty shall not preclude either Party from prescribing special formalities in connection with the establishment of investments in its territory of nationals and companies of the other Party, but such formalities shall not impair the substance of any of the rights set forth in this Treaty.

ARTICLE XI

TAXATION

1. With respect to its tax policies, each Party should strive to accord fairness and equity in the treatment of investment of nationals and companies of the other Party.

2.   Nevertheless, the provisions of this Treaty, and in particular Articles VII and VIII, shall apply to matters of taxation only with respect to the following:

(a) expropriation, pursuant to Article III;

(b) transfers, pursuant to Article V; or

(c) the observance and enforcement of terms of an investment agreement or authorization as referred to in Article VII (1) (a) or (b).

Matters by item by 2(c) shall not be covered to the extent they are subject to the dispute settlement provisions of a convention for the avoidance of double taxation between the two parties, unless such matters are raised under such settlement provisions and are not resolved within a reasonable period of time.

ARTICLE XII

APPLICATION OF THIS TREATY TO
POLITICAL SUB-DIVISIONS OF THE
PARTIES

This Treaty shall apply to political subdivisions of the Parties.

ARTICLE XIII

ENTRY INTO FORCE
AND
DURATION AND TERMINATION

1.   This Treaty shall be ratified by each of the Parties, and the ratifications thereof shall be exchanged as soon as possible.

2.   This Treaty shall enter into force thirty days after the date of exchange of ratifications. It shall remain in force for a period of ten years and shall continue in force unless terminated in accordance with Paragraph 3 of this Article. It shall apply to investments made or acquired thereafter.

3.   Either Party may, by giving one year's written notice to the other Party, terminate this Treaty at the end of the initial ten year period or at any time thereafter.

4.   With respect to investments made or acquired prior to the date of termination of this Treaty and to which this Treaty otherwise applies, the

provisions of all of the other Articles of this Treaty shall thereafter continue to be effective for a further period of ten years from such date of termination.

IN WITNESS WHEREOF, the respective plenipotentiaries have signed this Treaty.

DONE in duplicate at _____ on the day of _____ in the English and   languages, both texts being equally authentic.

FOR THE UNITED STATES OF AMERICA:

FOR

ANNEX

Consistent with Article II paragraph 3, each Party reserves the right to maintain limited exceptions in the sectors or matters it has indicated below:

The United States of America

Air transportation; ocean and coastal shipping; banking; insurance; government grants; government insurance and loan programs; energy and power production; custom house brokers; ownership of real estate; ownership and operation of broadcast or common carrier radio and television stations; ownership of shares in the Communications Satellite Corporation; the provision of common carrier telephone and telegraph services; the provision of submarine services; use of land and natural resources.

Investment Index

About the Editors and Contributors

BART S. FISHER, Partner, Patton, Boggs & Blow, Washington, D.C.; Adjunct Professor of International Relations, Georgetown University; J.D., Harvard Law School (1972); Ph.D., Johns Hopkins School of Advanced International Studies (1970); M.A., Johns Hopkins School of Advanced International Studies (1967); B.A., Washington University (1963).

JEFF TURNER, Associate, Patton, Boggs & Blow, Washington, D.C.; J.D./M.S.F.S., Georgetown University Law Center and School of Foreign Service (1982); B.A., Tulane University (1976).

STEVEN M. SCHNEEBAUM, Attorney, Patton, Boggs & Blow, Washington, D.C.; Adjunct Lecturer in International Trade Law, Columbus School of Law, The Catholic University of America; M.C.L. (A.P.), George Washington University (1978), B.A., Oxford (1976); M.A., Oberlin College (1970); B.A., Yale University (1969).

ALISON L. DOYLE, J.D./M.S.F.S., Georgetown University Law Center and School of Foreign Service (1983); B.A., University of Pennsylvania (1977).

CLAUDE G. B. FONTHEIM, Associate, Ginsburg, Feldman, Weil & Bress, Washington, D.C.; M.P.P., J.D., University of Michigan (1981); B.A., University of Michigan (1977).

R. MICHAEL GADBAW, Partner, Verner, Liipfert, Bernhard & McPherson, Washington, D.C.; J.D., University of Michigan (1974); M.A., The Fletcher School of Law and Diplomacy (1970); B.A., Fordham University (1969).

MARK P. JACOBSEN, J.D., Georgetown University Law Center (1983); B.A., St. Olaf College (1979).

WILLIAM E. COUGHLIN, J.D./M.S.F.S., Georgetown University Law Center and School of Foreign Service (1983); A.B., Georgetown University (1978).

GEORGE S. TRISCIUZZI, J.D./M.S.F.S., Georgetown University Law Center and School of Foreign Service (1983); A.B., Brown University (1978).